# North West England Walks

## by car, bus and train

**Published by** Sigma Leisure - an imprint of Sigma Press, Stobart House, Pontyclerc, Penybanc Road, Ammanford, Carmarthenshire SA18 3HP.

**British Library Cataloguing in Publication Data**
A CIP record for this book is available from the British Library.

**ISBN**: 978-1-85058-923-5

**Typesetting and Design by**: Sigma Press, Ammanford.

**Cover photographs**: top (left to right): Uppermill railway viaduct; 'The Childe of Hale' carved effigy in Hale Village; Hale Head Lighthouse; Back Tor. Main picture: The Macclesfield Canal at Nelson Pit Visitor Centre.

**Photographs**: © Ray Knapman unless stated otherwise.

**Maps**: Sigma Press

**Printed by**: Akcent Media Ltd

# North West England Walks

## by car, bus and train

Ray Knapman

SIGMA Leisure

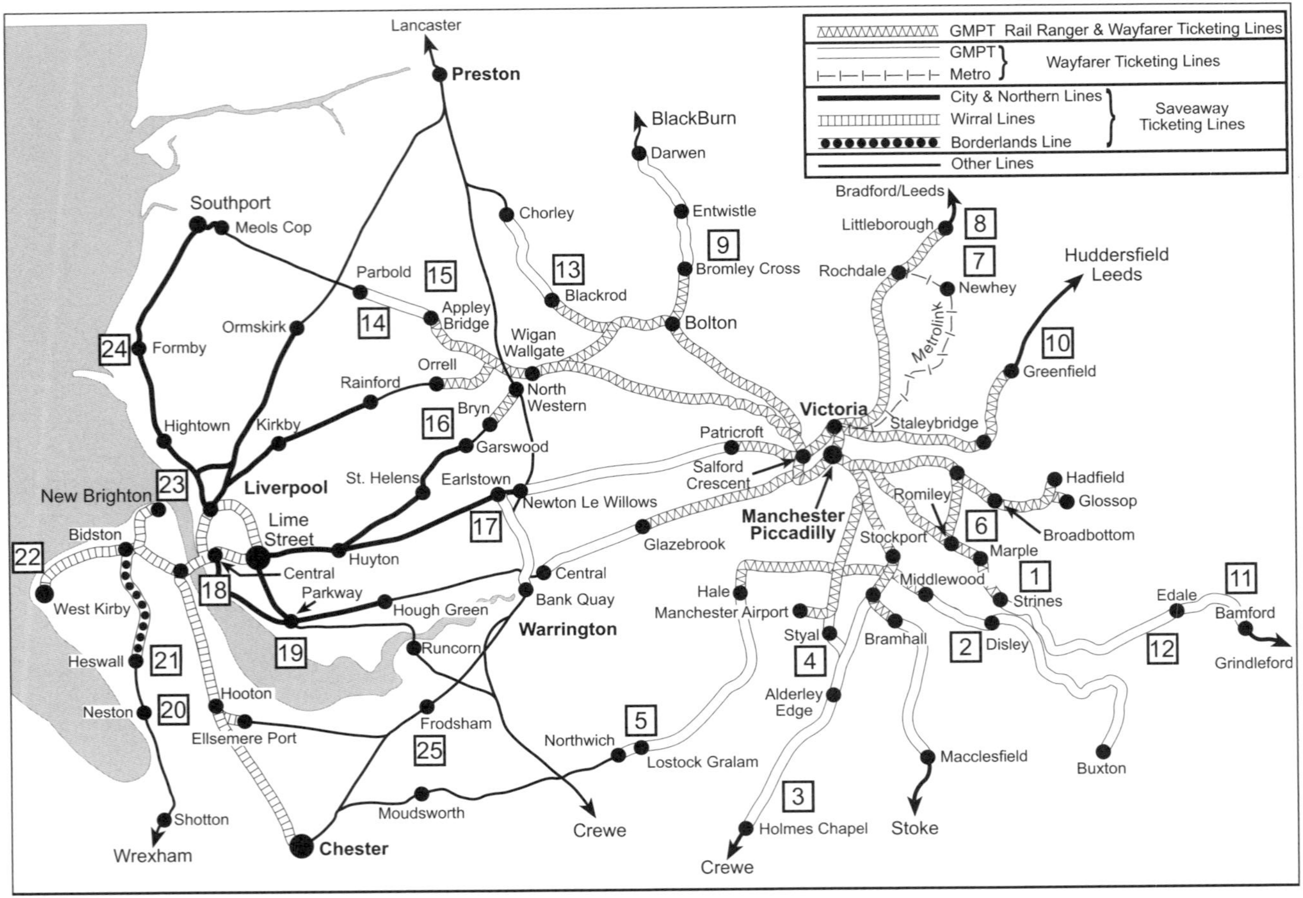

GMPT Rail Ranger & Wayfarer Ticketing Lines
GMPT
Metro
Wayfarer Ticketing Lines
City & Northern Lines
Wirral Lines
Borderlands Line
Saveaway Ticketing Lines
Other Lines
Lancaster
Preston
BlackBurn
Darwen
Entwistle
Bromley Cross
Bolton
Bradford/Leeds
Littleborough
Rochdale
Newhey
Metrolink
Huddersfield
Leeds
Greenfield
Southport
Meols Cop
Chorley
Blackrod
Parbold
Appley
Bridge
Wigan
Wallgate
Ormskirk
Formby
Orrell
Rainford
North
Western
Bryn
Garswood
Hightown
Kirkby
Liverpool
St. Helens
Earlstown
Newton Le Willows
Victoria
Staleybridge
Patricroft
Salford
Crescent
Manchester
Piccadilly
Hadfield
Glossop
Broadbottom
Romiley
Marple
Stockport
New Brighton
Bidston
Lime
Street
Central
Huyton
Parkway
Hough Green
Glazebrook
Central
Bank Quay
Warrington
Hale
Manchester Airport
Middlewood
Strines
Edale
Bamford
Grindleford
West Kirby
Runcorn
Styal
Bramhall
Disley
Heswall
Neston
Hooton
Ellsemere Port
Frodsham
Northwich
Lostock Gralam
Alderley
Edge
Macclesfield
Buxton
Shotton
Wrexham
Chester
Moudsworth
Crewe
Holmes Chapel
Crewe
Stoke
1
2
3
4
5
6
7
8
9
10
11
12
13
14
15
16
17
18
19
20
21
22
23
24
25

# CONTENTS

## MAP KEY

- Route of walk
- Bi-Diretional
- Detour
- Major Road
- Minor Road
- Tracks
- Railway
- Old Railway
- Tunnel
- Canal
- Viaduct
- Bridge
- Church with Spire
- Church with Tower
- Woodland (Broadleaf & Conifer)
- Viewpoint
- Trig. point
- Sand Dunes

# INTRODUCTION

The inspiration for this book came about when I discovered that many of the best walks in my locality could be reached by train and bus. I found public transport allows for linear walks following canals, rivers and lakes, making for more varied scenery and interest, and there is the added kudos of getting from A to B rather than walking in a circle. I often found that the return leg of circular walks are dull and are just a means of returning to the start without doubling back along the same route. Some of the walks do lend themselves to a circular route that maintain interest, and I have where possible included a shorter alternative route for more stroll type walkers.

I have compiled a list of walks from ones I have walked and chosen them for their beauty, variety and interest. The parameter I set when choosing the walks are that they must be within reach by the public transport network of the conurbations of Greater Manchester and Merseyside (and some surrounding parts of Cheshire, Lancashire, Derbyshire and Yorkshire). The range of the area of the walk locations are from the coastlines of the Wirral, Sefton and the Mersey, the hills and valleys of Lancashire, Cheshire and Greater Manchester with their canals and reservoirs, the West Pennine moorlands and the Dark Peak District.

For each of the walks, points of interest are indicated including noteworthy historical places, and places for refreshment. All but four of the walks start at a railway station and may be readily accomplished using the public transport system of these areas by most walkers living within the area. Most of the walks are not overly arduous and may be achieved by an average fit person and follow routes in the most beautiful, historical and interesting parts of this very diverse region. I have described walks that will suit stroll type walkers as well as provide routes which will appeal to those who prefer a lengthy walk. In fact, there is something for all types of walker! They will, I hope provide a new perspective of our area of North West England which has walks of beauty and interest here on our doorstep that are often overlooked when hurtling along the areas motorways to walks much further afield.

Many of the walks can be reached by using cheap off peak tickets. Because of the numerous tickets on offer in both the regions, a chapter is devoted to guidance on the tickets to use for reaching the walks in the book. The new network of electrified railway being built (at the time of writing) for the lines between Liverpool and Manchester/Wigan will enhance the service both in capacity, and journey time, making more reason to leave the car at home or at the rail station.

Were a car is preferred for convenience, car users are given detailed advice on reaching the walk locations including Sat Nav address. An alternative circular route for car users has been described for nearly all of the walks, and guidance given on public transport services to reach the start and end points for all the linear walks.

The advantages of using public transport may be summed up:

- Cheap and in some cases (if owner of a bus pass!) free transport to and from the start/finish points of the walk.
- Linear walks can be undertaken which enables a larger variety of scenery and interest and greater satisfaction in walking a route from A to B.
- Those with a liking of sampling the local brew and fare at hostelries may do so with no driving to consider.
- No parking problems.
- Less hassle in reaching the walks, no battling through the city traffic and conversely no steep and winding narrow country lanes. Many of the walks start from a rail station right on a scenic towpath or footpath.
- The environment benefits.
- With the ongoing electrification of much of the Liverpool to Manchester and Wigan lines, new more comfortable faster trains can be taken advantage of.

## Walk Categories

I have classified the walks into three categories:

| | |
|---|---|
| **Easy** | 3 to 6 miles on fairly flat ground |
| **Moderate** | 5 to 8 miles with some short climbs |
| **Hard** | 6 to 10 miles with some long or steep climbs |

Easy and Moderate walks are well within the capability of the average fit person. The hard walks are for the more seasoned, experienced walkers.

Most of the walks are on well-defined paths near to shelter but a few exceptionally good walks are on more remote hill type paths. Some walks do necessitate walking on tarmac but this has been kept to a minimum. I have indicated, on the longer walks, places where it is possible to shorten the walk and return to the start on public transport.

Although most of the walks are close to shelter and sustenance, all walking should be undertaken with appropriate walking shoes/boots and protective rainwear.

On all the walks muddy conditions may be encountered and should be prepared for. Young children and dogs must be closely supervised especially near railway lines and canals, and where there are farm animals.

I have purposely omitted an estimated time for each walk as there is a huge difference in people's outlook on walking, some like to ponder and absorb as they go, and the opposite extreme for some walkers is to do a walk as energetically as possible. There are of course other factors such as ability and stamina to consider, but if an estimate is required, a rule of thumb guide for the average walker I have found a rate of 2 mile an hour is a fair estimation.

Maps used are OS 1:25 000 Explorer for their more detailed interpretation of ground features and elevation. But for most walks the OS 1:50 000 Landranger series are more than adequate. These are OS Landranger Series: 108 Liverpool; 109 Manchester; 110 Sheffield; 117 Chester and Wrexham; and 118 Stoke on Trent and Macclesfield

So try leaving your car at home, catch a bus and/or train, and have a relaxing, enjoyable cheap day out in your local countryside with a new found appreciation.

## Acknowledgements

The ideas for my walks came from many sources, but the following need special mention for their invaluable help in the selection of walks for this book.

The TfGM and Merseytravel for their information on the rail network and guides on walks in their respective areas.

A special thanks to St Helens Local History and Archives Library for their kind permission to include the picture of the drawing of the Sankey Viaduct based on an engraving by I.VShaw.

I would like to thank my friends and family for their encouragement and help, especially my wife Helen for accompanying me on my reccys of the walks and keeping me sustained when working on my book at home.

## Notes on the off peak tickets of the Greater Manchester and Merseyside transport systems

This chapter should be read in conjunction with the location map showing the extent of the rail network that may be accessed using the Rail Ranger, Wayfarer and Saveaway off peak tickets.

### Greater Manchester

The basic **off peak rail fare** for any return rail journey within the GM region is a maximum of £4.30. The ticket may be bought at all manned stations and from the train conductor. As many of the walks in the book are within this region, this ticket may be all that is required by walkers travelling by train within the region.

The **Rail Ranger ticket** at £5.20 covers the same region and has the advantage of free use of the city centre Metrolink, useful for connecting travel between Victoria and Piccadilly stations. This ticket allows for more flexibility and can also be used on a train returning from a different location and/or multiple train journeys.

The **Wayfarer ticke**t provides for all GM transport systems - rail, bus and Metrolink with additional areas in Derbyshire, Cheshire and Lancashire. There are also concessionary tickets for over 60s and children. This is a useful ticket to have if bus, Metrolink and train travel is necessary, and for the walks starting from the Hope Valley line.

This ticket is especially useful for Merseyside walkers who may join the Wayfarer ticket region at Earlestown on the Liverpool to Manchester line where there is a large car park, or buy a train ticket from their local station to Earlestown station and then buy the Wayfarer ticket on the train for onward travel through Manchester.

**Directions to Earlestown Station**:

Sat Nav: Postcode WA12 9AU

From the East Lancs Road roundabout at junction 23 with the M6 take the A49 for Newton Le Willows and Warrington. Follow the road ¾ mile to a mini roundabout at The Oak Tree pub and turn right onto the A572 for St Helens, follow the road to the second set of traffic lights and turn left onto Victoria Road, follow the road to a mini-roundabout immediately before a railway bridge and turn right. After 300m. immediately before a road junction there is a car park for the station.

## Merseyside

Off Peak travel throughout the Merseyside region on Rail, bus and ferry can be made using the **Saveaway ticket**. The ticket may be bought at rail stations and retail outlets within the area. The cost varies according to which regions of Merseyside are used, but a maximum at £5.10 for all regions is a bargain. If just rail travel is needed then a Family Ticket for two adults and up to three children at £10.00 can be used. This ticket can be bought in advance and only at rail stations within the area. All but two of the Merseyside walks in this book may be reached by rail, so this ticket is the most economical one for walkers with children who live near a rail station in the Merseyside region.

Greater Manchester walkers who wish to take advantage of these tickets can travel by car to Lea Green rail station, park for free and buy the tickets for onward travel on the rail network. This saves tunnel and fuel costs when walking on the Wirral and parking costs when walking the Liverpool seafront. It also makes the linear walks more enjoyable without the need to return to your car.

**Directions to Lea Green Station:**

Sat Nav: Postcode WA9 3BZ

From the M62 Junction 7, take the A 570 towards St Helens, after one mile at the second roundabout turn right onto Elton Head Road and the station is in ½ mile on the right.

## Summary of the main off peak travel tickets of Greater Manchester and Merseyside

The summary on the following page is by no means the definitive list of the tickets available for off peak travel, and walkers are advised to check at travel centres and the websites in the ticket summary for other offers that may be more suited to their needs.

The most useful website for information on your trip is **www.traveline.info** This gives both bus and train times for all journeys in all areas.

Other websites are:

| | |
|---|---|
| **www.merseytravel.gov.uk** | for the Merseyside network |
| **www.tfgm.com** | for the TfGM network |

Weekday journeys must start after 9:30am, weekends and bank holidays no restrictions apply

Children under 5 are free in both regions.

## Summary of the main off peak travel tickets of Greater Manchester and Merseyside

| Ticket Type | Wayfarer | Rail Ranger | Saveaway |
|---|---|---|---|
| Network area | TfGM Area + parts of Cheshire, Derbyshire, and Lancashire | TfGM Area | Merseytravel Area + rail travel to Chester, Ellesmere Port and Ormskirk |
| Ticket availability | Stations and train conductors, Pay Point shops, in and around the TfGM area | Stations and train conductors in TfGM and on lines into the area | Stations and travel centres within the Merseytravel area |
| Rail travel | Ok in network area | Ok in network area | Ok in network area |
| Bus travel | Ok in network area | X | Ok in network area |
| Metro travel | OK | City centre only | n/a |
| Adult | £12.00 | £5.20 | £5.10* |
| Child aged 5 to 16 (Child aged under 5 travel is free) | £6.00 | £2.60 | £2.70* |
| Group (up to 2 adults + 2 children aged 5 to 15) | £23.00 | n/a | n/a (A Family Ticket for 2 adults and 3 children is available at £10.00 for the whole Merseyrail network) |
| Concession for Over 60s | £6.00 | X | X |
| Residents holding bus passes of respective ticket issuing areas | £6.00 | Free rail and bus travel In TfGM area | Free rail and bus travel in Merseytravel Area |

*Ticket prices correct at time of writing*

***The Saveaway ticket prices are for travel across all the Merseyside zones to reach the walks in the book. Residents of Merseyside may travel through fewer zones so may pay less.**

# LIVERPOOL WALKING ROUTES

Unlike Manchester, Liverpool isn't blessed with an overground tram system linking the railway stations. On arrival at Liverpool's main line station at Lime Street Station, passengers may use the escalators to access the Merseyrail system directly to the Wirral line, but to travel on the Northern Line (the starting points of two of the walks are in this book) to Southport entails a 10 minute walk to join trains at Central Station.

Walk number 18 starting at Albert Dock can be accessed by using the Wirral line to James Street Station, but some walkers may prefer to travel from Lime Street Station through the town centre and the Liverpool 1 Shopping precinct to Albert Dock on foot. There is a subway to access the Wirral Lines, and to cross the busy Lime Street for those wishing to reach Victoria Street bus stops.

Car users who are venturing to do these walks by train for the first time may find the need for these connections daunting, with these points in mind a map of the quickest and most convenient walking routes through the Liverpool town centre is shown on the following page.

The location of the bus stops for services to Heswall and Neston are also shown in Victoria Street.

A. Lime Street Station
   For trains to Walk number 22, West Kirby and Caldy

B. Central Station
   For trains to Walk number 23, Sefton Coast
   For trains to Walk number 24, Formby Point

C. James Street Station
   For trains to Walk number 18, South Liverpool Waterfront

D. Victoria Street bus stop VE
   For bus number 487 to Neston for Walk number 20, Neston and Parkgate
   For bus numbers 471 and 472 to Heswall for Walk number 21, Wirral Country Park and Thurstaston Common

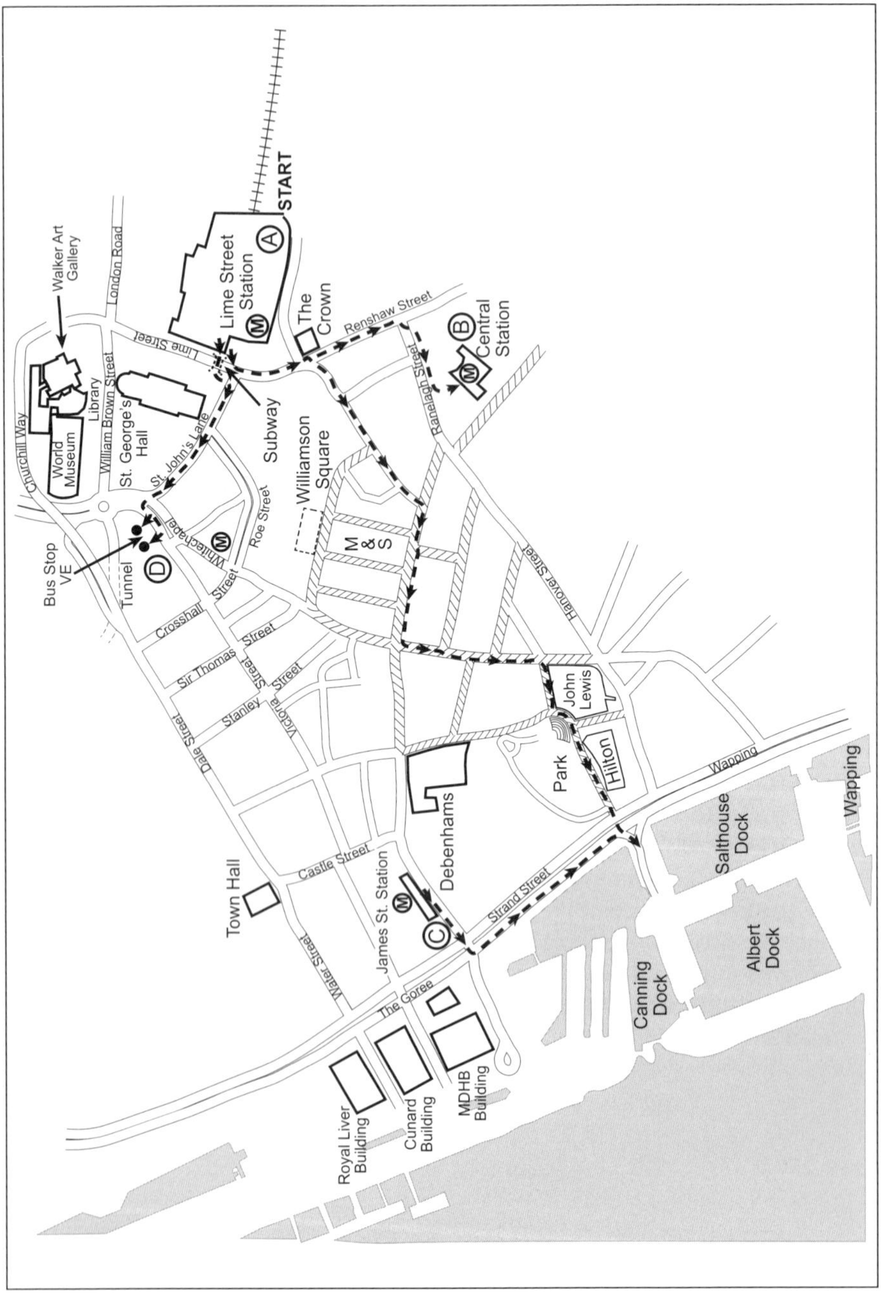
START
A
Lime Street Station
M
The Crown
Renshaw Street
B
Central Station
Walker Art Gallery
London Road
Lime Street
William Brown Street
Library
World Museum
Churchill Way
St. George's Hall
St. John's Lane
Subway
Williamson Square
Ranelagh Street
M & S
Roe Street
Whitechapel
Bus Stop VE
Tunnel
D
Street
Crosshall
Sir Thomas Street
Victoria Street
Stanley Street
Dale Street
Hanover Street
John Lewis
Park
Hilton
Wapping
Salthouse Dock
Wapping
Debenhams
Castle Street
James St. Station
C
Town Hall
Strand Street
Water Street
The Goree
Albert Dock
Canning Dock
Royal Liver Building
Cunard Building
MDHB Building

# WALK 1
# The Peak Forest Canal

*A simple linear riverside and canal towpath walk that is full of historical and scenic interest all the way.*

| | |
|---|---|
| Route | Strines – Roman Lakes – Marple – Peak Forest Canal – Marple Aqueduct – Romiley |
| Start | Strines Railway Station (car user's park at Romiley or Marple station car park) |
| Finish | Romiley Railway Station (or Marple Railway Station for the shorter walk) |
| Distance and grade | 5½ miles linear – 593 ft (180m) ascent – Moderate<br>3 miles linear (shortened route) – 350 ft (107m) ascent – Easy |
| Map | OS Outdoor Leisure 1 – The Dark Peak District |
| Terrain | Level paths on firm ground most of the way. One short steep stretch and some paved road side walking |
| Refreshments | Many pubs and cafés at both Marple and Romiley |

## Directions to the walk

**Public transport:** Travel to Manchester city centre, and then catch a train from Piccadilly Station to Strines. A two hourly (hourly on Saturday) frequency direct service, with intermediate trains running to Strines via New Mills from Sunday to Friday means you must check the timetable. The return journey from Romiley to Piccadilly has a much better frequency of three trains per hour.
**By car:** The best way to do this walk is to park your car either at Romiley railway station for the full route or Marple station for the shortened route before catching a train to Strines, and then follow the walk back to your car. An infrequent train service to return to the start of the walk means a check of the timetable is essential before setting out.
**Sat nav:** Postcode SK6 4BN will get you to Romiley Station, the station car park is off Guywood Lane; for the shorter walk, SK6 7DA will get you to Marple Station. The station car park is off Brabyn's Brow.

**Road directions:** From the M60 anticlockwise at junction 25 take the 2nd exit off the roundabout for A560 for Bredbury. At a second roundabout take the second exit to continue on the A560 for Bredbury. Follow the road for ½ mile then turn right for the A6017 towards Hazel Grove and Romiley. After ½ mile continue straight on to cross the A627 at traffic lights towards Romiley. Follow the road through Romiley under the railway bridge, the entrance to the car park is on the left off Guywood Lane.

## Walk description

The walk has lots of historical interest, it follows the River Goyt valley where water is never far away, be it canal river or lake, where wildfowl may be seen. Highlights being the 'Roman Bridge' and the flight of locks on the Peak Forest Canal in Marple. The route starts from the countryside station of Strines following tracks past old farmsteads and alongside the River Goyt, passing the 'Roman Bridge', which is actually an ancient packhorse bridge over the River Goyt.

The walk continues on past the Roman Lakes with its waterfowl before joining the Peak Forest Canal in the pretty village of Marple. The route then follows the towpath alongside an impressive series of locks before crossing the aqueduct running parallel to the railway viaduct and the glorious views high above the River Goyt. The route continues along the towpath through woodland, turning sharp right above Bredbury Green before the canal is left to join the main road through Romiley to arrive at the station.

The walk may be cut short to 3 miles by returning from Marple rail station.

## Walk Directions

1. Once alighting from the train and the train pulls away, the peace and tranquillity becomes apparent with only birdsong and wind in the trees. One wonders the purpose of the location of this station for there is no habitation in view; Strines is actually ½ mile away. From the station take the farm track under the railway bridge and turn right up a track which soon crosses the railway, turn left onto a track at a no through road sign.

2. Follow the track past the quaintly named Windy Bottom Farm, the track passes under the railway then follows the River Goyt. Look out for the Roman Bridge over the river on the left, this is definitely not Roman, it is a packhorse bridge given the name Roman in Victorian times when the area was very popular with excursion trains arriving at Marple with hundreds of visitors. Continue round a bend past Flood Gates Cottage,

then under the railway on a high viaduct and continue past Roman Lakes on the right.

3. The track is joined by other tracks from the right, at the second track bear left across the bridge over the Goyt and climb the road up to and over the railway. The road joins a main road at a cross roads, go straight on until the road joins Stockport Road at a canal bridge over the Peak Forest Canal.

   Look for the horse tunnel under the road, which was constructed to allow horses drawing barges to pass safely across. Marple town centre is straight ahead and it is well worth a visit to this pretty village, and perhaps some refreshment before continuing down the canal towpath.

The horse tunnel at Marple

4. Turn right to follow he towpath down the flight of locks. There are a total of 16 locks giving a raise in level of 254 ft. The canal passes under Station Road through a small tunnel, leave the canal towpath and cross the road to continue to follow the towpath which is on the opposite bank.

   The walk can be shortened here by leaving the canal and turning right along the road to Marple Station which is 150m on the left.

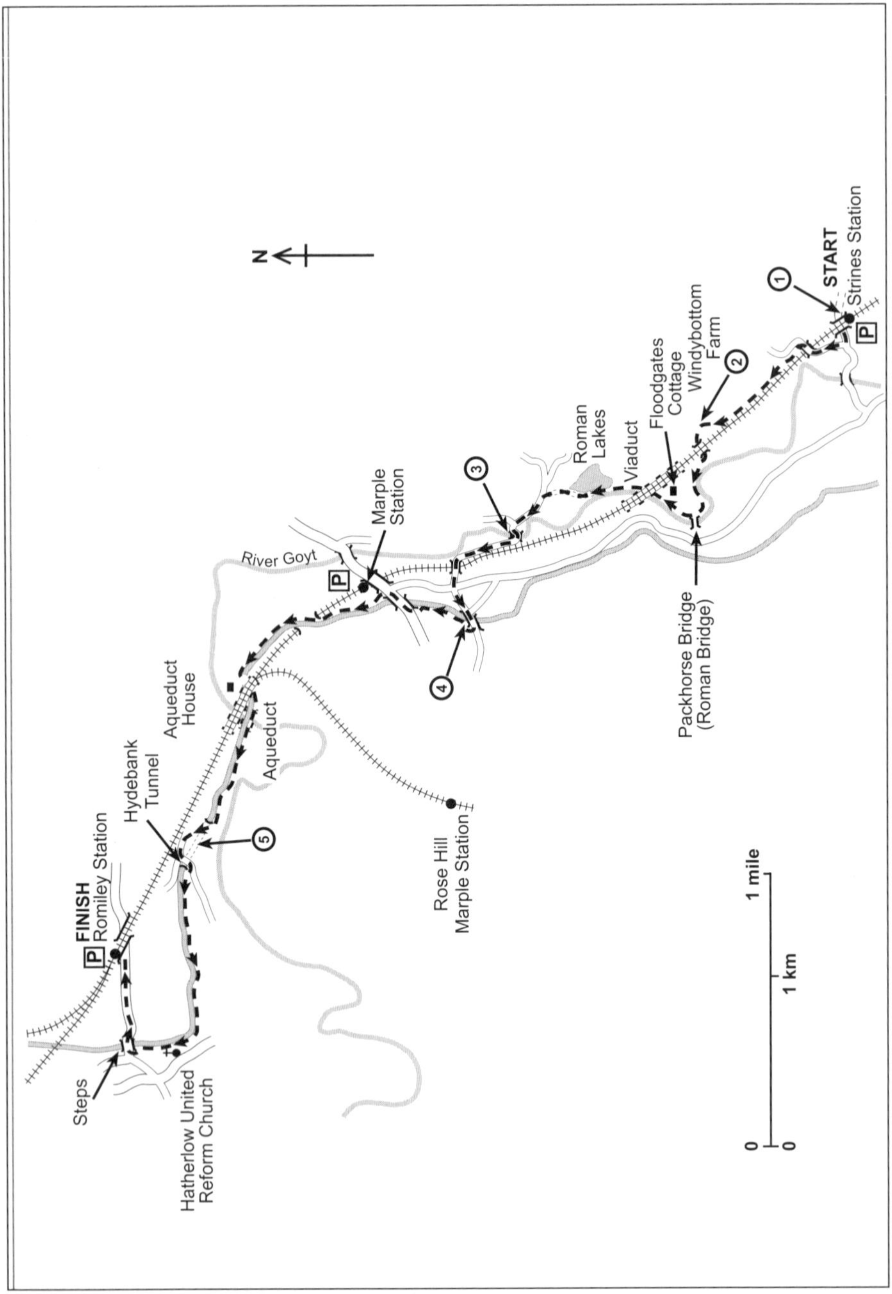
N
START
Strines Station
1
2
Windybottom Farm
Floodgates Cottage
Viaduct
Roman Lakes
3
Packhorse Bridge (Roman Bridge)
Marple Station
River Goyt
4
Aqueduct House
Aqueduct
Hydebank Tunnel
5
Rose Hill Marple Station
FINISH
Romiley Station
Steps
Hatherlow United Reform Church
1 mile
1 km
0
0

Aqueduct and viaduct span the River Goyt

This delightful wooded stretch of canal descends through four sets of locks then passes over the railway before descending another four sets of locks, then passing under the railway viaduct. At this point the towpath changes sides of the canal again at a grand looking Aqueduct House. Continue onward under the railway viaduct. The canal then crosses the aqueduct over the River Goyt. The view is impressive with the railway viaduct running parallel with the aqueduct crossing high above the River Goyt.

5. Continue following the canal until Hydebank tunnel forces towpath users to ascend a track over the canal. The track is joined by another on the right, bear left down to rejoin the canal bank. Follow the towpath through a heavily wooded stretch of the canal until Romiley Paper Mill comes into view on the opposite bank, they manufacture paper and cardboard tubes. Hatherlow United Reform church comes in view on the left on an elevated section overlooking Bredbury Green. The canal swings sharply right. Continue on to a road bridge over the canal, pass under the bridge and ascend the steps to the road, then turn left to walk up hill to Romiley town centre along Stockport Road. This is Romiley's main street. Look out for

the Wesleyan chapel of 1811 (MDCCCXI) with the star of Bethlehem above the door - it is now a Signol physiotherapy and acupuncture centre! The railway station is a little further along under the railway bridge on the left.

There are many pubs and other refreshments to be had here before catching the train home.

## Historical notes

**Marple Aqueduct** was built 1800, and is 103 yards (97 metres) long. There are three arches over the River Goyt, the highest being 100 ft (30.5m) above the river. The piers are built using red sandstone and are oval in section. The higher courses are in a white dressed stone and have holes built into either side of each arch to reduce the weight of the structure.

**The Peak Forest Canal** starts in Duckinfield where it joins the Ashton Canal and terminates at Bugsworth (since 1930 called Buxworth). This was once a busy transhipment basin for the canal company's Peak Forest Tramway. This six mile line was constructed to carry limestone from the High Peak area. The canal, tramway and aqueduct were designed by the Canal Company's consultant engineer Benjamin Outram.

The canal fell out of use when a part of the aqueduct collapsed in the winter of 1961-2. A campaign to reopen the Peak Forest and Ashton canals was set up to recreate the Cheshire Ring of waterways. The Inland Waterways Association held its National Rally at Marple in 1966 and the campaigning continued for five years, then in 1971 the British Waterways Board decided to refurbish Marple Locks and the Ashton Canal. The work was completed in May 1974 and celebrated by a grand reopening ceremony.
More information at**www.marple-uk.com/water2.htm**

More of the authors photographs can be found at:
**www.geograph.org.uk/search.php?i=46085187**
Press the tab key marked Map to get the locations

# WALK 2
# Lyme Park and the Macclesfield Canal

*A walk with a variety of landscapes which passes along a towpath, field paths, parkland, and a visit to one of the North West's greatest stately homes.*

| | |
|---|---|
| Route | Middlewood – Macclesfield Canal – West Parkgate – Lyme Park – Elmerhust Wood – Disley |
| Start/finish | Linear route A: Start: Middlewood railway station<br>Finish: Disley railway station<br>Circular route B: Start/Finish: Middlewood railway station<br>Circular route C: Start/Finish: Nelson Pit Visitor Centre |
| Distance and grade | Route A: 5¾ miles linear route for train users – 702 ft (214m) ascent – Moderate<br>Route B: 6 ¾ miles circular route for train users – 722 ft (220m) ascent – Moderate<br>Route C: 5¾ miles circular route for car users – 600 ft (183m) ascent – Moderate |
| Map | OS Explorer 268 Wilmslow Macclesfield and Congleton |
| Terrain | Fairly level walking on good paths most of the way, a few stiles and some field paths which may be muddy after rain. There are a couple of stretches of quiet country lanes |
| Refreshments | Nelson Pit Visitor Centre, Boars Head pub near the Nelson Pit Centre, Lyme Hall Park, Rams Head pub at Disley |

## Directions to the walk

**Public transport:** Travel to Manchester city centre, and then catch a train from Piccadilly Station to Middlewood station. A two hourly frequency direct service (intermediate trains run to Middlewood via Disley) for Monday to Sunday, means you must check the timetable. For the return from the linear route, there is an hourly direct service running from Disley to Manchester Piccadilly.

**By car**: **Sat nav**: Postcode SK12 1TH will get you to the Nelson Pit Visitor Centre (grid reference: SJ 945833).

**Road Directions**: From the traffic lights at the cross roads on the A523 in Poynton, go up Park Lane, after ¾ mile, fork left down Middlewood Road (signposted Davenport Golf Club). Take first right (with brown sign for Nelson Pit). The visitor centre is opposite the Boar's Head pub.

## Walk Description

This is a leisurely walk with a variety of landscapes from a pleasant canal towpath to the pristine parkland of Lyme Hall, and the foothills of the Peak District. It is at its best in late spring /early summer for the stunning displays of rhododendrons and the gardens of Lyme Hall.

Train users start the walk at Middlewood Station, which is conveniently located next to the Middlewood Trail, a former railway converted into a 'greenway' for walkers, cyclists and horse riders. This is followed to Nelson Pit Visitor Centre where car users join the route. A browse at the centre will give an insight to the local history of the area, then a stretch of the Macclesfield Canal is followed by a woodland walk into Lyme Park, with all its attractions including its formal gardens, herd of deer and Hall used by the BBC for its *Pride and Prejudice* series. The walk continues along a brook side

The Macclesfield Canal at Nelson Pit Visitor Centre

in a wooded valley below Cage Hill, Route A ends with a country lane to the village of Disley. Routes B and C return along field paths and tracks through woodland to the Macclesfield Canal. Car users follow this back to the visitor centre, train users return to Middlewood Station from the canal.

## Walk Directions

### Route A: 5¾ miles Linear route for train users

1. From Middlewood Station, climb the ramp to the track of the Middlewood Way, which is a dismantled railway line converted into a 'greenway', cross the railway bridge and follow the wood lined track under three bridges until reaching a bridge at the site of Higher Poynton Station.The platforms to this station have been preserved, making a pleasant picnic area. Climb the steps up to the road bridge and turn right to follow the road to Nelson Pit Visitor Centre.

### Car users join the route here.

2. It is well worth a browse at this centre, which has loads of information on the area, refreshments and toilet facilities. Carry on past the car park at the centre to a second larger car park where there is a gap stile onto the Macclesfield Canal towpath, turn right over a footbridge which crosses the neck of a basin (Mount Vernon Wharf) which was once used for loading barges with coal from the mine. Follow the path past the many boats moored on this busy stretch of canal. The canal widens after the road bridge, this was caused by subsidence due to the coal mining. Further on there is a smaller widening (winding hole) for turning barges around. At a footbridge (No. 16) a pivot point for a dismantled swing bridge can be seen next to the base. The canal turns right over an aqueduct crossing a small valley. Shortly after a farm access bridge (No. 17) is reached, leave the towpath and cross this bridge, turn left to follow the track beside a row of cottages which comes out onto a narrow lane (Shrigley Lane). Turn right to follow the lane which runs alongside a brook. Pass the entrance to Redacre farm and carry on to a layby on the left with a kissing gate, pass through this and take the path uphill which comes out onto a track next to a bridge over a brook.

3. Turn left over the stone bridge then turn right through a gate in front of West Parkgate Lodge, onto the National Trust estate (no charge) and follow the track as it winds up through the mixed woodland of Hase Bank Wood.

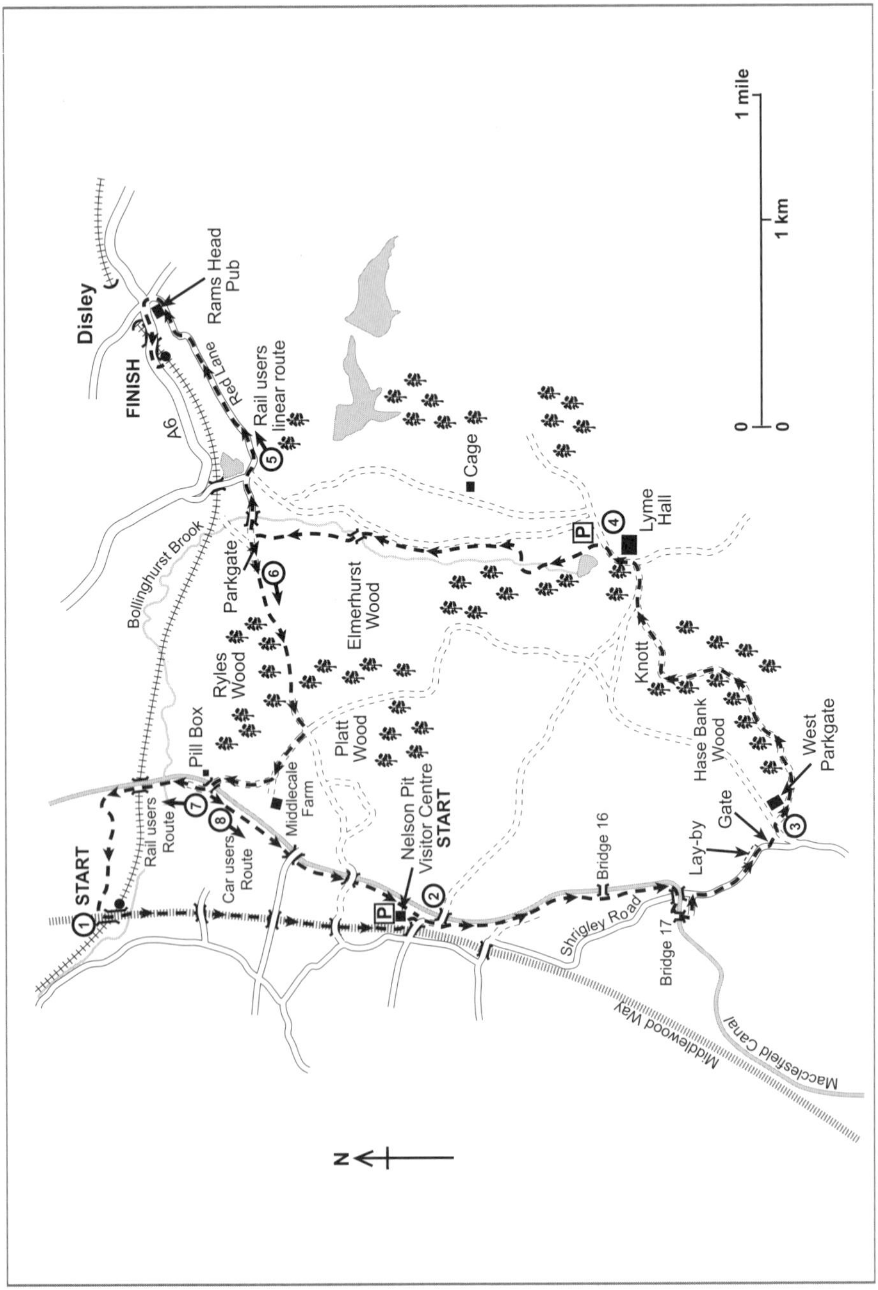

START
Rail users Route
Car users Route
Pill Box
Middlecale Farm
Nelson Pit Visitor Centre
START
Platt Wood
Ryles Wood
Elmerhurst Wood
Parkgate
Bollinghurst Brook
A6
FINISH
Disley
Rams Head Pub
Red Lane
Rail users linear route
Cage
Lyme Hall
Knott
Hase Bank Wood
West Parkgate
Gate
Lay-by
Bridge 16
Bridge 17
Shrigley Road
Middlewood Way
Macclesfield Canal
N
0
1 km
1 mile

The formal gardens at Lyme Hall in spring

This path is beside a brook and passes through mixed woodland which is exceptionally beautiful in early summer when the rhododendrons are at their best. The track climbs to come out past a gate onto what appears to be wild moorland, the contrast of scenery is striking. The path continues around a hillock called the Knott then slowly descends down to a more wooded area then onto Lyme Hall.

4. Here there is a chance to visit the formal gardens and house (payment charge) and a refreshment break before carrying on the walk. Restart the walk by taking the drive by the car park signed 'The Timber Yard' past the mill pond. Carry straight on past the Yard to a gate marked as a play area leading into Crow Wood, follow the track then shortly bear right across the mill stream. Follow the path alongside the stream, then leave the wood by crossing a ladder stile and continue on uphill on steps and swinging left. The monument known as the Cage comes into view above on the right. Follow the path which runs parallel to the drive briefly on the right before dropping down back to another wall stile, cross this to

enter Elmerhurst Wood. The path descends back to the stream which is crossed by a footbridge and a couple more plank bridges before another stile leads you out of the wood onto a track.

5. The linear route continues by turning right onto the track, pass over a stream and a lodge then cross Bollinghurst Brook onto Red Lane. This tree lined narrow lane is followed past a residential area to a fork, bear left along the lane between stone walls to arrive at the Rams Head in Disley. Turn left at the traffic lights, the railway station is 100m on the left.

**Route B: 6 ¾ miles Circular route for train users**

Follow points 1, 2, 3, and 4 then:

6. The circular routes return to the Macclesfield Canal by turning left over a cattle grid past Elmershurst Cottage, straight onto a path with a sign for Middle Wood through a small gate, then follow the track beside a stone wall. Pass alongside a wooded area, cross a wall stile and at the corner of the field carry straight on into the wood before descending and crossing a bridge over a stream. Soon the path emerges from the wood into a field, climb up and stay next to the hedge on the left until a stile onto a farm track is reached, turn right and follow the track. Turn right just before Middlecale farm. The track soon crosses the canal next to a World War II pillbox, which has been decorated and been turned into a workshop of distinction!

7. Go straight ahead up the tow path away from the bridge, crossing the railway bridge then leaving the tow path by bearing left, then turning sharp left on a track marked Ladybrook Valley. Pass through a wooded area then emerge onto a field, cross the field path parallel to the railway on the left to a track, bear left and follow the path which comes out onto Middlewood Way, turn left and the station is a few steps away.

**Route C: 5 ¾ miles Circular route for car users**

Follow points 2, 3, 4 and 6, then point 8.

8. Car users turn alongside the tow path on the opposite side, and then turn right to pass back under the bridge. Follow the tow path along this picturesque stretch of the canal for ¾ miles, past a marina packed with boats back to Nelson Pit.

## Historical Notes

### The Macclesfield Canal

The Macclesfield Canal (Maccy) was one of the last to open in the country in 1831 and was nearly built as a railway. It linked up the Peak Forest and Trent and Mersey canals. The canal was very busy in its heyday, carrying coal, silk and cotton, and stone from the quarries of the Peak District. It also carried fertilizer and night soil from the towns and Manchester for the farmers to use as fertilizer! It closed to commercial traffic in the 1950s. It is now a very popular leisure waterway and forms part of the Cheshire Ring.
More information at: **www.macclesfieldcanal.org.uk/history/index.htm**

### The Nelson Pit Visitor Centre

The centre was built on the site of a former colliery with the assistance of a Heritage Lottery Fund grant, and opened in spring 1999. The colliery was part of the extensive Poynton coal field with 74 pits being sunk. All coal mining ceased in the 1930s.
More information at: **www.brocross.com/poynton/collieries/shaft.htm**

### The Lyme Park Estate

The estate was granted to Sir Thomas Danyers in 1346 and passed to the Legh's of Lyme by marriage in 1388. It remained in the possession of the Legh family until 1946 when it was given to the National Trust. The house dates from the latter part of the 16th century. Modifications were made to it in the 1720s. The house, gardens and park have been used as locations for filming the BBC's *Pride and Prejudice* series.

The monument called The Cage stands on a hill to the east of the approach road to the house. It was originally a hunting lodge and was later used as a park-keeper's cottage and as a lock-up for prisoners.
More information at: **http://en.wikipedia.org/wiki/ Lyme Park**

More of the authors photographs can be found at:
**www.geograph.org.uk/search.php?i=46085442**
Press the tab key marked Map to get the locations

# WALK 3
# Mystical Alderley Edge

---

*Circular walks in this fascinating area of myths and historic interest, together with a visit to a great viewing rocky platform, makes this a good walk for any season.*

| | |
|---|---|
| **Route** | **Alderley Edge – Wizard's Well – Stormy Point – Clock House Wood – Artist's Lane – Castle Rock** |
| **Start/finish** | **Routes A and B: Alderley Edge Railway Station**<br>**Route C: The National Trust car park and public conveniences (pay and display) next to The Wizard restaurant. Alternative free parking is on a layby next to the path entrance to Castle Rock path on Macclesfield Road one mile from Alderley Edge town centre** |
| **Distance and grade** | **Route A: 5½ miles for train users – 852 ft (260m) ascent – Moderate**<br>**Route B: 4½ miles for train users – 774 ft (236m) ascent – Easy**<br>**Route C: 4¼ miles for car users – 688 ft (210m) ascent – Easy** |
| **Map** | **OS Explorer 268 Wilmslow Macclesfield and Congleton** |
| **Terrain** | **Mostly good fairly level woodland paths with a couple of long steep stepped stretches. Field paths have a few stiles and may be muddy after rain. Parts of the train user's route require some walking on quiet suburban roads** |
| **Refreshments** | **The Wizard Tea Room next the National Trust car park. The Drum and Donkey pub/restaurant down Moss Rose off Heyes Lane. Many bars and restaurants in Alderley Edge** |

## Directions to the walk

**Public transport:** Travel to Manchester city centre then catch a train from Manchester Piccadilly. There are 3 trains per hour from Monday to Saturday, and 1 train per hour on Sunday.

**By car**: **Sat Nav**: Postcode SK10 4UB will get you to the Wizard restaurant, the National Trust car park is next door (grid ref: SJ 860772).

**Road Directions**: From the M60 junction 3, follow the A34 to Alderley Edge, then turn left onto the B5087 Macclesfield Road. The Wizard is 1½ miles on the left. The layby is 1 mile on the left. The start of the walk from the NT car park is at point 4. Alternatively from the layby at point 6C.

## Walk Descriptions

This walk is one for all seasons, beautiful in spring and summer and full of birdsong, colourful during the autumn fall, stark and revealing in winter. Despite its modest elevation of 215m (705 feet), the Edge gives a panoramic view eastward over the flat Cheshire Plain. The route follows the eroded, exposed buttresses of red sandstone among mature woodland. There are wonderful views towards the Peak District from Blackstone Edge and Kinder Scout in the north to Sponds Hill, Cats Tor, Shining Tor and the Macclesfield Forest to the southeast. The route takes in such evocative place names such as Wizards Well, Castle Rock, Holy Well, Stormy Point and Clock House Wood, all this together with the remains of ancient copper mines and a site of an ancient beacon, there is something of interest all along the way.

The longer route A walk continues along the lower side of Macclesfield Road on lanes and tracks through farm lands, parts of which are owned by the National Trust, including a small stretch of the aptly named Artists Lane. The route B follows most of route A, but takes a more direct route back to the station. Car users on route C also follow much of route A covering all the main interesting features of this magical area.

## Walk Directions

### Route A: 5½ miles for train users only

1. Leave the station approach road and turn left, then immediately right onto Trafford Road and follow this road through the pleasant suburbs for 300m to a cross roads at Chapel Road and turn left. The road is now named Mottram Road. Continue along until the quaintly named Squirrel's Jump on the right, take this road and follow until the National Trust sign for Alderley Edge. Follow the path through a wooded area, the view steadily opens up on the left to show the first glimpses of the Cheshire Plain. There follows a steep stone and wooden stepped path. I counted 107 steps! At the top the path joins another path from the right, turn left to follow along this terraced path past outcrops of sandstone above the path. Look out for the Wizards Well which lies at the foot of an inscribed buttress of rock. Follow this path then after the outcrops are passed bear right and climb the steps by a pair of posts and go to the left, this is the

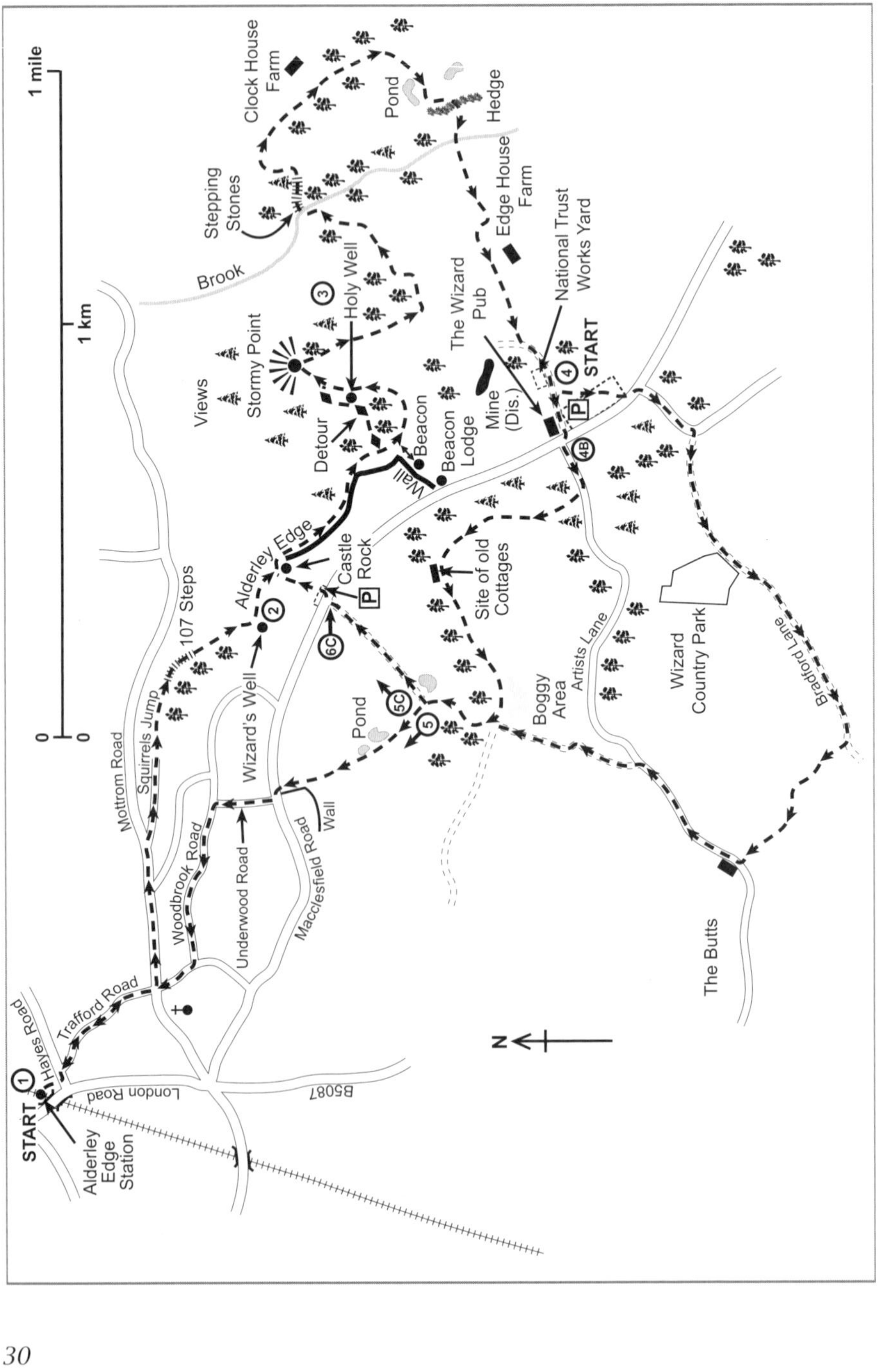

0
0
1 km
1 mile
START
Alderley Edge Station
Hayes Road
Trafford Road
London Road
B5087
Woodbrook Road
Mottrom Road
Squirrels Jump
Underwood Road
Macclesfield Road
Wall
Wizard's Well
107 Steps
Alderley Edge
Castle Rock
Pond
Views
Stormy Point
Detour
Holy Well
Beacon
Beacon Lodge
Wall
Brook
Stepping Stones
Clock House Farm
Pond
Hedge
Edge House Farm
National Trust Works Yard
The Wizard Pub
Mine (Dis.)
START
Site of old Cottages
Boggy Area
Artists Lane
Wizard Country Park
Bradford Lane
The Butts
N

site of Castle Rock, a prominent outcrop with commanding views over Cheshire's plain.

**This is where car users join the route to complete the circuit from point 6C.**

2. Descend again to follow the path along the edge of crags then keep on ahead past a path descending left.

   (This path is an alternative route which goes down steps and crosses a footbridge then past the Holy Well before ascending back to the main path.)

   Climb up to a level path past a castellated wall on the right, turn right to follow the wall, climbing up to the highest point of the edge where the site of a long-gone beacon was located. An engraved tablet set on a stone proclaims this as the Armada Beacon, almost certainly used in 1588 to warn of the sighting of the Spanish Armada. Descend back to continue along the main path and bear left following the path past waymarkers.The path ascends a few steps then emerges out onto a large clearing of flat sandstone, this being a natural viewing area called Stormy Point. Take in the views and spot the landmarks of Taxal Edge and the Shining Tor/Cats Tor ridge.

The view from Stormy Point

3. Having had a break, bear right on a broad level track, ignoring the track off to the right, to a junction of paths at a gate, turn left and follow the signs for Hare Hill. The path is now in Dickens Wood where Tree Creepers may be seen around here spiralling up tree trunks looking for insects in crevices on the bark. The path descends steadily down into a small gorge with a brook running through it. Ignore the path off to the left, the path gradually descends to the brook then crosses it by stepping stones.

The stepping stones in Dickens Wood

Keep right to ascend again up the steep stepped path through the woodland, the path twists and turns then descends to pass Clock House Farm before ascending once again past a National Trust sign to emerge next to kissing gate onto a field. Turn right through the gate and cross the field to a gate with a waymarker near a pond. Pass through the gate and walk between two ponds, then go left along the hedge. Look out for a stile on the right where the path bends left, cross the stile and take the path along the fenced path. At the next stile, cross and join a track following a hedge and at a gate go over a stile on the right. Turn left at the next stile then follow the path up to another stile and fenced track past Edge House Farm. Cross a gravel track onto a narrow fenced path and turn left onto a broad track at the end. Follow the track to the National Trust works yard where a path on the left through a gate leads to the car park or continue straight on for the tea room.

**This is the start of the walk for car users from the NT car park.**

4. Turn left to follow the far side of the car park and bear right behind the public conveniences along a path through the wood onto the main road almost opposite Bradford Lane. Carefully cross the road and follow the lane to a junction, turn right to follow Bradford Lane. After passing the Wizard Caravan Park on your right the lane becomes a bridleway. Follow the path past a few farm houses on the right then at a waymarked footpath sign on the right, turn right to follow the path. This follows the

hedge alongside a field, then through a tunnel of dense woodland to emerge onto Artists Lane, turn right up the lane. After 250m a broad gated waymarked path is on the left. Turn down this path through woodland then past an open sandy area, to a crossroads of footpaths in a wooded area. Carry straight on into the wood, to emerge at another crossroads of paths, turn left to a gate and National Trust sign.

**Car users continue onto point 5C.**

5. Pass through the gate and bear 45 degrees left to follow the path across the open field towards a small copse of gorse around a pond. The path passes on the left of the pond and continues towards a wall around a residential area. A pair of posts on the right of the wall show the entrance to a ginnel which leads through to Macclesfield Road, almost opposite Underwood Road. Cross over and follow this very attractive road to its end, then turn left down Woodbrook Road which is even more attractive as it is cobbled for much of its way, passing large properties with beautiful gardens. The road ends at Trafford Road, cross over and turn right. Follow the road through more attractive residential areas with more gorgeous gardens, at a crossroads continue straight on Trafford Road which comes out onto Heyes Lane. Turn left, Alderley Edge Station is a few metres on the right.

## Route B: 4½ miles for train users

Follow points 1 to 3 then continue on from point 4B.

4B. Turn right in front of The Wizard, cross the road carefully and turn into Artists Lane. Follow the road for 80m and turn right onto a path into the woods, follow this alongside a field boundary, shortly after the path bends left, turn right through the woods to emerge in a clearing. Turn left downhill back into the woods and descend the unmarked path to emerge into a chaotic area of disturbed ground, an interpretation board gives the history of Hagg Cottages c.1930 which are now totally demolished. Pass this and continue on, bearing right at a marker post past a boggy area until a crossing of paths, turn right before a gate back into the wood and follow the path to emerge at another crossroads of paths, turn left to another gate and National Trust sign. Follow the walk back to the station from point 5.

## Route C: 4½ miles for car users

From the NT car park the start is from point 4. Continue onto the following points 5C and 6C.

Layby users start from point 6C. Continue onto points 2, 3, 4, followed by 5C.

5C. Turn right before the gate, and continue along the path with a narrow border of trees, between fields. The path emerges at a stile onto the main Macclesfield Road opposite the layby and the access path to Castle Rock. Cross the road carefully.

6C. From the layby follow the path past the National Trust sign up to the open flat top of Castle Rock. Descend down to the terraced level path and turn left to follow the path around the buttress of sandstone, after 100m look out for The Wizards Well at the foot of an inscribed buttress of rock. Return the way you came back to Castle Rock. From here follow the directions for points 2 and 3, to return to the NT car park.

## Historical Notes

**Alderley Edge** is a unique place with many myths and legends which are reflected in the names given to the rock formations and wells. This is probably due to the copper and lead mining activity which has gone on here for centuries, the greatest era was in the 19th century. Working in the labyrinth of mine workings, with only candlelight for illumination, no doubt helped invoke stories of the supernatural. The most famous of these legends conjured the name of the Wizard given to a natural spring (well) and a cave hidden on the Edge which is reputably guarded by a wizard. This has never been found, but an effigy of a wizard has been etched in the rock above the Wizards Well.

More information at **www.alderleyedge.org**

More of the authors photographs can be found at:

**www.geograph.org.uk/search.php?i=46085468** and

**www.geograph.org.uk/search.php?i=47678970**

Press the tab key marked Map to get the locations.

# WALK 4
# Styal Country Park and the River Bollin

*Circular walks following the course of the River Bollin through Styal Country Park with a visit to Quarry Bank Mill.*

| | |
|---|---|
| Route | Styal – Northern Woods – River Bollin – Morley – Twinnies Bridge – Quarry Bank Mill |
| Start/finish | All routes: Quarry Bank Mill car park |
| Distance and grade | Route A: 5½ miles full Circular route – 462 ft (141m) ascent – Moderate<br>Route B: 3¾ miles Northern Woods route – 390 ft (119m) ascent – Moderate<br>Route C: 3¼ miles Twinnies Bridge route – 242 ft (74m) ascent – Easy |
| Map | OS Explorer 268 Wilmslow Macclesfield and Congleton |
| Terrain | A and B are mainly level, but have several stretches of steep steps, and some parts of the route can be muddy after rain. Route C is an easy level route most of the way on well-defined footpaths and tracks. All routes follow short stretches of roadside |
| Refreshments | The National Trust Quarry Bank Mill Café and ice cream vans. The Honey Bee pub at Morley |

## Directions to the walk

**Public transport:** Travel to Manchester city centre, and then catch a train from Piccadilly Station, where a frequent train service runs to Manchester Airport, some of which run directly from Wigan, Bolton and Liverpool. The number 200 bus service runs from the airport station which conveniently travels the short distance to Styal and the Quarry Bank Mill car park. These services are from Monday to Sunday. There are fewer direct Sunday train services but there is frequent service from Piccadilly to the airport. Check traveline for the services in your area.

**By car: Sat Nav**: Postcode SK9 4LA will get you to the National Trust Quarry Bank Mill car park (grid ref: SJ 836830).
**Road directions**:From the M56 junction 5, follow the signs for Cheadle and Styal past the airport. Turn right onto B5166 for Quarry Bank Mill. Follow the brown signs through Styal, the turning for Quarry Bank Mill is on the right.

## Walk Description

The full circular route is a lovely walk which is especially attractive in late spring when bluebells may be seen along much of the way. It follows a stretch of the River Bollin which meanders through the National Trust Styal country estate where the fascinating Quarry Bank Mill may be visited. Routes A and B both pass by the picturesque Styal village, then on paths that follow the meandering River Bollin, crossing it via Oxbow Bridge and Chapel Bridge. There is always something of interest as the routes pass through a varied landscape with mixed woodland, open fields and the beautiful estate park.

The shorter route C route avoids the steep steps and follows a more level route. It takes in the south part of the route A through the Styal estate past farms and a 'Green Lane' then along the bank of the attractive wooded Pigginshawe Brook before passing over Twinnies Bridge, followed by the path alongside the River Bollin back to Quarry Bank Mill.

## Walk Directions

### Route A: 5½ mile full circular route

1. From the entrance to the car park, turn left down the drive towards the Mill, in a few steps a sign indicates the path to Styal Village. Follow this gravelled path to pass through a gate then between fields to another gate, cross a track then continue on through another gate and carry on down the path alongside woodland. The path emerges next to Styal Village Cross. The mill workers housing called Oak Cottages, with their cobbled streets and former village shop, can be seen straight ahead and are well worth a visit before returning to the cross. Take the path alongside the entrance to Norcliffe Chapel, passing an information board, before entering the Northern

Styal Village Cross

Woods. At a fork in the path keep right of a small gulley on the left which deepens as the path slowly descends. Pass a metal bridge that spans the gorge, but do not cross. The path comes to the first of many stone steps, descend these then turn to descend two more flights of steps, which leads onto Chapel Bridge.

Cross the bridge and walk steeply uphill to a junction of paths, turn right to climb steeply for a short distance, the path bends left. Hereabouts is the overgrown Folly Bridge that may be seen below the path, soon after a Giant Redwood tree comes into view.This was planted by the Greg family, the mill owners, and is one of many exotic species planted at Styal. Carry on through the broad leaf woodland, then descend a flight of steps which drops down through evergreen larch trees to emerge alongside the river on the right at a junction. Carry on straight ahead following the river upstream to the Oxbow Bridge.

Riverside path in Styal Country Park

2. Cross over the bridge and bear left then up a steep flight of steps through dense woodland and rhododendrons, this is quickly followed by equally steep descending steps through Giants Castle Wood. Soon the path comes

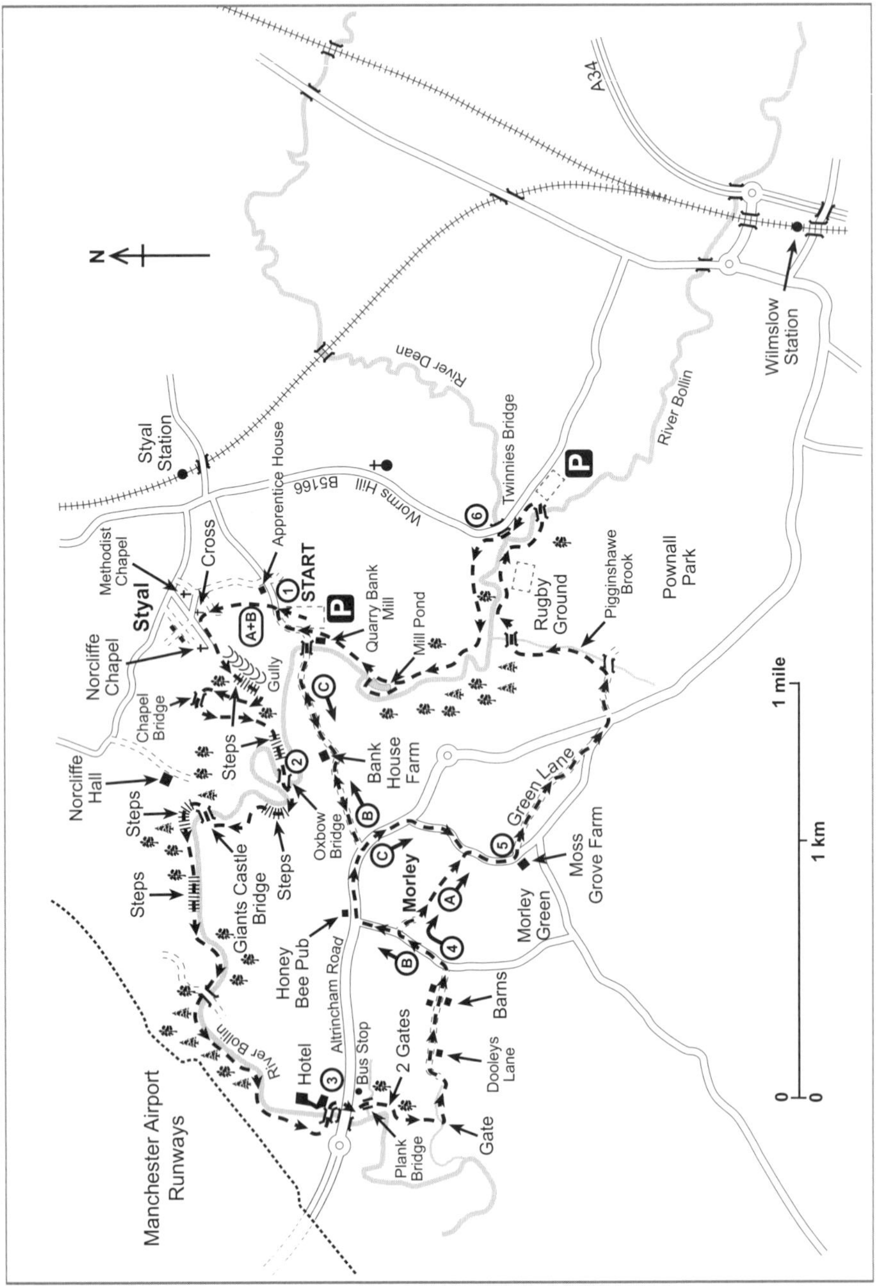

N
A34
Styal Station
Styal
Methodist Chapel
Cross
Apprentice House
Worms Hill B5166
River Dean
Twinnies Bridge
River Bollin
Wilmslow Station
1 START
A+B
Quarry Bank Mill
Mill Pond
Norcliffe Chapel
Gully
Chapel Bridge
Steps
Norcliffe Hall
Giants Castle Bridge
Oxbow Bridge
Bank House Farm
Rugby Ground
Pigginshawe Brook
Pownall Park
Green Lane
Moss Grove Farm
Morley Green
Morley
Honey Bee Pub
Altrincham Road
Barns
Dooleys Lane
2 Gates
Bus Stop
Hotel
Plank Bridge
Gate
Manchester Airport Runways
1 mile
1 km
0
0

to Giant's Castle Bridge near a small weir. Look out for the bricked archway on the left far bank; this is the tailrace tunnel from Greg's waterwheel. Cross over the bridge and climb yet another flight of steep steps, and then descend once again to a nice level path which follows the river before emerging from the wood to pass alongside field boundaries. Follow the path which re-enters a wooded area at a broad farm access bridge over the river, carry on past this to follow the delightful riverside path. The path climbs away from the river to emerge at a bridleway. Keep to the riverside path which runs parallel to the bridleway and follow alongside the river, taking care at a slippy eroded section. The path emerges onto a road, turn left to cross the bridge which leads to the Holiday Inn on Altrincham Road.

3. Walk through the hotel car park and cross the busy A538, turn right past a bus stop then pass through a waymarked kissing gate. Follow the path across a field towards a wood, cross over a plank bridge through a boggy area with Gunnera-like wild plants, then pass through another gate, then up a bank through the wood to another gate and straight cross another large field. The path comes out at a brook and a footbridge. Cross this and pass through another gate and turn left across the field. Keep to the left boundary and turn left at a muddy patch to round a fence corner which leads on to a stile where the Bollin Way sign indicates the way towards Shady Grove. Follow the path between hedges to arrive at a track past a house onto Dooley's Lane. The track passes three large impressive brick barns where a flock of house martins were seen.

4. Follow the lane to the main road and turn left and follow the road for about 250m to a waymarked sign on the right, with a sign for Chelsea cottage.

**At this point the shorter Northern Woods route is followed by going to point B.**

Turn down the drive, which becomes cobbled then pass a set of white cottages. To the right of the last garage at the end of the road cross a stile and cross a large field in the direction indicated. At the far side another stile is crossed. Carry on ahead crossing another field to another stile onto a lane (Nansmoss lane). Turn right to follow the lane to a junction with a track opposite Moss Grove Farm.

5. Turn left to follow the waymarked 'Bollin Way' an ancient 'green lane' track, which passes through gorse bushes, and a gate is passed before emerging onto Mobberley Road. Turn left then at a junction with the busy A538, cross the main road straight onto the waymarked Bollin Way track.
   Follow the track to just before a footbridge where the waymarked Bollin Way is taken on the left. This lovely path follows the winding course of Pigginshawe Brook through a wooded steep ravine with the pungent smell of wild garlic, and carpeted in bluebells in late spring. This stretch of the walk is one to savour. Eventually the path descends to a boggy area where boardwalks have been conveniently laid where many bog plant species can be seen. The path then passes through the woodland between a sports field and the course of the River Bollin to a footbridge over the river, which is crossed before turning left to another footbridge alongside the road bridge over the River Dean. This is called Twinnies Bridge and spans the confluence of the rivers Dean and Bollin.

6. Take the path to the left to follow the river, this passes through woodland then at a mill pond alongside the river a path on the left may be taken to skirt the mill pond. Carry on past a weir before re-joining the main path which emerges at the mill yard of Quarry Bank Mill where a well-earned rest and refreshments can be had. The mill has many attractions such as a fully working waterwheel, steam engines, weaving machinery and demonstrations, museum pieces, and a fascinating history of the mill is told with of the working lives of those who worked here. There is also a garden which is being extended and revised, all in a lovely setting in the valley of the River Bollin. To return to the car park walk up the cobbled drive beside the Mill.

## Route B: 3¾ mile Northern Woods route

Follow points 1 to 4 then continue on from point B.

B. This route continues from point 4 by walking straight on past the sign for Chelsea Cottage along Morley Green Road to the major Altrincham Road, where opposite the road junction is the Honey Bee pub. If not visiting the pub turn right and stay on the tarmacked path and follow the road for around 200m and cross the road carefully at a lowered kerb crossing. Opposite the crossing, pass a 'Restricted Byway' sign that marks the entrance to a rough track, pass through a gate to follow the track which leads on past Bank House Farm. Pass through a gate then turn left, then right behind the last building where the track becomes a delightful path leading downhill with views over the Styal Country Park. The final stretch leads on through a gate with the river in view and the Quarry Bank Mill gardens on the opposite side. Finally the path passes the entrance to the gardens and crosses the stone bridge next to the Mill. The car park may be reached by crossing the bridge turning left up the driveway which brings you back to the car park entrance on the right.

### Route C: 3¼ mile Twinnies Bridge route

The route starts at point C.

C. The Twinnies Bridge route starts at the car park entrance, turn left to descend the drive down to the mill. Turn right immediately before the Mill and follow the road over the stone bridge, pass the entrance to the gardens and follow the path uphill, continue on and pass through a gate. The views over the gardens and the river in the Styal Country Park to the right open up as you climb. The path emerges next to Bank House Farm, turn left and right then pass through a gate and continue on alongside the farm onto a rough track. Pass through another gate and follow the track to the main Altrincham Road. Cross the road carefully and turn left to follow the tarmacked path for about 150m then turn right onto Nansmoor Lane. Follow the lane for 300m to a waymarked Bollin Way 'green lane' track on the left opposite Moss grove Farm.

**Continue on to finish the walk by following points 5, and 6.**

## Historical Notes

**Quarry Bank Mill** has been featured in the BBC's drama *The Mill* and is a fine example of Britain's industrial revolution. It was located in Styal because of the availability of a reliable source of water supply from the River Bollin, essential for driving a waterwheel. The first wooden wheel was installed in 1784 and could generate 10 horsepower. The Mill was built to spin cotton yarn using the waterframe, which was the latest technology of the time.

The Gregs were forward thinking mill owners and experimented with all the latest innovations, they introduced power looms in 1838 in weaving sheds, production peaked with over 400 looms in use, weaving coarse cotton cloth.

From the beginning, the Mill was highly dependent upon child apprentices, employing up to 100 who lodged at the Apprentice House. With mechanisation the apprentice system became less economical and numbers began to decline with the apprentice system finished 1847.

Although by today's standards working conditions were very severe, at the time they were undoubtedly better than average, with the Gregs being regarded as good employers.

The mill, like the whole spinning and weaving industry, suffered from competition of cheap imports and, in 1959, the mill closed for commercial production.

The mill was bequeathed to the National Trust by the Gregs in 1939, and remains a working Cotton Mill producing over 9,000m (10,000 yards) of cloth each year, where visitors can observe the 19th Century textile machines working and meet skilled cotton workers.

More of the history of the mill can be found at **www.spinningtheweb.org.uk** published by Manchester City council.

More of the authors photographs can be found at:
**www.geograph.org.uk/search.php?i=46085628** and
**www.geograph.org.uk/search.php?i=46085707**
Press the tab key marked Map to get the locations

# WALK 5
# Anderton and Great Budworth

*Linear and circular walks along a canal towpath, visiting historic heritage sites, country parks and a village of character.*

| | |
|---|---|
| **Route** | **Lostock Gralam – Lion Salt Works – Great Budworth – Marbury Country Park – Anderton Lift Visitor Centre – Anderton Nature Park – Northwich** |
| **Start/finish** | **Linear Routes A and B: By train: Start: Lostock Gralam Railway Station. Finish : Northwich Railway Station. By bus number 45: Start: Manchester Road, Lostock Gralam. Finish: Northwich Bus rank in Watling Street**<br>**Circular Route C: By car: Start/Finish: Anderton Boat Lift Visitor Centre. By bus number 46: Start: New Road, Anderton. Finish: Northwich Bus rank in Watling Street** |
| **Distance and grade** | **Route A: 8½ miles by train (7½ miles by bus) – 380 ft (116m) ascent – Moderate**<br>**Route B: 5¾ miles by train (5 miles by bus ) – 239 ft (73m) ascent – Moderate**<br>**Route C: 6½ miles by car ( 8 miles by bus) – 370 ft (113m) ascent – Moderate** |
| **Map** | **OS Explorer 267 Northwich and Delamere Forest** |
| **Terrain** | **Routes A and C follow level, well defined and marked paths, with few stiles. Some field paths may be muddy and care is needed in navigating through Marbury Park. There are a couple of stretches of roadside walking. Route B follows easy, level, well marked paths and a couple of stretches of roadside walking** |
| **Refreshments** | **Anderton Lift Visitor Centre, the George and Dragon pub at Great Budworth, many pubs and cafés in Northwich. Public conveniences and picnic area in Marbury Park** |

## Directions to the walks:

**By train**: Travel to Manchester city centre, then catch a train from Piccadilly Station for the hourly service to Lostock Gralam. This service runs from Monday to Saturday, on Sunday there is a two hourly service. Return from Northwich station to Manchester Piccadilly on the same service. This rail service may also be used by walkers joining trains from the Chester direction.

**By bus**: Travel to Warrington bus station then catch either bus number 45 or 46, which together have an hourly service to Northwich, Monday to Saturday. The number 45 goes via Lostock Gralam, where routes A or B may be joined at point 1, by alighting at Manchester Road in Lostock Gralam and continue to follow the road to the canal. Bus number 46 goes via Anderton where route C may be joined by alighting at New Road in Anderton, continue to follow the road over the canal bridge and turn left on a path down to the towpath. Follow the canal to the Anderton Visitor Centre, continue onto the circular route from point C. In all cases it is best to finish the walk in Northwich town centre at Watling Street to catch either bus back to Warrington.

**By car**: **Sat Nav** : Postcode CW9 6FW will get you to the Anderton Boat Lift Visitor Centre (grid ref : SJ 648754).

**Road directions**: From the M56, junction10, take the A49 for Northwich, turn left onto A533 for Barnton. Follow the brown signage. There is a charge for parking. The walk starts at point C.

## Walk Description

The Anderton Lift Visitor Centre is a fascinating, well organised and deservedly popular venue which merits a day out in itself. The circular route C starts from the centre along the towpath of the Trent and Mersey Canal which is followed to the old Lion Salt Works, then along mainly field paths to the picturesque village of Great Budworth and the George and Dragon pub. From here more field tracks are followed with views over Budworth Mere, then on to Marbury Country Park, an ideal spot for a picnic in the woodland next to the mere and to check out its renowned bird life. From here paths leading through Hopyards Wood, part of the Mersey Forest, are followed back to the canal and on to Anderton. The walk is on flat, mostly good paths and few stiles, but lots of kissing gates!

Walkers on linear route A follow much the same as route C but an additional extension on paths through Anderton Nature Park and Carey Park is made to reach Northwich railway station, or the bus stand in Watling Street.

The shorter linear route B follows the canal, visiting the highlights of the Lion Salt Works and The Anderton Lift Visitor Centre, before returning via the canal towpath and paths through the aforementioned parks back to Northwich railway station or Watling Street bus stands.

## Walk Directions

### Route A: 8½ mile Linear route for train users (7½ miles for bus users)

1. Following the scenic rail route through Knutsford from Manchester, alight at Lostock Gralam and from the station access road, turn left over the railway bridge to follow Station Road to the traffic lights on Manchester Road and turn left.

   **Bus users start their walk at the first bus stop past the Slow and Easy Pub on Manchester Road.**

   Follow the road for 350m to the canal bridge, cross the road carefully and descend the steps to the towpath of the Trent and Mersey Canal and proceed straight ahead. The canal crosses an aqueduct over the Wincham Brook then bends left, the rural scenery soon gives way to light industry, then Northwich Football Club is passed near a footbridge. Continue on, passing under a road bridge, then at the next road bridge No.193, pass under the bridge and leave the canal bank via the steps up to the road.

2. Turn right, cross and follow the road for 50m to the brown signed Lion Salt Works. These are the remains of the old Lion Salt Works, allegedly the last in Britain to produce salt by the traditional evaporation method using brine pans. It was closed in 1986 and was featured on a television programme about worthy sites for spending money on to preserve them. It seemed to lie in limbo for some years, but on their website are plans to turn it into a museum in spring 2015.

   Return to the canal bridge, and follow the road to pass between two meres and the memorable Loony Lins furniture outlet. Just past this turn left at the waymarked sign onto a farm track, then onto field path via a metal kissing gate. This is the first of many passed on the route. Follow the path which passes alongside first a hedge then across a field then through gap in another hedge and between fields across a farm track, then alongside a hedge backing a residential estate to emerge onto a main road (Marston Lane). The path passes through about seven gates on its way.

   Turn left and stay on the verge then, where possible, carefully cross the road to the pathway on the opposite side. Follow the road for about 300m and take a footpath via another metal kissing gate in the right hand hedge and cross the field path which climbs then follows alongside a hedge. At a break in this hedge, turn left to emerge on the High Street of the characterful village of Great Budworth. Turn right towards the church to

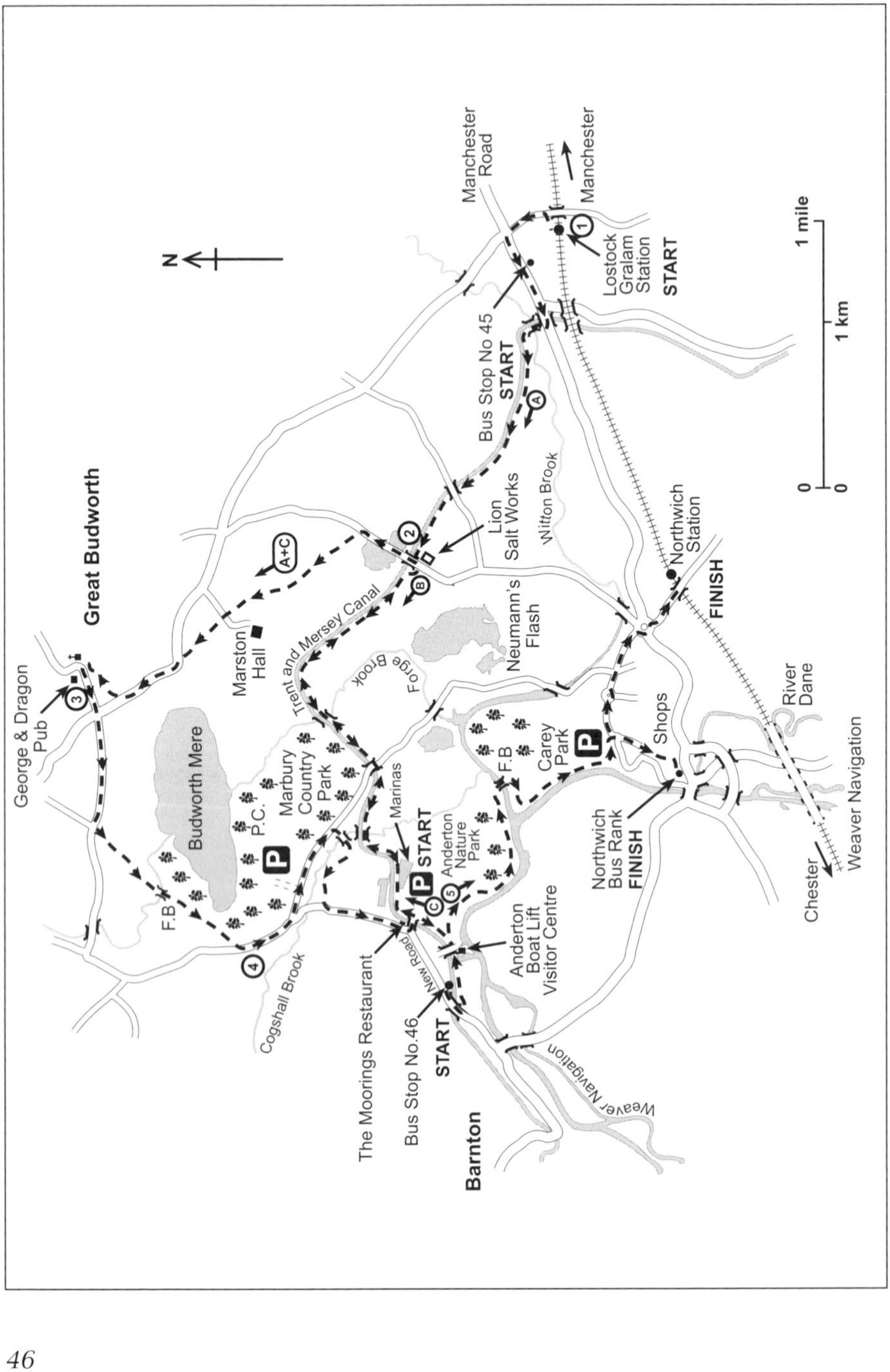
N
Great Budworth
George & Dragon Pub
3
Budworth Mere
F.B
4
Cogshall Brook
P.C.
P
Marbury Country Park
Marston Hall
A+C
Trent and Mersey Canal
Forge Brook
Neumann's Flash
B
2
Lion Salt Works
Witton Brook
Bus Stop No 45
START
A
Manchester Road
Manchester
1
Lostock Gralam Station
START
1 mile
1 km
0
0
Northwich Station
FINISH
River Dane
Weaver Navigation
Chester
Northwich Bus Rank
FINISH
Shops
P
Carey Park
F.B
Marinas
P
START
Anderton Nature Park
5
C
Anderton Boat Lift Visitor Centre
The Moorings Restaurant
New Road
Bus Stop No.46
START
Barnton
Weaver Navigation

where the George and Dragon will be found in a lovely setting in the centre of the village. Trestle tables are provided, a good place to soak up the atmosphere and for a spot of refreshment.

3. On leaving the pub retrace the route through the village, taking in the views of the black and white houses and cobbled side roads, at the end is Warrington Road at a crossroads. Cross and go straight on and follow Budworth Lane, until a waymarked path opposite a road junction signed Budworth Heath. Turn left and follow this path into a wood. On emerging from the wood pass a kissing gate into a field, cross this and maintain the same direction, cross a small footbridge and continue onward across more fields dotted with trees. Budworth Mere is in view on the left for much of the walk along this stretch, which has a further three more of the ubiquitous kissing gates before emerging onto Marbury Road.

4. Turn left and continue on Marbury Road past Marbury Hall Nurseries entrance, carry on another 200m to reach the entrance to Marbury Country Park on the left. A short walk leads to a left turn and a barrier with a Marbury Country Park sign, carry on to toilet facilities and an information centre next to the lake. There are picnic tables, perhaps a good spot for lunch. It is particularly noted for birdwatching and the variety of birdlife recorded here. There are numerous paths and tracks in the park, so following a visit to the lake, make your way back to the entrance sign and turn left down the No Entry signed lane. Follow this tarmacked lane, look out for a path on the right, turn onto the path which steps down into the wood then follow Marbury Brook (on some maps called Cogshall Brook). The path is joined by another path, turn right onto this to cross the brook via a wooden footbridge. Follow the path out of the wood up to a newly made path that skirts around an open area. Turn left and follow the path as it twists and turns, until it emerges onto Marbury Road, turn left then left again past The Moorings Restaurant. The road

Wood carved bench in Marbury Country Park

crosses the canal, descend down the path on the right and follow the towpath ahead to the Anderton Visitor Centre.

The visitor centre is well worth browsing with a lot of information and lots to see. The history and workings of the Anderton Boat Lift is well explained, this together with the facilities on offer could take a good deal of your time! There are boat trips through the lift where a descent on a boat to the River Weaver and back up to the canal may be made, but I suspect time would not allow completing the walk and time to appreciate all that's on offer here. Perhaps this calls for another days outing!

**This is the start and finishing point for car users.**

5. To complete the walk for train/bus user's, return along the towpath to the large car park, turn right to the back of the car park where a wide path leads into Anderton Nature Park, keep right at the giant ornamental dragonflies, follow this path as it descends down alongside the River Weaver. Where it turns away from the river follow a smaller path alongside the river to a footbridge, cross this and follow the path up to a wide path and turn right. This is Carey park, continue alongside the river, the path

The Anderton Boat Lift

bends left away from the river then at a T-junction of paths turn right to an entrance to a car park on the main road.

**Bus users** turn right onto Leicester street and follow the road to the pedestrianized precinct, continue straight on, following signs for the market through to Watling Street, where the bus stands will be found on the right.

**Train users** turn left onto Leicester Street, follow this road to a roundabout and carry straight on, then at a large roundabout go straight on following the sign for Northwich Station, the station is 100m on the left.

### Route B: 6¼ mile linear route for train users (5 miles for bus users)

Follow point 1 and point 2 up to the Lion Salt Works, then instead of following the road over the canal bridge, return to the towpath and carry on alongside the canal. The canal passes an open stretch then passes farmland on one side and mixed woodland on the other. The canal bends sharp left and enters a more densely wooded stretch where a footbridge is reached giving access to Marbury Country Park. Carry on under a small road bridge then shortly the canal bends left and right, past large marinas on both sides of the canal. After another bend and a couple more bridges the Anderton Boat Lift Centre is reached with all its attractions. The route then follows on from point 5.

### Route C: 6½ mile Circular route for car users (8 miles for bus users)

From the car park, turn right along the canal towpath under the car park access bridge and walk past the two large marinas on either side of the canal. The canal skirts around Marbury Park and under a road bridge and then a footbridge, where the canal passes through pleasant woodland on either side. A more open stretch follows past farmland on one side and mixed woodland on the other before reaching bridge No. 193 at Marston. Join point 2 of the walk by climbing the steps to the road.

Follow on to points 3 and 4 to return to the car park at the Anderton Lift Visitor Centre.

**Bus users** complete their walk by following on to point 5 to catch a bus in Watling Street.

## Historical Notes

### Marbury Country Park

A former residence of the Smith-Barry family, Marbury Country Park is now managed by Cheshire West and Chester Council as a country park. The walks

and trails take visitors through the historical landscape which includes the magnificent lime avenues, arboretum and raised terraces, which provide glimpses of Budworth Mere.
More information at
**www.northwichwoodlands.org.uk/woodland/marbury.shtml**

## Anderton Boat Lift

The Anderton Boat Lift is an ingenious piece of engineering, towering above the banks of the River Weaver, it resembles a monstrous iron insect. It was built by Edwin Clark in 1875 to lift barges the 50 feet between the River Weaver and the Trent & Mersey Canal. It makes use of the counterbalancing of the water filled sealed tanks, to avoid the loss of water necessary when using conventional locks, and minimising the power required to raise and lower canal boats.
More information at **www.canalrivertrust.org.uk/Anderton-boat-lift**

## Lion Saltworks

See **www.lionsaltworks.org**

More of the authors photographs can be found at:
**www.geograph.org.uk/search.php?i=46085951**
Press the tab key marked Map to get the locations

# WALK 6
# Etherow Valley Woodland Walk

*A walk of great variety through the peaceful wooded valley of the River Etherow with its artefacts of the cotton industry, and the viewing points from a country park.*

| | |
|---|---|
| Route | Broadbottom – Great Wood – Idle Hill – Werneth Low Visitor Centre – Back Wood – Botham's Hall – Cown Edge Way – Lymefield Visitor Centre |
| Start/finish | Circular route by train: Broadbottom railway Station<br>Circular route by car: Lymefield Visitor Centre |
| Distance and grade | Circular routes for both train and car users:<br>7 miles – 1508 ft (460m) ascent – Moderate/Hard<br>4 miles – 715 ft (218m) ascent – Easy |
| Map | OS Outdoor Leisure 1 The Dark Peak District |
| Terrain | Mostly good well marked but undulating paths with a stiff climb up Idle Hill. Some field paths have stiles and are steep and slippery when wet. The short route avoids the steepest parts up to Lower Higham Visitor Centre |
| Refreshments | Lymefield Visitor Centre and Lower Higham Visitor Centre, Lymefield Garden Centre and the Cheshire Cheese pub in Broadbottom outside the entrance to the visitor centre |

## Directions to the start of walks

**By train**: Travel to Manchester city centre. There is a daily, half hourly service from Manchester Piccadilly for the half hourly service to Broadbottom.

**By car**: **Sat Nav**: Postcode: SK14 6AG will get you to Lymefield Visitor Centre (grid ref: SJ 996935).

**Road directions**: From the end of the M67 towards Glossop, take the second exit onto the A57/Hyde Road, after ½ mile turn right onto Market Street. Keep straight on at Broadbottom Road. Follow this road for 2 miles past the railway station then under the railway bridge, the visitor centre is on the right. Start the walk at point A.

## Walk Description

Broadbottom station is conveniently placed for the start of this walk, sited to serve this stone built village. With a chequered history of mills; first there was corn, then wool, followed by cotton mills, these were powered by the waters of the River Etherow. This is a great countryside walk which passes stone farmsteads and cottages along woodland paths with good views, belying the fact that it's so close to Manchester's suburbs.

The route starts near the River Etherow and follows it for a short distance, then, after passing the timeless hamlet of Hodgefold, soon enters The Great Wood. After a stretch along farm tracks with fine views, the route passes through Back Wood before a steep path through heather up to Idle Hill and the view point called Windy Harbour. A short stretch of the Tameside Trail is followed up to the Cenotaph and a viewing point at Werneth Low Country Park where a refreshment break can be taken. The route then returns by another path through Back Wood, across the River Etherow and a lovely stretch of the Cown Edge Way with more superb views, then by way of a small wooded valley back across the River Etherow. Finally there is a visit to the Broad Mill Heritage and Lymefield Visitor Centre. The short route omits the path through Back Wood and the steep climb up Idle Hill to the Werneth Low Visitor Centre.

## Walk Directions

**Car users** start at point A. Leave the car park and turn left then right in front of Lymefield Terrace. Carry on along the gravel path through the Broad Mills Heritage site to the footbridge over the River Etherow. Do not cross the river but carry on up the track to follow the signs for Hodgefold. Turn left in front of the terraced houses, then climb up a track above the river gorge, past an outstanding row of terraced housing called Summerbottom Terrace, then continue onto point 1 where indicated.

1. **Train users** leave Broadbottom station by the exit from Manchester bound platform and turn left on Moss Lane. Go down a tree covered path to a row of terraced cottages, turning right down onto a wide track at Summerbottom Terrace next to the river Etherow in a gorge on your left.

   **Car users join the route here.**

   Follow the unmarked lane (Hodge Lane) which is an old packhorse route for carrying salt from Cheshire to Yorkshire. The path descends to the river. Look out for the vats on the left once used for dyeing the cloth made at Hodge Print Works, then on past a row of cottages to a cross roads, carry straight on past another row of cottages. This is Hodgefold. Carry straight on past the last cottage to follow the signposted path into the Great Wood. Cross a metal bridge to follow the path straight on through the wood up some steps and over a planked bridge. Follow the path out of the wood alongside a fenced field to a gate on the left of a cattle grid on a broad track.

2. Turn left onto the track and cross two cattle grids, follow the track to Botham's Hall, For the short route go past the hall and turn left then follow onto point 4.

   Just before the Hall turn right through a gate past a pig sty to take the grassy path into Back Wood, carry straight on ignoring the path on the left. The delightful woodland path follows and crosses a brook on footbridges a couple of times before emerging from the wood. Keep to the left hand side of the field to a track, turn right along the track to a gate and stile, cross the stile and bear left to cross a field to a narrow lane (Apple Street). Turn right and follow this for a few metres, then turn left up an unmarked track, cross a stile on the left into a field. Keep to the right hedge and climb steeply up to a boundary wall stile at a signpost, cross this to climb up a partly sunken path through heather to Idle Hill. Near the top, pass a large bungalow to reach Windy Harbour at a narrow lane (Cock Brow).

3. Stop here to admire the view over Tameside, Broadbottom, Longdendale, and the Dark Peak District. Turn right after a few steps to follow the track between two old stone gateposts on the right down to the cenotaph and the toposcope viewpoint indicating all the landmarks around. Then if you wish to pay a visit to the visitor centre carry on, forking right over a stile to the Lower Higham visitor centre. It's worthwhile to have a browse and perhaps have some refreshment before retracing your steps to Windy Harbour.

   Otherwise retrace your steps from the cenotaph to Windy Harbour. From here go left down the narrow lane 'Cock Brow', follow it as it bends left steeply until it levels out. Just before Howards Barn look out for the hidden track on the right where a large growth of pink flowering Himalayan Balsam (which occurs frequently in summer on this walk), is passed before going down a muddy path through a fantastic tunnel of holly bushes. At the end cross another track to a stile, cross this and follow the sunken path down to another broad track and turn right

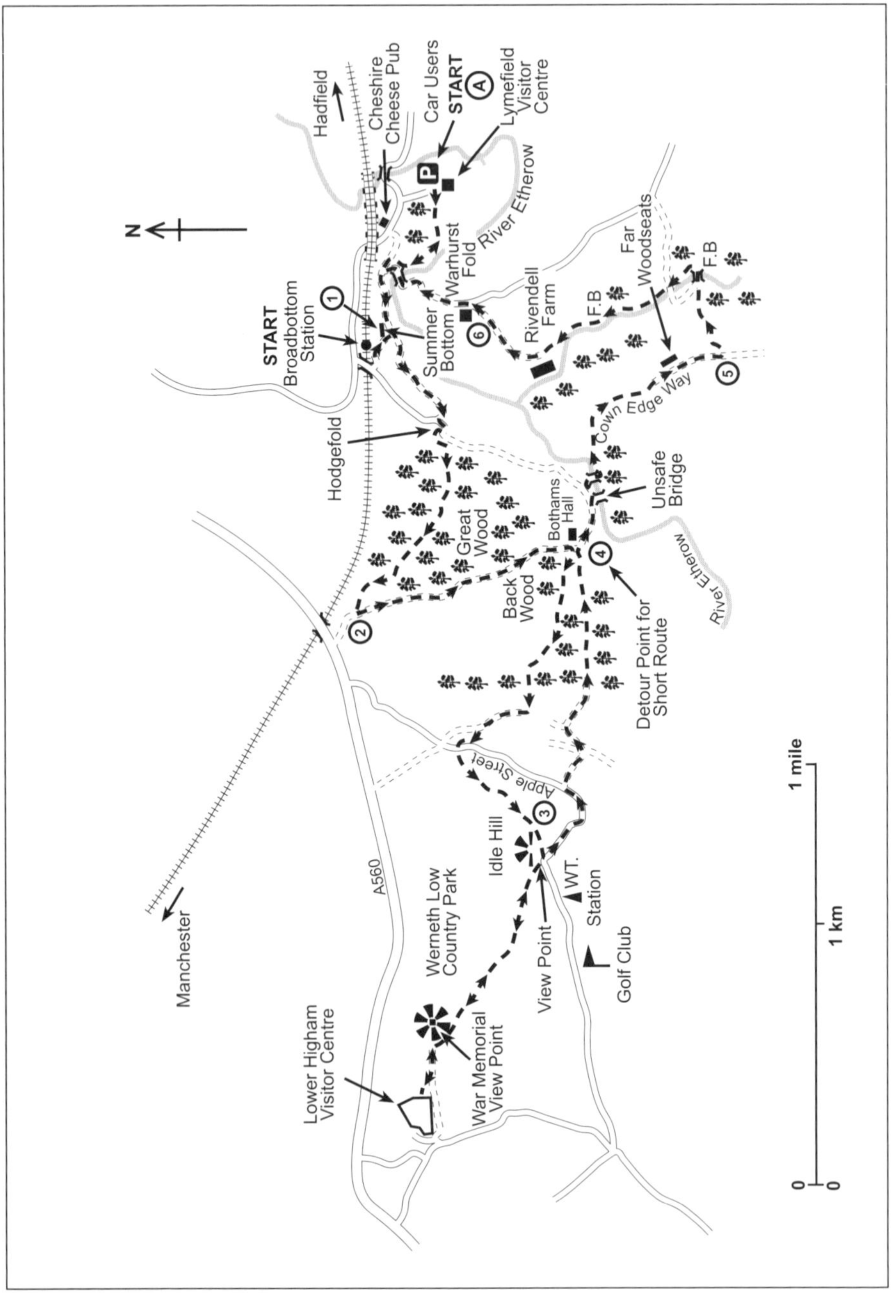
N
Hadfield
Cheshire Cheese Pub
Car Users
START
A
Lymefield Visitor Centre
P
River Etherow
Warhurst Fold
START
Broadbottom Station
1
Summer Bottom
6
Rivendell Farm
F.B
Far Woodseats
F.B
5
Cown Edge Way
Hodgefold
Unsafe Bridge
Bothams Hall
4
Great Wood
Back Wood
Detour Point for Short Route
River Etherow
2
Apple Street
3
Idle Hill
WT. Station
View Point
Golf Club
Werneth Low Country Park
A560
Manchester
Lower Higham Visitor Centre
War Memorial View Point
1 mile
1 km
0
0

downhill past a five barred gate. Follow the track to a metal gate, pass through this and cross a field bearing right past an isolated tree to a stile and a waymarker, cross this to enter Back Wood. The path passes through the wood then down a long flight of neat twisting steps to a bridge over a brook, then up more steps before reaching a junction of paths. Turn right, then through a gate to Botham's Hall, turn right then bear left around the Hall.

Botham's Hall

4. Follow the track past the delightful gardens of Lower Barn, carry on alongside the river, go past an unsafe bridge over the river, then cross a stile on the right. Where a path leads to a narrow footbridge over the river, cross over and bear left and continue left alongside a fence. Follow the path as it swings left high above the river then bear right uphill through the woods. The path becomes unclear here. Continue on uphill through the wood, crossing a small plank bridge on the way before reaching a fence at the top edge of the wood. This is the Cown Edge Way, turn right to follow the fence, pass a large stone marker post. Then cross a stile at the end of the wood and carry straight on, follow the path as it passes along the top of a field. Great views can be seen from here over the

Etherow Valley and beyond. Cross a stile by a gate at 'Owd House' at Far Woodseats and continue straight on along the track to Far Woodseats Lane. Follow the lane until an isolated bungalow on the left.

5. Look out for a hidden stile in small gap in a holly hedge to your left about 25m after the bungalow on the left. Cross the stile and go straight ahead and cross another stile beyond the outbuildings. The path follows the fence on the right downhill past a large tree on the left. The path becomes indistinct here. The way is steeply downhill into a grassy hollow towards a house, the steep slope is best negotiated by zig-zagging down towards the house, bear right in front of the house to a stile. Cross this then down wooden steps and bear right along the path to cross a footbridge over a stream. Ascend steps then turn left onto a track and pass the house.

   Follow the track which turns into a path through the wooded valley with stream down below. Continue on until a footbridge, cross this and pass through a small wooden gate. Follow the path as it skirts the boundary of a field to another small gate, on the left is another large growth of Himalayan Balsam, then follow on to a track. Turn left, passing immediately through a five-bar gate, with a trough on your right. This is Rivendell Farm, follow the track past the farm to a gate by a cattle grid with a duck pond on the right. In spring there is heady aroma of hawthorn from the many bushes around the farm. Follow the track, pass through a gate and turn left along the road.

6. The road becomes a path at Warhurst Fold Farm, continue on the path which is shortly joined by the River Etherow at the bottom. Cross the footbridge admiring the view of the river as you pass and turn right at the signpost for Lymefield Visitor Centre.

   The remains of the vast Broad Mills can be seen in the form of the large circular gasometer, mill race and wheel pit. Continue along the gravel path to the Lymefield Visitor Centre where

The River Etherow near Lymefield Vistor Centre

information, public conveniences and refreshments may be had, or if closed the café at the garden centre.

**Rail users** return to the station by returning to the footbridge over the River Etherow, then follow the signs for Hodgefold, carry on up the track. Turn left in front of the terraced houses then climb up a track above the river gorge, then past an outstanding row of terraced housing called Summerbottom Terrace. At the end of the terrace turn right to walk up the path where the station ramp for the platform to Manchester is on right.

## Historical Notes

### The Mills in the Etherow Valley

The River Etherow once powered three mill complexes along this short stretch of river. Moss Mill started out as a woollen mill in 1798, it was converted to Hodge dye works in 1805 and their dye vats can be seen on the walk. They remain in good condition and it is easy to imagine the heavy work involved in putting the cloth through the bleaching and dying processes. The dyed cloth was of such high quality that some pieces are still on display in the Victoria and Albert Museum.

Broad Mills was a collection of mills owned by the Sidebottom family who by 1860 employed 1,200 people running 25,000 spindles and 1,500 looms. There was also a calico printing mill. The mills changed ownership many times before going into liquidation in 1934. The final blow was a fire in the 1940s which led to its demolition in 1949.

There is one remaining textile mill still currently operating. Named Lymefield Mill, it stands near the Lymefield Visitor Centre and the River Etherow. It is currently occupied by Tiviot Prints Ltd.

More of the history of Broadbottom at:
**www.marplelocalhistorysociety.org.uk/trips/trips-2011-2012/81-may-2012-broadbottom-and-mottram.html**

More of the authors photographs can be found at:
**www.geograph.org.uk/search.php?i=46107110** and
**www.geograph.org.uk/search.php?i=46109338**
Press the tab key marked Map to get the locations

# WALK 7
# The Piethorne Valley

*Moorland valley walk following reservoir and open moorland tracks, with great views, natural and historic interest at every turn.*

| | |
|---|---|
| **Route** | **Newhey – Ogden Reservoir – Piethorne Reservoir – Rochdale Way – Rag Hole Farm – Hollingworth Lake – Littleborough** |
| **Start/finish** | **Circular route A: Newhey Metrolink Station**<br>**Circular route B: Ogden car park**<br>**Linear route C: Start: Newhey Metrolink Station**<br>**Finish: Littleborough Railway Station** |
| **Distance and grade** | **Route A: Circular 5¼ miles route for train users – 821 ft (252m) ascent – Moderate**<br>**Route B: Circular 3½ miles route for train users – 505 ft (154m) ascent – Easy**<br>**Route C: Linear 6½ miles route for train/tram users – 902 ft (275m) ascent – Moderate. Route C is linked to Walk 8 to make a great ,satisfying linear station to station walk between Newhey and Littleborough railway stations** |
| **Map** | **OS Explorer OL21 South Pennines** |
| **Terrain** | **Generally good firm, level paths with few stiles but there are some short steep stretches. Some quiet road walking** |
| **Refreshments** | **The Bulls Head pub, a walker friendly pub with good food and ale, on Lane Bottom off Ogden Road, and the Bird in Hand pub on Huddersfield Road, Newhey. There are toilet facilities at Ogden car park** |

## Directions to the Walk

**Public transport**: Travel to Manchester city centre, and then catch a Metrolink tram from Victoria Station on the Rochdale line to Newhey station. A frequent service runs from Monday to Sunday.

**Car users**: **Sat Nav**: Postcode OL16 3TQ will get you to the Ogden car park on Ogden Lane (grid ref: SD 952122).

**Road directions**: Exit junction 21 on the M62 eastbound towards Milnrow. Follow the signs for the A640 south for Huddersfield. After about 2 miles and after passing through Newhey, turn left at a fork with a sign for the Bulls Head pub. This is Ogden lane, the car park is 500m on the left. The walk is joined at point 2.

The Bulls Head pub at Ogden

## Walk Descriptions

Newhey lies at the foot of the Piethorne Valley and its station on the Metrolink Victoria Station to Rochdale line is a convenient start point for this great walk with magnificent expansive moorland scenery and wildlife.

The circular walks are a circuit of the reservoirs in the beautiful Piethorne Valley on the Pennine foothills below Windy Hill. The paths follow a network of walled tracks and paths across moorland with atmospheric ruins of ancient farmsteads, a waterfall, and four reservoirs to view on the way. The Victorian stone works of water channels, water treatment and pump houses are a feature of the walk and can be admired for their longevity and the way they seem to blend into the rugged moorland landscape.

## Walk Directions

### Route A: 5¼ mile circular route

**Cautionary note**: this route can get flooded at Carr Lane after heavy rainfall. In this case it is advisable for walkers to complete the walk by following point 3 onto point 5 back to Ogden car park, and then retrace their steps through Haugh to Newhey Station.

1. From the Rochdale bound platform at the Metrolink station at Newhey, walk up the ramp to Huddersfield Road, turn right to cross the bridge then right again into Railway Street, follow the road to the end then continue along a path which crosses a brook and emerges at another road (Two Bridges Road). Turn left to follow this through a small residential area, where the road bends left,turn right to pass the Cedar Tree restaurant on Haugh Fold.

   This is a pretty stone hamlet with a cobblestone road, at a fork in the road bear left towards Haugh Square then at another fork bear left again.

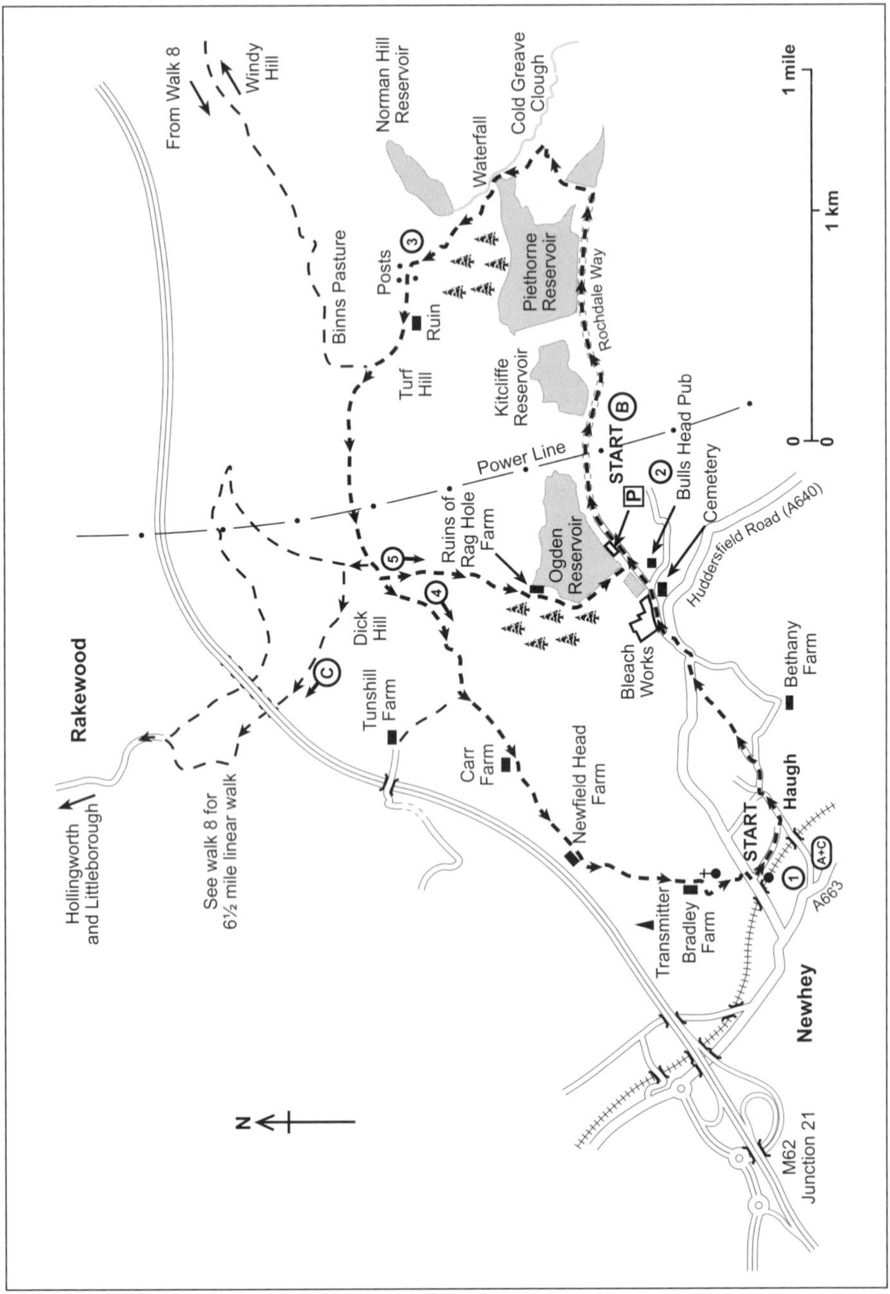

From Walk 8
Windy Hill
Norman Hill Reservoir
Cold Greave Clough
Waterfall
Binns Pasture
Posts
3
Ruin
Turf Hill
Piethorne Reservoir
Rochdale Way
Kitcliffe Reservoir
START B
Bulls Head Pub
Power Line
2
P
Cemetery
Huddersfield Road (A640)
Ruins of Rag Hole Farm
5
4
Ogden Reservoir
Dick Hill
Bleach Works
Bethany Farm
Rakewood
C
Tunshill Farm
Carr Farm
Newfield Head Farm
Haugh
START
1
A+C
A663
Hollingworth and Littleborough
See walk 8 for 6½ mile linear walk
Transmitter
Bradley Farm
Newhey
N
M62 Junction 21
0
1 mile
1 km

Follow the rough track which passes a paddock with friendly horses, the track narrows and leads to Huddersfield Road, turn right to follow this for 50m then turn left at a fork onto Ogden Road. Continue past the Bleach and Dye works, and then at a lychgate on the right, bear left to follow the road past a small reservoir, then the dam of Ogden Reservoir. Soon after the reservoir dam the car park is passed.

**This is where the route is joined by car users. Turn left at the car park entrance to join the walk at point 2.**

2. The route from here follows the Rochdale Way. Carry on gently uphill, passing the entrance to Kitliffe Farm, then a pylon. The water treatment works is passed alongside Kitcliffe Reservoir then up to the high dam of Piethorne Reservoir. Continue straight on the track alongside the reservoir and pass through a kissing gate. Ignore the track off to the left and continue straight on to follow the track to the dam wall of Hanging Lees Reservoir. Turn left to cross this, grand views open up here over the

Piethorne Reservoir with transmission mast on Windy Hill in view

Piethorne Reservoir and the surrounding moorland. Bear right at a junction of tracks, then turn left at a waymarker for the Reservoir Trail and follow the track downhill, passing a stone building which was once used to store lime to reduce the acidity of the water. There follows an impressive man-made waterfall from Norman Hill Reservoir. Ignore the path to the left and continue straight on to a gate.

3. Pass through the gate, carry on uphill following the track as it winds between broken stone walls. Pass two large stone posts either side of the track. Shortly after, look out for a benchmark on a stone post on the left where there appears to be a ruined farmstead. Continue uphill, the track passes between Binns Pasture and Turf Hill before descending gently to a junction of tracks and signpost. Take the track for Hollingworth Lake to the left. The track passes through a deep cutting before the M62 comes into view to your right, shortly the track passes beneath a pylon line before another junction with a signpost and a large concessionary notice board is reached.

**Car users on the circular route B turn left at point 5.**

**Walkers on the linear route C continue onto Walk 8 at point 5.**

4. Carry straight on to pass through a gate and take the track (Tunshill Lane) to ascend over the flank of Dick Hill. Fine views open up over the Piethorne Valley towards the distant hills of North Wales. Cross a nifty lifting bar stile, ignore a turning on the left, then after about 200m at a sharp right hand bend, turn left at a marker post to descend a grassy track between stone walls. The track gets steeper and rougher past Carr Farm. Shortly after the track levels out, carry on along the track past Newfield Head Farm, where the track becomes cobbled. Take a hidden left fork onto an unmarked path, cross a stile then follow the grassy path alongside a fence past a ruined farm to another stile and carry on to a track leading to Bradley Farm.

   The track passes the peculiar hillock viewed on the right topped by a telecommunications mast. The farm access road is joined then followed past a church on a fine cobbled track. Look out for a short cut to the station on the right down steps past a school to join the main road (Huddersfield Road), a few metres on the left is the Bird in Hand pub. Newhey Metro Station is 100m to the right.

## Route B: 3½ mile circular route for car users

Follow points 2 and 3 then onto point 5.

5. Turn left at the signpost down towards Ogden Reservoir, after 350m Turn right off the main track and pass the ruins of Rag Hole Farm. This is a beautiful location set in a small wooded valley with views over the reservoir, a place to savour and perhaps to enjoy a well-earned break. Following the second remains of the farm, turn down the paved path and down steps to a small stone slab bridge over a brook and turn left to follow the cobbled path alongside a brook. Pass through a kissing gate, then pass through a gap on a stone wall on the left to descend steps onto the path across the dam to return to the car park.

## Route C: 6½ mile Linear route for tram /train users

Follow points 1, 2 and 3 then onto point 5 on walk number 8 which follows the linear route to Littleborough railway station.

Ogden Reservoir dam

## Historical Notes

**The Piethorne reservoirs** were built in the 1800s to satisfy the demand for a constant water supply by the increased population needed for the cotton mills and to feed the canals built during the industrial revolution. The steep valleys of these South Pennine moors provided the means to build dams to provide the water needed by the cotton industry. The nearby town of Oldham was transformed into the cotton spinning capital of the world. Farming settlements were cleared to make way for the reservoirs which are great feats of typical Victorian engineering and were built to last.

More of the authors photographs can be found at:
**www.geograph.org.uk/search.php?i=46114081**
Press the tab key marked Map to get the locations

# WALK 8
# Hollingworth Lake and Blackstone Edge

*Circular walks on the South Pennine moorlands, with great views in wild open scenery, taking either the high road over the watershed of Blackstone Edge or the low road round Hollingworth Hill.*

| | |
|---|---|
| Route | Littleborough – Lydgate – Roman Road – Aiggin stone – Blackstone Edge – Windy Hill – Rochdale Way – Sykes Nab – Hollingworth Lake |
| Start/finish | By train: Littleborough railway station<br>By car: Hollingworth Lake Visitor Centre |
| Distance and grade | Route A: 9¾ miles for train users – 1731 ft (528m) ascent – Hard<br>Route B: 8¾ miles for car users – 1460 ft (445m) ascent – Hard<br>Route C: 4½ miles for car and train users – 646 ft (197m) ascent – Moderate/Easy |
| Map | OS Explorer OL21 South Pennines |
| Terrain | The long A and B routes follow generally good well marked paths and tracks with a steady but long climb and a few steep stretches. The short C route follows mainly good paths and tracks that are fairly level with some gentle ascents, and a couple of stiles |
| Refreshments | Hollingworth Lake Country Park Visitor Centre, The Wine Press pub on Rakewood Road. There are no facilities on the routes other than at the start and beginning |

## Directions to the Walks

**Public transport:** Travel to Manchester city centre, and then catch a train from Victoria station to Littleborough station. A half hourly service runs from Monday to Saturday, hourly on Sunday. The station is conveniently located for both of the walks, being adjacent to the Rochdale Canal where the towpath may be taken to reach tracks and paths to either of the routes.

**By car**: **Sat Nav**: OL15 0AQ will get you to the Hollingworth Lake Country Park Visitor Centre (grid ref: SD 939152).
**Road directions**: Exit junction 21 on the M62. Join the A640 towards Milnrow, after ½ mile turn right at traffic lights for Milnrow onto the B6225. Follow the signs for Hollingworth Lake, and turn right on sharp left hand bend at the end of the lakeside road onto Rakewood Road at the Wine Press Pub. The visitor centre and car park is 100m on the left.

## Walk Descriptions

### For the routes over Blackstone Edge (A and B)

The walk over Blackstone Edge is steep in places and as there are no facilities on the route, this requires you to take all the sustenance needed for about a five hour walk. It is essential to have good walking boots and good outdoor clothing for any change of weather conditions.The weather on the ridge can be much more severe than lower levels. This walk is best done on a fair day with the better chance of good visibility, as once the climb to the ridge has been accomplished, the views are exceptionally good. The stretch following the Pennine Way over the summit is fairly level with a great feeling of space and openness in all directions as you stride across the top of the moor.

From the start points, good easy level paths are followed up to part of the Rochdale Way, which is followed climbing steadily to reach Lydgate where the Peak district sign indicates the boundary of the National Park, then continuing steadily up to where the famous enigmatic 'Roman Road' is reached where the climb begins in earnest. The Blackstone Edge ridge looms ahead on the right and the path thankfully levels out at the Aiggin Stone where the route turns right onto the Pennine Way. From here the route gradually ascends the Edge to the trig-point where no doubt a well-earned rest is taken to take in the views and savour the achievement of reaching the highest point on the walk. From here a fine stretch of the Pennine Way is followed to the M62 crossing. There follows a steady descent over moorland paths via Windy Hill, with fine views all along the way. The route then follows the Rochdale Way under the M62 to return past Hollingworth Lake and the visitor centre.

### For the short circular route (C)

This route is a short 'taster' of the Pennine moors, with lots of interest, following paths with a couple of stiles and modest climbs. Tracks and paths gently ascend to Whittaker Moor which lies below Blackstone Edge where a level walk along a stretch of the Rochdale Way is followed with good views over Hollingworth Lake. Then onto a winding path down to Syke Nab farmstead, where another level path is joined which follows a water feed channel around Hollingworth Hill and more elevated views can be enjoyed before reaching the Lake at Hollingworth Fold. The circuit is completed by crossing the dam to reach the visitor centre car park where a path alongside a brook leads back to the Rochdale Canal and the station.

## Walk Directions

### Route A: The 9¾ mile route for rail users

1. From Littleborough Station descend the steps to walk through the subway onto Canal Street, cross over to the canal side and turn left alongside the canal, pass a car park onto the towpath to the locks and a footbridge over the canal. Cross over the canal, turn left to follow the path alongside the canal, follow the path as it swings right alongside a row of terraced houses, and carry on through a small wooded area to emerge onto Ealees Road. Turn right to follow the left branch of the road, sign posted for Hollingworth Lake. Go past a mill and follow the track which becomes unmade. At a right hand bend look out for steps on the left leading up to a small waymarked gate and a path.

   **This is the point car users join the route.**

2. Take this path to pass through the gate and enter a wood, soon the path turns sharp left at a small gate, ignore this and continue along the path through the wood alongside a small brook. Cross a footbridge over the brook. The path ascends a wooded bank and emerges at a junction of paths near a large concrete slab. Cross the slab, which is actually a bridge over a feeder canal for the Rochdale Canal. Pass through the small gate with the warning sign 'Beware of Flying Golf Balls,' then continue forward across a grassy patch to a broad gravel path crossing between greens on the golf course. The path is joined by a track from the left, continue on the track with the objective of Blackstone Edge directly ahead. The track passes Shore Lane farmhouse and emerges at a gate with an access track on the left for the farm. Pass through a kissing gate onto the track into the farm, the track swings left and is joined by another track from the right, this is the Rochdale Way.

3. Follow this to a road at Lydgate, turn right along a dirt track to pass a row of cottages and the boundary stone with High Peak engraved on it. Straight ahead on the horizon can be seen the profile of Blackstone Edge. Carry on the track alongside a drystone wall until a tarmacked road is

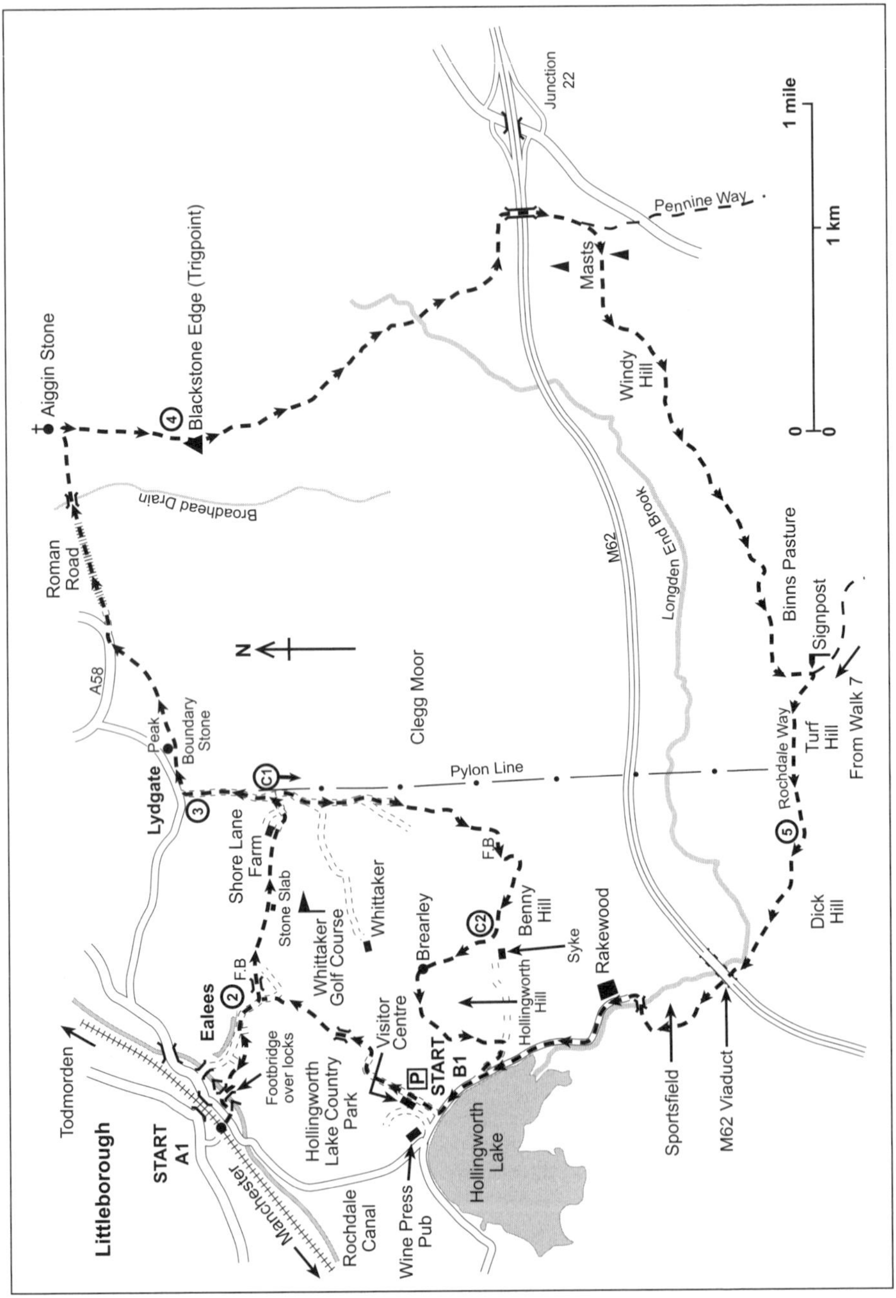
Littleborough
START
A1
Todmorden
Manchester
Rochdale Canal
Wine Press Pub
Hollingworth Lake
Hollingworth Lake Country Park
Footbridge over locks
Ealees
2
F.B
Visitor Centre
P
START
B1
Whittaker Golf Course
Whittaker
Stone Slab
Shore Lane Farm
Lydgate
3
C1
Peak
Boundary Stone
A58
N
Clegg Moor
Pylon Line
Brearley
C2
Benny Hill
F.B
Hollingworth Hill
Syke
Rakewood
Sportsfield
M62 Viaduct
Dick Hill
5
Rochdale Way
Turf Hill
From Walk 7
Signpost
Binns Pasture
Longden End Brook
M62
Windy Hill
Masts
Pennine Way
Junction 22
Roman Road
Broadhead Drain
Aiggin Stone
4
Blackstone Edge (Trigpoint)
0
0
1 km
1 mile

Lydgate, the gateway to the High Peak

reached and crossed, the path is joined by the stone setts of the 'Roman Road'. Follow the track as it ascends, crossing a drainage channel then onward to arrive at the watershed and an ancient stone boundary marker, The Aiggin Stone with some markings and a cross engraved. On the right pass through a stile and follow the well worn steep path of the Pennine Way up to the Trig-point at 472m (1548ft) elevation. The pillar stands rather improbably on a huge boulder, on the edge of the rocky outcrop. The views over the East Lancashire landscape towards the distant hills of Wales are superb, a good place for a break and to soak up the ambience of the open moorland.

4. From here the broad path descends down to a couple of fords draining the moors then suddenly the M62 comes into view,this is followed to a large footbridge crossing, the sight of the motorway as it cleaves its way through the moorland is impressive. Having crossed the bridge, continue along the track leading to pair of masts, bear right on the path to pass between the masts. The path from here on has extensive views over east Lancashire and on clear days right up to the Welsh mountains. Follow the broad path then on through a broken stone wall, shortly the path joins

another wall on the left, follow this for 200m then pass through the wall. Look out for wheatear as they flit along the wall showing off their white rumps. Continue to follow the main path keeping the wall on the right and maintaining the higher ground. The path enters a track between drystone walls, follow this as it bends left to emerge at a gate at a junction of tracks and a signpost. Take the track on the right for Hollingworth Lake, follow this to another junction of tracks and a signpost.

**Walkers on the station to station route C from Walk 7 join the route here.**

5. Turn right through a gate on the track for Hollingworth Lake, in a few metres turn left up steps off the main track to a stile onto the waymarked path (The Rochdale Way), follow this path as it descends then passes under the motorway. After 200m pass through a gap in a wall on the right, then turn left to skirt around a sports field and turn right onto a track. Follow the track and cross a flat bridge, turn left onto a tarmacked road and follow the road past an old mill into the hamlet of Rakewood. Continue on past Hollingworth Lake to the entrance to the visitor centre and car park.

   Walkers wishing to visit the Wine Press pub carry straight on past the visitor centre for 100m.

Rakewood Viaduct carries the M62 over the Rochdale Way

**Rail users** carry on past the visitor centre and car park, keep to the left on a track and pass through a gate, then at a right hand bend turn left onto a path through a picnic area. Pass over a footbridge, turn left onto the broad path alongside Hollingworth Brook, then through several kissing gates to a road and signpost. Turn left and follow this to bring you back to Ealees Road and return along the unmarked path on the left back to the canal and Littleborough Station.

## Route B: The 8¾ mile circular route for car users

B1. From the visitor centre follow the track to the rear left of the car park on a track, and pass through a gate, then at a right hand bend turn left onto a path through a picnic area. Pass over a footbridge then turn left onto the broad path alongside Hollingworth Brook, then through several kissing gates to a road and signpost. Turn left onto the road, follow this to a sharp left bend, look out for steps on the right, and ascend these to a small waymarked gate and a path. Continue onto points 2, 3, 4 and 5.

## Route C: 4 mile circular route (4½ miles for train users)

Train users follow point A1, car users B1, then follow point 2, and onto C1.

C1. Turn sharp right almost back on yourself and follow the broad tarmacked bridleway of the Rochdale Way, with its great views over Hollingworth Lake. Soon a forked junction is reached. Take the left fork onto the unmade track and continue to follow the bridleway alongside a powerline. Shortly after a kink left and right in the track, nearly opposite a pylon, look out for a well defined path winding down on the right towards a plantation in the distance. Take this path which descends and crosses a plank bridge and emerges onto a track. Turn right and follow the track to follow a walled plantation down between stone pillars before arriving at the isolated farmstead of Sykes Nab.

The Rochdale Way on Whittaker Moor

C2. This pleasant spot nestles between the Hollingworth Hill and Benny Hill, good for a ponder before moving on across a grassy patch to the right where a faint path runs off to the left of a track to run between Hollingworth Hill and a canal feeder channel. The path contours around the hill where a stile is crossed, then on towards Brearley Farm and a stone slab bridge. Cross this before turning left at a yellow arrowed waymarker and a gate. Continue alongside the channel passing through a kissing gate, then a plantation of mountain ash trees full of berries in the autumn. The view towards the lake opens up before the path bears left. Follow the path and shortly cross the channel at a stile, continue on to another dilapidated kissing gate before emerging at Hollingworth Fold on Syke Road.

A steam pump near Hollingworth Fold was used to draw water from the lake into the channel for the four mile journey to the summit of the canal.

Turn right and follow the road down to Rakewood Road and continue on across the dam to the visitor centre and the car park.

**Rail users** carry on through the car park, keep to the left, leaving it at the rear left end on a broad path to pass a picnic area, passing over a footbridge. Turn left alongside Hollingworth Brook, then through several kissing gates to a road and signpost. Turn left and follow this which brings you back to Ealees Road and return along the unmarked path on the left back to the canal and Littleborough Station.

## Historical Notes

### Hollingworth Lake Visitor Centre

Information on the visitor centre may be found at
**www.rochdale.gov.uk/parks_and_countryside/hollingworth_lake.aspx**

### The Roman Road

I have checked several websites for the authenticity of the claim that this is indeed a Roman road, but it seems the jury is out, as there is a lot of disagreement as to its age. But it is agreed that this was a main route for packhorse transport over the Pennines in medieval times. It is thought likely it is a turnpike road of around 1735 with the central trough being a channel for working cables to haul vehicles up the incline.

### Hollingworth Lake

The lake was originally built as the main water source for the Rochdale Canal, but developed as a tourist resort from the 1860s, and became known as the Weighver's Seaport. There is a scenic, 2.5 miles (4.0 km) walk around the lake, which passes a nature reserve with a bird hide in the south-western corner of

the lake, in an area from which boats and watersports are excluded. The lake provides habitat for a variety of wildlife.
Attributed to **en.wikipedia.org/wiki/Hollingworth_Lake**

**The Aiggin Stone**
These marker stones or waymarkers were used for religious purposes. Some of these stones were even used by people carrying coffins; the coffin rested here and prayers for the dead would be recited, perhaps a stone or two placed on top of the cairn as well. The letters I and T obviously have some religious significance, possibly IN TEDIUM or 'In the Lord we trust' or 'In praise of the Lord'.
Attributed to **http://northernantiquarian.forumotion.net/t285-the-aiggin-stone-on-blackstone-edge**

More of the authors photographs can be found at:
**www.geograph.org.uk/search.php?i=46109536**
Press the tab key marked Map to get the locations

# WALK 9
# Entwistle and The Three Reservoir Walk

*Walks following reservoir, brook side and moorland paths, in beautiful scenery, together with a variety of wildlife, and a visit to Turton Tower.*

| | |
|---|---|
| **Route** | **Entwistle Reservoir – Wayoh Reservoir – Turton Bottoms – Jumbles Reservoir – Bromley Cross – Jumbles Reservoir – Turton Tower – Witton Weavers Way – Entwistle Reservoir** |
| **Start/finish** | **Linear route A: Start: Entwistle railway station.<br>Finish: Bromley Cross railway station<br>Circular route B: Bromley Cross station (Shortened linear route finish: Entwistle railway station)<br>Circular route C: Batridge Barn car park** |
| **Distance and grade** | **Route A: 5 miles for train users – 577 ft (176m) ascent – Moderate<br>Route B: 8 miles for train users – 950 ft (290m) ascent – Moderate/Hard (this may be shortened to a 4 mile linear route by finishing at Entwistle Station – Easy)<br>Route C: 7 miles for car users – 940 ft (287m) ascent – Moderate** |
| **Map** | **OS Explorer 287 West Pennine Moors** |
| **Terrain** | **The walks are on mainly good paths with some gentle hills and a little road walking on minor roads** |
| **Refreshments** | **The Strawbury Duck pub, picnic area and café at Jumbles Park, The Black Bull Inn at Turton Bottoms and The Railway pub at Bromley Cross** |

## Directions to the Walks

**public transport**: travel to bolton railway station; there is a frequent service from manchester and wigan from monday to saturday, hourly from wigan on sunday, then catch a train to entwistle or bromley cross station from bolton. there is an hourly service monday to sunday. note: entwistle station is a request stop, please inform the conducter if you wish to alight here, if catching a train from here please indicate to the driver you wish to board the train.

**Car users**: **Sat Nav**: Postcode BL7 0NF will get you to Nabbs Cottage on the B6391. Batridge Road is just past this on the right going north, and going south look out for well marked signs for the car park on your left just before reaching Nabbs Cottage.

**Road directions**: From the A666 going north after passing through Egerton from Bolton, turn right onto the B6391 and then turn left onto an unclassified road with Batridge Barn signage, follow road to car park (grid ref SD 722172).

## Walk Descriptions

There are two routes for train users, Route A that follows paths from Entwistle Station down one side of Wayoh and Jumbles Reservoirs to Bromley Cross Station, and a longer circular route B starting from Bromley Cross Station which allows for a complete circuit of both Jumbles and Wayoh reservoirs and a part of the moorland walk on the Witton Weavers Way. For those wishing to succumb to the delights of the Strawbury Duck they can shorten the walk here and return home from Entwistle Station. The circular route C, for car users follows much the same route round both reservoirs.

Entwistle is a moorland village at the head of Wayoh reservoir which is known for its great variety of birdlife. Following the path around the reservoir, the linear route passes through the stone village of Turton Bottoms, and on to a cobbled lane, then a beautiful path alongside a babbling brook. This leads on to Jumbles Reservoir where refreshments at the information centre are available. The route then rounds Jumbles Reservoir dam onto a tree lined lane to Bromley Cross Station.

The Strawbury Duck at Entwistle

Car and train users on the circular routes follow much of the linear route, but complete the circuit by following a tree lined lane at the south end of Jumbles Reservoir skirting round the west side, passing stables and a sailing club. The route follows onto Turton Tower, then a fine stretch of the Witton Weavers Way, with wonderful moorland views, before descending back to the car park or Entwistle station.

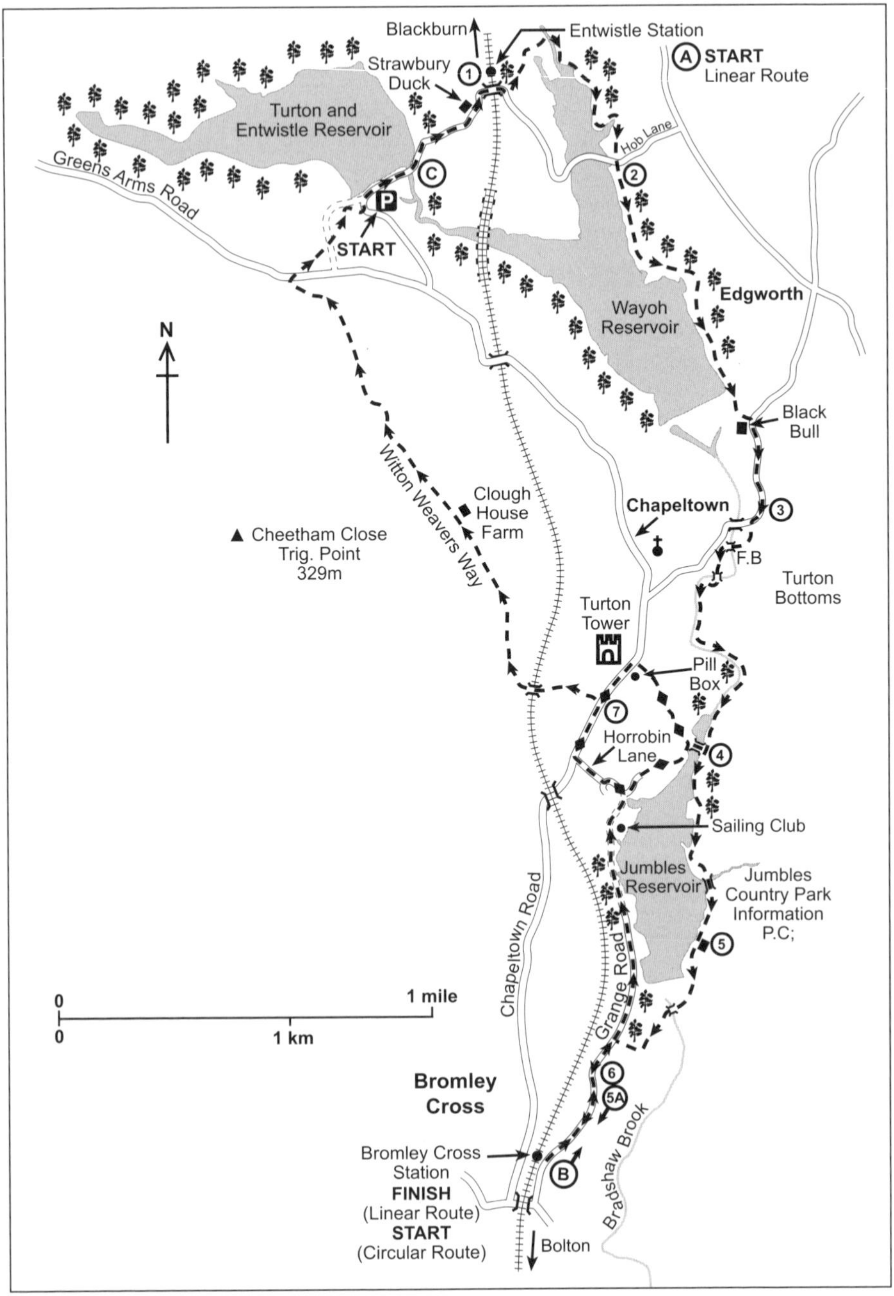

Blackburn
Entwistle Station
A START
Linear Route
Strawbury Duck
Turton and Entwistle Reservoir
Hob Lane
Greens Arms Road
C
P
START
Wayoh Reservoir
Edgworth
N
Black Bull
Witton Weavers Way
Clough House Farm
Chapeltown
Cheetham Close Trig. Point 329m
F.B
Turton Bottoms
Turton Tower
Pill Box
Horrobin Lane
Sailing Club
Jumbles Reservoir
Jumbles Country Park Information P.C;
Chapeltown Road
Grange Road
0
1 mile
0
1 km
Bromley Cross
5A
B
Bradshaw Brook
Bromley Cross Station
FINISH
(Linear Route)
START
(Circular Route)
Bolton

## Walk Directions

### Route A: 5 miles linear route for train users

A foretaste of the route to be followed is given on the scenic train journey through the Bradshaw Valley, especially from the Armsgrove Viaduct over the Wayoh Reservoir. Entwistle station seems to have been ideally sited for walkers. It is situated in wonderful walking countryside between Turton and Entwistle Reservoir and Wayoh Reservoir where very little habitation is apparent. From the station platform climb the ramp to the road and turn left over the bridge, then bear right.

**Car and train users following circular routes B and C join the linear route here.**

1. Look out for the gated, waymarked path on the left a few metres on, and take the path which descends steeply to a kissing gate and a wood. Continue on to a broad track and cross two footbridges over streams which take the path to the eastern side of Wayoh Reservoir, the path follows this side to Hob Lane.

2. From Hob Lane follow the path around the reservoir, this area has a recorded count of over 140 bird species, and parts of the water's edge have been given conservation status to protect wildfowl nesting here. Follow the path up a gentle rise, the views of Armsgrove Viaduct which straddles an inlet of the reservoir can be seen to the right, with the moorland of Cheetham Close and Turton Heights above. The path continues around the reservoir ending at the dam which is bypassed and a short climb brings you to a kissing gate near the Black Bull pub on Bolton Road.

3. Turn right to walk down Bolton Road for 400m and turn left up the cobbled Birches Road, as the road bends left, bear right onto a gravelled track. A path is soon reached which leads onto a delightful stone footbridge over Bradshaw Brook, continue along

Bradshaw Brook at Turton Bottoms

the ascending path which comes out onto a lane, turn left and follow the lane which becomes cobbled. Follow this lane to a bridge over the Bradshaw Brook again and turn right immediately to follow the brook side path. This delightful path continues through a wooded gorge with lovely sights and sounds along the way.

4. The path comes out at Jumbles Park Quarry and a footbridge across the head of Jumbles Reservoir.

   Walkers on the linear route who wish to visit Turton Tower must do a short detour here by crossing the bridge and follow the path uphill through woodland, then a meadow ,passing a pillbox on the left. The path emerges onto Chapeltown Road, turn left and follow the road to the driveway up to Turton Tower. Having paid a visit to the tower, return to the road, turn right and follow the road for 200m to Horrobin Lane. Turn left down the lane and bear left at a sign for the sailing club and follow the cobbled lane. Where the cobbles finish continue on the lane alongside the reservoir past a small car park, then a path brings you back to the footbridge at the head of the reservoir, cross over and rejoin the route along the well-marked path on the eastern side.

   Pass a bird hide and look out for the wildfowl on the reservoir, pochard, goldeneye, and tufted duck as well as the common species may be seen. The path crosses a bridge over an inlet and comes out at the information centre café and picnic area.

5. Following a break, carry on along the path past a plaque unveiled by the Queen. Turn right and go down steps to a bridge with the weir on the right. Water flows from here to fill Bradshaw Brook and on to the river Croal and then the Irwell. After crossing the bridge go over a stile, bear left and then curve right to come out at a gate onto Grange Road.

**Car users on the circular route C turn right onto Grange Road at point 6.**

5a. At this point train users on the linear route (A) turn left to follow the road for 300m to Bromley Cross station. Turn right at a small triangular patch of grass on the right past a row of houses, the station is a few steps away.

## Route B: 8 miles circular route for train users

From Bromley Station, cross the lines to the opposite platform and exit the station by turning right down a short road to a triangle of grass and turn left down the lane (Grange Road).

6. Follow the road past the Grange where horses may be seen, as there are stables nearby. Carry on through a set of gates, closing them before proceeding. This is an attractive wooded area alongside the reservoir, where wildfowl such as great crested grebe may be spotted. Soon the boat club is passed. Cross a footbridge and turn left onto Horrobin Lane and follow this cobbled lane up past many attractive gardens to Chapeltown Road.

7. Turn right to follow this major road for 200m to the entrance on the left to Turton Tower. Turn up the drive and, if minded, pay a visit to this famous medieval building.

   Carry on up the stony track to cross the railway on an ornate bridge which seems to match the tower just passed. The track comes to a junction; bear right through a kissing gate and follow a broad track across the open moors. This is the Witton Weavers Way, a fine stretch with great views. Soon Clough House Farm is passed, carry on until a small path which short cuts towards Green Arms Road. Cross the road and pass through a gate and descend down the path to a lane which crosses the path, continue on the path opposite which comes out at the car park on Batridge Barn Road. Continue to follow the lane across the dam with great views over Turton and Entwistle Reservoir. Bear right at a fork after crossing the dam, the lane becomes unmade and passes first a camping barn then (if you can resist temptation) the Strawbury Duck pub, before crossing the railway bridge and bearing right at Entwistle Station.

**The walk can be shortened here by returning home from Entwistle station.**

The circular route B is completed by following points 1,2,3,4,5,and 5a to return to Bromley Cross Station.

### Route C: 7 mile circular walk for car users

From the car park walk along the road towards the lake, crossing the dam then follow the lane past the Entwistle camping barn where the road becomes unmade, then continue past the Strawbury Duck and over the railway bridge, then follow points 1, 2, 3, 4, 5, 6 and 7 back to the car park.

## Historical Notes

### Turton Tower

The tower was built in the Middle Ages as a stone pele tower and is a rarity as these towers are more usually found nearer the Scottish borders. The present

appearance of the house is mainly resulting from James Kay who acquired ownership in 1835 and refurbished the rooms with 17th century panelling. His son designed the nearby castellated railway bridge in keeping with the Tower's appearance. It is now owned by Lancashire County Council who maintains it as a museum. Times of opening and charges telephone: 01204 852203
More information at **en.wikipedia.org/wiki/Turton_Tower**

## Turton Bottoms

During the 19th century the area around Turton Bottoms was a hive of industry which included Springside Spinning Mill, Black Rock Bleachworks, Turton Colliery and the Stone Mill in Turton Vale.

## The Reservoirs

The Turton and Entwistle Reservoir was completed by 1838 to serve the needs of the bleachers and mill owners along Bradshaw Brook, to maintain a continuous water supply in the dry periods for their industrial operations. As the population of Bolton and district grew, the domestic water capacity was increased by the construction of Wayoh Reservoir, built in 1876, followed much later by the Jumbles Reservoir which was opened in 1971.

More of the authors photographs can be found at:
**www.geograph.org.uk/search.php?i=46109734**
Press the tab key marked Map to get the locations

Winter sunshine at Turton and Entwistle Reservoir

# WALK 10
# Uppermill, Diggle and the Tame Valley

*A canal towpath walk up to the historic Standedge tunnels followed by scenic moorland tracks and paths visiting hamlets of the upper Tame Valley.*

| | |
|---|---|
| Route | Greenfield – Huddersfield Canal – Uppermill – Diggle – Standedge Tunnel – Pobgreen |
| Start/finish | By train: Greenfield railway station.<br>By car : Wool Road canal side car park |
| Distance and grade | A 6 mile Circular route for both train and car users – 938ft (286m) ascent – Moderate |
| Map | OS Outdoor Leisure 1 The Dark Peak District |
| Terrain | The paths are flat and mostly on firm ground with gentle ascents, there are a number of stiles, and some muddy ground may be encountered |
| Refreshments | Brownhill Countryside Centre, the Diggle Hotel, and Church Inn at Pobgreen. Many pubs in Uppermill and Greenfield |

## Directions to the walk

**Public transport**: Travel to Manchester city centre, then catch a train from Manchester Victoria. An hourly service runs from Monday to Sunday to Greenfield.

**By car: Sat Nav** : Postcode OL3 5QR will get you to the car park on the A670, Wool Road (grid ref: SD 995065).

**Road directions**: From the M62 eastbound at junction 21, exit toward Milnrow then take the A640 towards Huddersfield for about 3 miles until Denshaw and the Junction Inn. Go straight across the offset junction onto the A6052 for Delph. Follow this road 4 miles through Delph, taking the New Delph Road (A6052) at the offset crossroads. After 1 mile to a mini roundabout at Uppermill, turn first left, the car park is 150m on the left. The walk starts at point 2.

## Walk Description

The railway station at Greenfield is conveniently located near the canal towpath for the start of the walk. Following a figure of eight route, many feats of engineering are to be seen, including the Huddersfield Narrow Canal with its chain of locks as it climbs towards the famous Standedge canal and railway tunnels and the massive Saddleworth Viaduct. The towpath route has views and interest all the way, passing through pleasant rural countryside to the small town of Diggle. Then onto country lanes and paths up to Pobgreen with a popular pub on the moors. From here paths and lanes are followed back to Uppermill, before returning to the station along paths and a country lane with more great views over the Tame Valley.

## Walk Directions

1. On alighting from the train, cross the station bridge and turn downhill to pass The Railway pub and at a road junction, turn sharp left downhill following the road to the canal bridge and take the steps to the towpath. Follow the towpath across the entrance to a new basin, carry on to a bridge and the first of many locks. Notice how narrow these are, some locks have a single leaf. The canal passes under the High Street in Uppermill where the towpath crosses to the opposite bank and the Saddleworth Museum is located. There is a cruise boat usually moored alongside the museum. Carry on to cross the canal again at Moorgate Street, then follow this very scenic stretch of canal until the magnificent Saddleworth Railway Viaduct with 23 arches, coincidently, at lock 23. The site of the Brownhill Countryside Centre is just past the viaduct on the right, where seats are provided on the towpath. This is a good spot to rest and admire the view.

Uppermill railway viaduct spans the Huddersfield Narrow Canal

2. Carry on following the towpath, the canal bends right and widens. Shortly the car park which lies opposite a large Transhipment Warehouse is passed.

**Car users start the walk here.**

Continue to follow the canal as it passes through many locks as it climbs towards the Pennine watershed. There are basins between the locks to allow barges to pass each other. Soon the landscape becomes more rural and open with views over the moors. Cross the canal at lock 32 to see the paving slabs with engraved historical stories in amusing Monopoly game form. Shortly after this the tunnel entrance is reached.

There is a stone etched 1893, the date of a short extension, the tunnel was actually opened in 1811 and is over 3 miles long. Follow the path from the canal side up to a car park and turn right into Sam Road. Follow the road as it climbs then crosses, the railway. From the bridge you can see the Standedge railway tunnels, two older unused, and the later dual tracked one which all re-emerge the other side of the Pennine watershed at Marsden. Just after the bridge is the Diggle Hotel which has a beer garden and pub meals.

Standedge tunnel entrance at Diggle

3. Turn right down Lee Side, crossing a babbling brook by attractive gardens, and follow the lane as it climbs up towards the moors, look out for a waymarked track for Fairbanks Farm on the left. Turn up the track and pass by the fine old mullion windowed stone farm houses. Follow the track to where it turns right through a gate, keep left of the stone wall and cross a stile, follow the path up between fence and wall to the next stile. Cross this and pass alongside gardens to emerge at Running Hill Lane and cross the road directly onto another waymarked path at a kissing gate. Follow the faint grassy path to the left of a gulley. The path drops steeply down to marshy ground. Cross this on stepping stones, then continue onto a

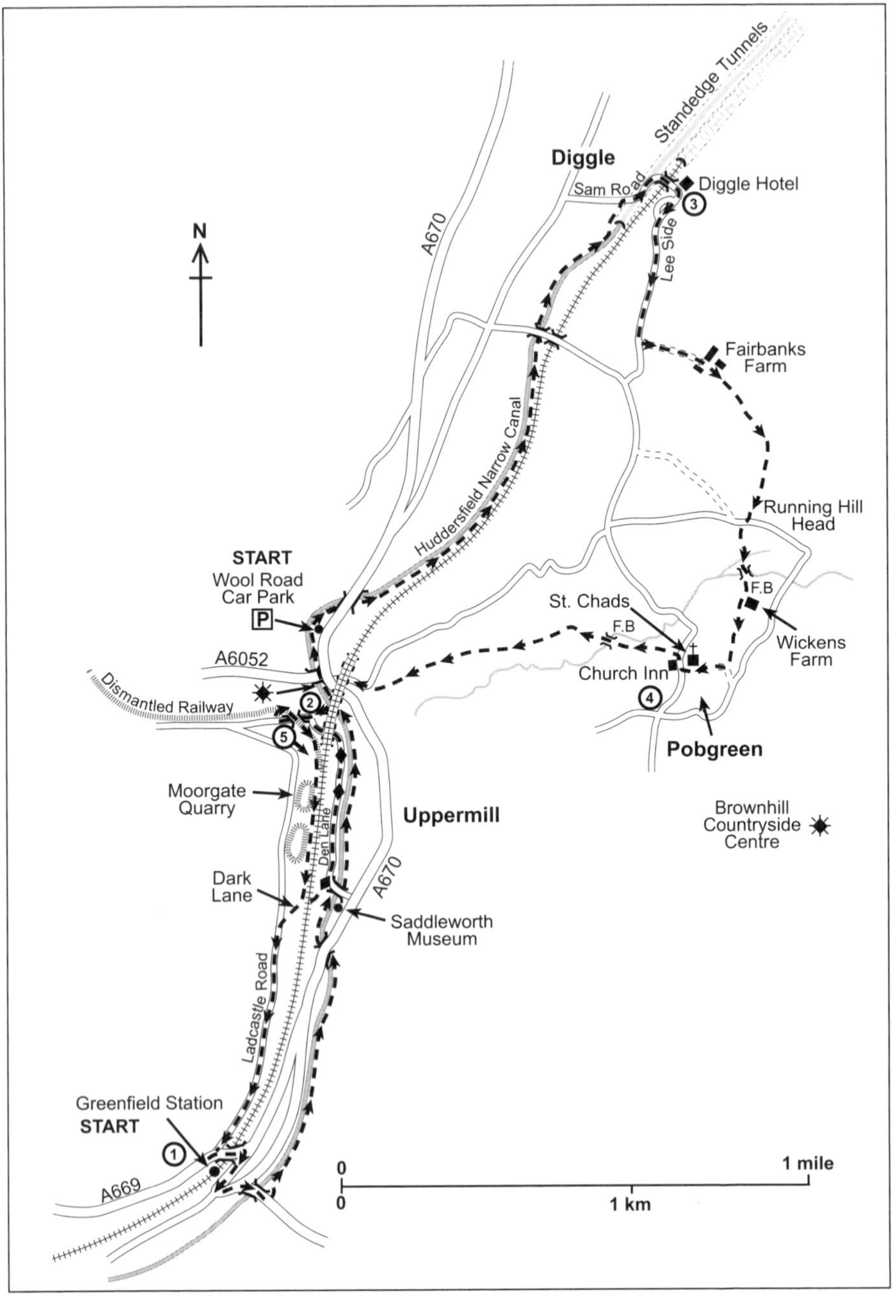
Standedge Tunnels
Diggle
Sam Road
Diggle Hotel
3
Lee Side
A670
N
Fairbanks
Farm
Huddersfield Narrow Canal
Running Hill
Head
START
Wool Road
Car Park
P
F.B
St. Chads
Wickens
Farm
F.B
A6052
Church Inn
Dismantled Railway
2
4
5
Pobgreen
Moorgate
Quarry
Uppermill
Brownhill
Countryside
Centre
Den Lane
Dark
Lane
A670
Saddleworth
Museum
Ladcastle Road
Greenfield Station
START
1
0
1 mile
A669
0
1 km

small stream with more stepping stones before crossing a field, bear right on a faint path below a farmhouse (Wickens Farm). Continue on the path, crossing a stile then cross another field to a footbridge, before a further couple of stiles and a gate leads you to steps down to a track. Turn right past Ivy Bank Farm, pass through a gate and down a gravel path, which comes out at a car park next the St Chads Church.

4. Opposite the church is The Church Inn which brews its own ale and serves great food, a good place for a break! Once refreshed turn towards the church and turn left at a waymarked path and follow it down to a gap stile and then a footbridge. Continue on to pass through a further two stone gap stiles. Follow the path to the left of a plantation. There is a good view of the transmission mast above Greenfield from here. The path emerges onto a track at a gate. Follow the track to another gate, then follow the track to where a waymarked path on the right leads to a pasture behind a row of houses, and this emerges onto a lane which continues down to High Street opposite the Brownhill Countryside Centre.

   **Car users can shorten the walk here by turning right to follow the canal back to the car park.**

   **Train users can shorten the walk by turning left to follow the canal towpath back to Greenfield Station.**

5. From the centre turn left on the canal towpath and cross the canal via the stone bridge under the viaduct to take a track to Den Lane.

   (For a shorter walk on firm ground, turn left onto Den Lane and follow the road and after passing a row of terraced houses turn right onto a waymarked path to cross the railway on a level crossing onto Dark Lane to rejoin the route.)

   Turn right and follow the lane which passes under a stone bridge of the dismantled railway branch line to Delph. Turn right onto the railway trackbed and turn right and follow the sign-posted track over the bridge you have just passed under towards Moorgate Quarry.

   The path follows the branch line used by the steam train affectionately known as the 'Delph Donkey'. Shortly the path passes through a cutting and then emerges between the main line railway and a heather clad hill. Ignore the path off to the left, continue on past a large disused quarry. There are great views over the Tame Valley with the Pots and Pans Memorial prominent. After passing through woodland the path emerges onto a broad track (Dark Lane). Turn right to follow this uphill which leads to Ladcastle Road. Continue left with more great views all the way back to the railway station. Turn sharp left at the main road and the station is on the right.

**Car users carry on from here at point 1 to return along the canal back to the car park.**

## Historical Notes

### Brownhill Countryside Centre

The centre has a nature garden, café, and toilet facilities. For further information:
**www.oldham.gov.uk/info/200393/parks_countryside_and_canals/678/brownhill**

### Huddersfield Narrow Canal Standedge Tunnel

This three mile tunnel, runs between Diggle and Marsden, and is the longest canal tunnel in Britain. The canal was built with 74 locks over its 20 mile route and at its highest point is 645 feet above sea level, which makes it the highest stretch of canal in Britain.

Construction of the canal started in 1794 and was due to be completed in 1799. It was finally opened in 1811 after many construction problems, not least of which was that the two ends did not line up, resulting in bends in the tunnel having to be made. It was built without a towpath, the horses being led over the moor from the ends of the tunnel whilst the bargees legged the boats through the tunnel, propelling the barge by lying on their backs and 'walking' along the tunnel roof. The canal fell into decline once the railway that runs alongside it was built, and finally closed in 1944. But after many years of hard work by many interested bodies the canal was reopened for traffic in 2001.

The fascinating history of the Huddersfield Narrow Canal can be found at:
**www.penninewaterways.co.uk/huddersfield/standedge3.htm**

### Saddleworth Museum

Website: **www.saddleworthmuseum.co.uk**

More of the authors photos at:
**www.geograph.org.uk/search.php?i=53286619**
**www.geograph.org.uk/search.php?i=53286675**
Press the tab key marked Map to get the locations

# WALK 11
# Win Hill and Vale of Edale

*A steep hill walk with an exhilarating viewpoint is followed by a gently descending ridge walk with fantastic views all the way, and a satisfying finish at the unique atmospheric village of Edale.*

| | |
|---|---|
| **Route** | **Bamford – Win Hill – Hope Cross – Jagger's Clough – Lady Booth Brook – Edale** |
| **Start/finish** | **Start: Bamford Railway Station (car users use station car park)<br>Finish: Edale Railway Station** |
| **Distance and grade** | **8 mile linear route – 2243 ft (684m) ascent – Hard** |
| **Map** | **OS Outdoor Leisure 1 The Dark Peak District** |
| **Terrain** | **Some very steep rough paths and a few stiles, but mainly firm and level with a few steep stretches on a well-marked route** |
| **Refreshments** | **The Penny Pot next to the station; The Rambler Inn and Old Nags Head Pub in Edale** |

## Directions to the walk

**Public transport**: Travel to Manchester city centre then catch a train from Manchester Piccadilly for the 2 hourly service from Sunday to Friday, or hourly on Saturdays to Bamford.

**By car**: **Sat Nav**: Postcode S33 0BN will get you to Station Road, Bamford.

**Road directions**: From the M67 towards Glossop take the A57 through Glossop and follow the road through the Snake Pass and Woodlands Valley to Ladybower Reservoir. Turn right onto the A6013 towards Bamford. Follow the road through Bamford, turn off on the left for Bamford station and park in the station car park.

## Walk Description

The Vale of Edale is a beautiful valley which benefits from its remoteness, not having major road access. Only the railway provides direct access from

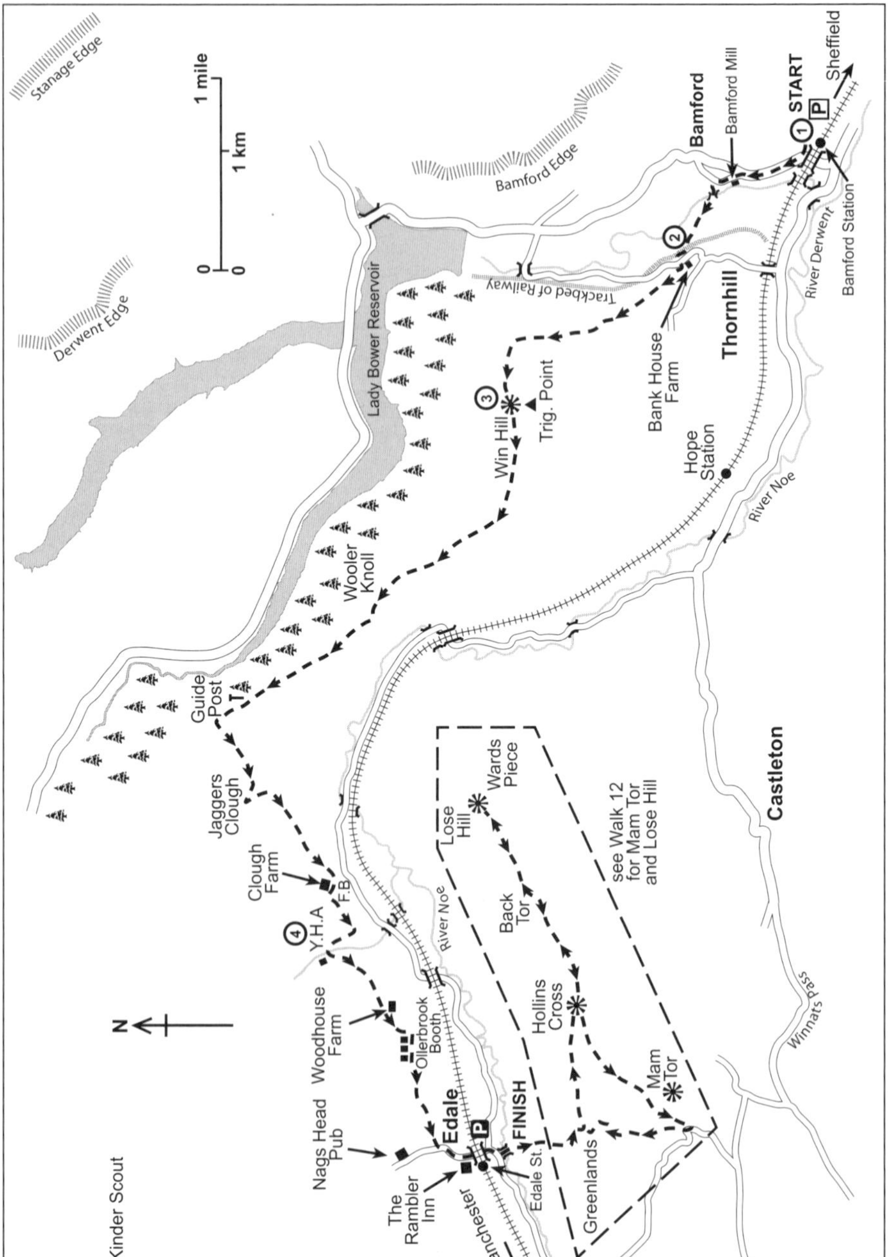
Stanage Edge
Derwent Edge
Bamford Edge
0
0
1 km
1 mile
N
Bamford
Bamford Mill
START
P
Sheffield
Bamford Station
River Derwent
Trackbed of Railway
Lady Bower Reservoir
Bank House Farm
Thornhill
Win Hill
Trig. Point
Hope Station
River Noe
Wooler Knoll
Guide Post
Jaggers Clough
Clough Farm
F.B.
Y.H.A
Woodhouse Farm
Ollerbrook Booth
River Noe
Lose Hill
Wards Piece
Back Tor
Hollins Cross
Mam Tor
see Walk 12 for Mam Tor and Lose Hill
Castleton
Winnats Pass
Kinder Scout
Nags Head Pub
Edale
P
FINISH
The Rambler Inn
Edale St.
Greenlands
Manchester

Manchester. Consequently there is a timeless feeling here with little commercialism and unspoiled countryside and grand mountain scenery.

It is a rambler's delight with great walking routes, which are focussed on Edale, the start point for The Pennine Way. With its two atmospheric walker's pubs, this is a great end point for this exhilarating walk, which starts at the old village of Bamford before a challenging climb up to the heady heights of Win Hill with its commanding panoramic views over the northern Peak District edges and Ladybower Reservoir. The walk continues along the ridge to Wooler Knoll before descending along the lower slopes of the valley, passing Hope Cross, Jagger's Clough and Nether Booth, ending at the favourite walker's watering hole of Edale.

This is a long hill walk which is steep in places and as there are no facilities on the route you will need to take all the sustenance required for about a five hour walk. It is essential to have good walking boots and good outdoor clothing for any change of weather conditions. The weather on the ridge can be much more severe than at lower levels. A fair day with a better chance of good visibility is essential to get the full benefit of the great views.

## Walk Directions

1. From the station approach road, turn right to follow the main road towards Bamford. After about 500m take the left fork onto Mill Lane, follow this past the entrance to the huge Bamford Mill, now converted into residential apartments. Turn left past a 'Touchstone Trail' marker and in 20m, turn left again at a finger post sign through the complex to the delightful stone slab causeway and footbridge across the River Derwent. At the end of the bridge bear right to take the path across the field to a gate in the corner, cross another field and pass a barn, then turn left at a waymarker up to a stile, cross this onto a track. This is the track bed of the railway used for transporting material during the construction of the dams in the Derwent Valley. Cross the track and continue on the path to cross another two stiles before emerging onto a lane.

2. Cross the lane and follow the waymarked sign at Bank House Farm, and in a couple of steps pass through the gate on the left and climb the path above the gardens to a crossroads of paths, follow the path for Win Hill by ascending the steps, at another farm house turn right onto a track and follow this to a gateway which marks the boundary for open access land. Climb steadily up the path through mixed heathland of gorse and bilberry. The path follows a drystone wall on moorland where the views open up

The author at the Trig point on Win Hill

over the Derwent Valley and Bamford Edge beyond. The path then enters a conifer plantation where at a crossroads of paths a signpost indicates the direction left for Win Hill. Follow this broad path uphill until emerging from the woods where a stile is crossed before the path becomes steeper, with steps, leading up to the rocky summit of Win Hill and the trig point. The views are outstanding over Stanage Edge, Ladybower Reservoir and Lose Hill. There are usually resident sheep that prey on walker's lunch's on the top. It is a good place to catch your breath and appreciate this lofty viewing point.

3. From the top climb down to gain the path westward, the views along this path are stupendous on both sides of this broad ridge. Continue to follow the main upper path, shortly a wall is joined on the left, at the end of which the path swings northwest. Continue on this lovely path steadily descending across the moor towards another wall surrounding a forest. This is Wooler Knoll. Continue alongside the wall until the path descends and is joined by another broad path coming up from the left. This is a Roman Road, bear right to pass through a gate at a drystone wall, the path

gradually runs back towards the wall around the forest where the Hope Cross stands. Check out the quaint ancient spellings of place names on its four sides. Carry on to the crossroads of tracks at a stile and turn left to follow the path which shortly turns right and descends sharply into Jagger's Clough (named after the men who once led pack horses across the moors before the turnpikes were built). Cross the brook and almost double back to climb out of the clough. The path then descends down to Clough Farm. Follow the path signed Edale Youth Hostel, this path skirts around above the farm and crosses a brook and stile. Follow the path which is joined by a drystone wall.

4. Continue along the path as it turns away from the wall to skirt past the red roofed Youth Hostel and then cross Lady Booth Brook before turning left to meet the access road at the front of the hostel. Cross the car park, then pass through a gate and continue along the grassy path along the flank of the hillside, crossing several fields then through a copse and bear left down to a broad gravel path by Woodhouse Farm. Turn right and follow the path past a gate to Nether Ollerbrook. Pass between the buildings and bear left to follow the track, pass through a couple of gates then cross Grinds Brook in a small wood and emerge onto the road next to a cemetery. Turn left for the station, Rambler Inn and the Moorlands Visitor Center, right for the Old Nags Head

## Historical Notes

### Bamford Mill

The mill was originally a corn mill in the 17th century but at the turn of the 19th century it was converted to produce cotton by the Moore family. A weir was constructed across the River Derwent alongside the mill to increase the power required for the mill's waterwheel. By the mid 19th century the mill employed 170 workers and provided the main employment for Bamford. The mill closed as a working mill in 1965. Following several smaller industrial businesses, the mill complex was converted to residential apartments. The legacy of the Moore family and their influence in the village may be seen to this day in the form of the church, church hall, school, and the mill houses. More information at **www.peakdistrictinformation.com/towns/bamford.php**

### The Derwent Dams

The dams were constructed due to the huge increase in demand for water resulting from the Industrial Revolution and urbanisation of the 19th century

of the industrial cities of the East Midlands and South Yorkshire. During World War II the reservoir was used by pilots of the 617 Squadron for practising the low-level flights needed for Operation Chastise (commonly known as the 'Dam Busters' raids), due to its similarity to the German dams.
See: **http://en.wikipedia.org/wiki/Derwent_Reservoir_ (Derbyshire)**

## Hope Cross

The cross is 7 feet high and bears the names of Edale, Glossop, Hope and Sheffield on its faces. The date 1737 is carved below the Hope face, this being the date it was restored or replaced. It is located at an important ancient packhorse route known as 'Doctors Gate' through the Peak District.
More information at:
**www.derbyshireheritage.co.uk/Menu/Ancient/crosses/Hope-cross.php**

# WALK 12
# Lose Hill and Mam Tor

*An exhilarating classic ridge walk taking in two peaks with fantastic views all the way, starting from the walker's Mecca of Edale.*

| | |
|---|---|
| Route | Edale – Hollins Cross – Lose Hill – Mam Tor |
| Start/finish | By train: Edale railway station<br>By car: Public pay and display car park near station |
| Distance and grade | 6 miles circular route – 1646 ft (502m) ascent – Moderate/Hard |
| Map | OS Outdoor Leisure 1 The Dark Peak District |
| Terrain | Some steep rough stretches with stiles, but mainly on good easy to follow undulating paths, and a little quiet road walking |
| Refreshments | The Penny Pot next to the station; The Rambler Inn and Old Nags Head Pub in Edale |

## Directions to the walk

**Public transport**: Travel to Manchester city centre then catch a train from Manchester Piccadilly for the 2 hourly service from Sunday to Friday, or hourly on Saturdays to Edale.

**By car**: **Sat Nav**: Postcode: S33 7ZN will get you to Edale station (grid ref: SK 124853),

**Road directions**: From the A6 southbound take the slip road following a roundabout to exit at Chapel en le Frith onto unclassified road on left and follow directions for Edale. Follow the road 3½ miles over Rushup Edge and fork left to follow the sign for Edale. This narrow, steep winding road passes through Mam Nick and then Barbers Booth before arriving at Edale. A large pay and display car park is on the left just beyond a junction for the station on the left.

## Walk Description

The Vale of Edale is a beautiful valley which benefits from its remoteness with only the railway providing direct access from Manchester. Consequently there is a timeless feeling here with little commercialism and unspoiled countryside and grand mountain scenery. It is a rambler's delight with great walking routes, which are focussed on Edale, the start point for the Pennine Way.

With its two atmospheric walker's pubs, this is the starting point for this classic ridge walk, which arguably must rank as the best English ridge walk outside the Lake District. The walk along the ridge between Mam Tor and Lose Hill gives a wonderful uplifting experience of spaciousness and wellbeing. The walk involves some steep rocky paths and some degree of exposure but as long as the paths are followed the route is safe. The walk follows a path which has a gradual ascent up to the saddle of Hollins Cross, then follows the exhilarating walk along the ridge over Back Tor to Lose Hill. From the top there is a magnificent 360 degree view over the Hope Valley, Kinder Scout, Win Hill and the Eastern Peak district edges. Then returning to Hollins Cross with the grand perspective of the ridge in view all the way to the massive bulk of Mam Tor. The walk continues along the ridge to the summit of Mam Tor before descending to Mam Nick, then by a path descending past farms and to the lower slopes of the Vale of Edale to the characterful village of Edale.

This is a challenging hill walk which is steep in places and as there are no facilities on the route, it requires you to take all the sustenance needed for about a four hour walk. It is essential to have good walking boots and good outdoor clothing for any change of weather conditions. The weather on the ridge can be much more severe than at lower levels. A fair day with the better chance of good visibility is essential to get the full benefit of the great views.

## Walk Directions

1. From Edale station turn right to pass under the bridge to a road junction, turn right (**car users join the route here**) and walk 50m, turn left past a National Trust sign for Hardenclough Farm. Follow this narrow lane over a stone bridge spanning the River Noe, then past the farm where the lane narrows and bends left then right. Look out for a small gate and signpost in the hedge on the left just before a five barred gate at the entrance to a farm. Turn left to pass through the small gate onto a gravel path turn left to follow the path, pass through a gate and over a small brook then through a small wooded area. Cross a stile at a drystone wall then a second stile where there is a marked change from cultivated land to moorland. The path gets steeper here and more rutted, towards the top it is joined by another path from the left before reaching the saddle of Hollins Cross. The view opens up to reveal the Hope Valley on the other side of the ridge. There is a memorial stone to a walker at the crossing

point. This was once the route followed by mourners following the coffins of people who were passing from Edale to be buried in Castleton.

2. Facing towards the Hope Valley bear left and carry on along the broad path alongside the broken drystone wall eastward towards Lose Hill. The views either side along the ridge are superb. Further on the rocky knoll of Back Tor is reached, where the path passes a stile then twists steeply up and continues along the ridge passing a cairn. Follow the now paved path up to the summit at 476m elevation of Lose Hill or Ward's Piece, so called after Mr G.H.B. 'Bert' Ward in 1945 by the Ramblers' Association in appreciation of his support and promotion of rambling. A toposcope built at the summit helps identify the surrounding landmarks.

Back Tor presents a challenge to walkers on the way to Lose Hill

3. After sufficient time to rest and absorb the superb views, turn and retrace your steps back along the ridge. The return gives a further dimension to the views as the path heads towards Mam Tor, the so called 'shivering mountain', seen in the far distance with its massive easterly facing slope which gave way in 1979 to cut off the main road into Castleton. Follow the path back over Back Tor, with more great views, on to Hollins Cross and then cross a stile to continue along the paved path, gradually ascending the ridge to gain the summit of Mam Tor at 517m elevation. This has a Trig point and is the site of an ancient Bronze Age hill fort, traces of the ditch and rampart may be seen. There are also flattened areas around the summit which are the remains of the dwellings of the people who lived here 3,500 years ago.

The toposcope on Lose Hill, Win Hill can be seen in the distance

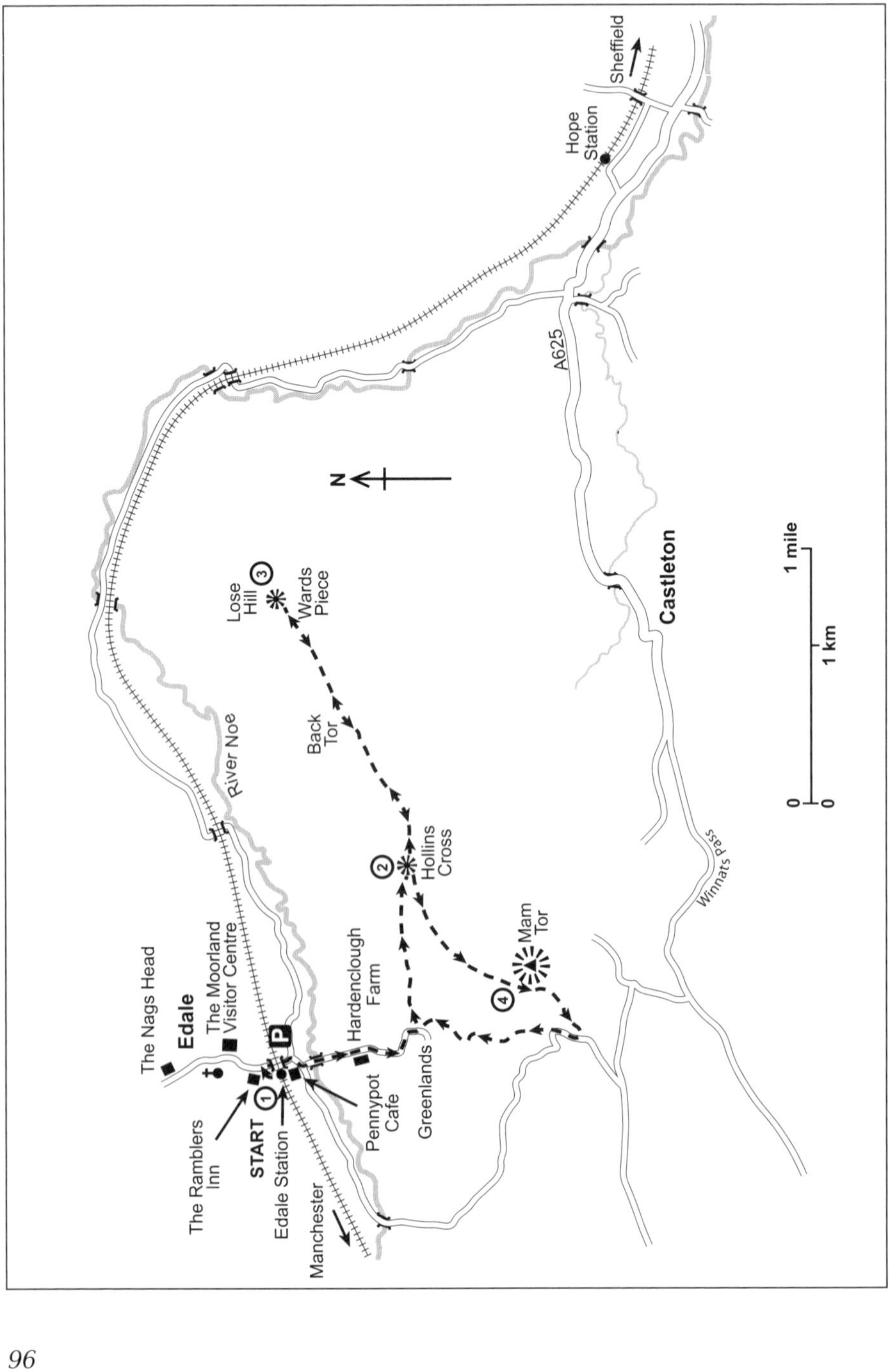
The Nags Head
Edale
The Moorland Visitor Centre
P
The Ramblers Inn
START
1
Edale Station
Manchester
Pennypot Cafe
Greenlands
Hardenclough Farm
2
Hollins Cross
Mam Tor
4
River Noe
Back Tor
Lose Hill
3
Wards Piece
N
A625
Castleton
Winnats Pass
Hope Station
Sheffield
0
0
1 mile
1 km

Mam Tor viewed from Back Tor

The views from here across the Vale of Edale towards Kinder Scout with its flat moorland top are excellent. This view of the Dark Peak can be compared with the White Peak with its deep gorges and grassy hill tops towards the south over Castleton. The Winnats Pass and Cave Dale which can be seen in this direction are typical of this kind of limestone landscape. This summit is a very popular spot and can get crowded with people out for a picnic on a fine summers day, this is in part due to the car park not far away giving easy access up the paved path from Mam Nick. Nevertheless it is a good spot on the walk to join them, enjoy the views and have a picnic before the descent down to Edale.

4. Having had a break, the way down is by way of a paved path past reminders of the prehistoric significance of the Bronze Age fort with artistic interpretations in the form of pottery, implements and dwellings. Pass through a gate onto the road through the high pass of Mam Nick, turn right and follow the road for 110m,then pass through a stile by a bus

stop on the right and bear left to follow the path descending next to a fence. Continue to follow this path alongside a wall which twists and turns down as it approaches a farm (Greenlands). Skirt around the farm boundary to a small gate on the left and a signpost indicating Edale. Pass through the gate which leads onto the narrow lane from which the walk started. Follow the lane back past Hardenclough Farm over the River Noe, turn right at the T-junction then left to Edale. The railway station is on the left. Straight on under the railway bridge is The Rambler Inn, and further up the lane is the Moorland Visitor Centre and the Nags Head pub.

## Historical Notes

### Win Hill and Lose Hill

There is a legend that Win Hill gets its name from the Battle of Win Hill and Lose Hill in 626. Prince Cwichelm and his father, King Cynegils of Wessex gathered their forces on neighbouring Lose Hill and marched on the Northumbrians based on Win Hill. Despite their superior numbers, Wessex was defeated by the Northumbrians by building a wall and rolling boulders down upon them. As there is no record of this battle in any Anglo-Saxon source it should best be regarded as a myth.

### Mam Tor

The hill is a 517m (1,696 ft) elevation. Its name means 'mother hill', so called because frequent landslips on its eastern face have resulted in a multitude of 'mini-hills' beneath it. These landslips, which are caused by unstable lower layers of shale, also give the hill its alternative nickname of shivering mountain. In 1979 the A625 road (Sheffield to Chapel en le Frith) was blocked by the crumbling eastern side of the hill, and has remained closed ever since. Nearby are four show caves: Blue John Cavern, Speedwell Cavern, Peak Cavern and Treak Cliff Cavern where lead, Blue John, fluorspar and other minerals were once mined.
More information at **en.wikipedia.org/wiki/Mam_Tor**

More of the authors photographs can be found at:
**www.geograph.org.uk/search.php?i=46114962**
Press the tab key marked Map to get the locations

# WALK 13
# Angelzarke and Rivington Reservoir

*Linear and circular walks following a line of reservoirs and waterways in a wooded and moorland landscape full of historical and natural interest.*

| | |
|---|---|
| **Route** | **Horwich – Rivington Country Park – Anglezarke reservoir – White Coppice – The Goit – Brinscall** |
| **Start/finish** | **Linear Route A: Start: The Crown Hotel, Horwich; Finish: Brinscall<br>Circular Routes B and C: By bus: The Crown Hotel, Horwich<br>By car: Great House Barn car park, Rivington Lane** |
| **Distance and grade** | **Route A: 7¾ miles for bus users – 85332 ft (193m) ascent – Moderate<br>Route B: 7 miles for bus users – 740 ft (201m) ascent – Moderate; 4½ miles for car users – 593 ft (181m) ascent – Easy<br>Route C: 10 miles for bus users – 1085 ft (331m) ascent – Hard; 7 miles for car users – 902 ft (275181m) ascent – Moderate** |
| **Map** | **OS Explorer 287 West Pennine Moors** |
| **Terrain** | **The paths are generally well marked and are mostly on firm ground with gentle slopes. There are some stiles and field paths that can be muddy. The bus user's routes entail some roadside walking** |
| **Refreshments** | **The Great House Barn at Rivington during the summer, ice cream vans near car parks, the Yew Tree pub on Knowsley Lane, the Cricketers Arms and the Oak Tree pubs at Brinscall** |

## Directions to the start of walks

**Public transport**: Travel to Bolton or Wigan then catch bus No. 575 to the Crown in Horwich, there is a frequent service Monday to Sunday (except for an hourly Sunday service from Wigan).

**By car**: **Sat Nav**: BL6 7S will get you to The Great House Barn (grid ref: SD 628138).

**Road directions**: Take the M61 to Junction 6 then take the A6027 for Horwich. Follow the signs for Horwich, turn left onto the A673 at the Beehive Roundabout, continue until The Crown pub at a roundabout, take the first exit of the roundabout and then turn right in 50m at the next junction. This is Lever Park Avenue which leads onto Rivington Lane; the Great House Barn car park is one mile on the left.

## Directions from the finish of the linear walk

From Brinscall School Lane, bus No. 24 to Chorley, half hourly frequency Monday to Saturday, hourly on Sunday. Then catch a train for Bolton and Manchester, or to return to the Wigan/Merseyside area connect at Chorley with bus No. 362 to Wigan, quarter hourly service Monday to Saturday, half hourly on Sunday.

## Walk Description

The linear walk follows the paths of the reservoirs from the southern dam of Rivington at Horwich up to the northern tip of Anglezarke, and then follows The Goit onto picturesque White Coppice and on past farmsteads and pasture land to the tranquil village of Brinscall. The first half of the walk is quite busy at weekends, being easily accessible by car users, but beyond Anglezarke the paths are quieter and the scenery more rugged.

The linear route and the longer circular routes enable walkers to see these less trodden paths through beautiful tranquil countryside. At the start of the walk there is the honeypot of Lever Park with all its attractions including the Great House Barn, the landscape is partly moorland with mixed woodland as the paths skirt around Winter Hill and Anglezarke Moor. Water is in view nearly all the way with waterfowl including great crested grebe, and because of the diverse habitats on the route there is a chance of seeing a large variety of species of birds. The circular walks follow much of the linear route but return along fairly level paths with great views over Anglezarke and Yarrow Reservoirs.

## Walk Directions

1. **Route A: 7¾ mile Horwich to Brinscall Linear Route**
   Alighting from the bus at the Crown Hotel walk past the roundabout, follow the road past Lever Park Avenue, then where the main road bends left turn up Dryfield Road on the right to follow this road. After a sharp bend right and a bridge over a stream take the waymarked footpath on the left, carry straight on until a broad path crosses diagonally in woodland, and take this path left to The Castle. This is Lord Leverhulme's replica of Liverpool Castle built in 1912. Work on it was abandoned following his

death in 1925. Having explored round the castle continue the walk by following the broad tree lined path north from the northeast tower of the castle. Ignore the path left along the lakeside. The path comes out onto Rivington Lane, turn left and follow the path alongside to the Great House Barn, a popular watering hole with tourist information and refreshments.

2. From the Great House Barn, carry on following the road for 200m and turn left onto a broad path that crosses the road diagonally. Follow the path which bends to the right and passes the old stone Rivington primary school, then joins Horrobin Lane. Turn left and follow the road across the dam, turn right at a waymarker on the other side of the lake, beside a stone house. Follow this road alongside the lake and past a plantation of very attractive rhododendrons, then at a quaintly named mansion called 'The Street' the road comes out onto Knowsley Lane.

3. Cross over the road and pass through a kissing gate to continue following the field path alongside a wall. Bear left on the grassy path and ascend a low hill then turn left onto a rough path which skirts around a dam to a stile, cross this to arrive at small car park, go through another stile next to a gate onto Back Lane. Follow the road for 500m past some attractive ivy covered cottages and take the waymarked track on the right for Heath Fold Farm. Walk down the track and turn left just before the farm onto a broad path. This is soon joined by a farm track, continue straight on, taking in the views over the reservoir and Pennine moors on this quiet country track. After 500m look out for a waymarker and stile on the right, cross this and a small field, continue to another stile and path into the woods alongside the reservoir. Descend a set of steps, cross a footbridge and continue along the woodland path. Birdsong and squirrels usually accompany you along this path, which gives fine views across the reservoir over to Waterman's Cottage. The path comes out through a kissing gate and steps onto Moor Road. Turn right to cross the dam and follow the road past Waterman's Cottage.

4. Turn left through a kissing gate next to a gate and follow the track through mixed wooded area below the steep Stronstrey Bank. This is a good place to see a variety of birds such as curlew, raptors and woodpeckers as well as the usual species. Follow the track over to a bridge, cross this then turn left to cross over the Goit at White Coppice, a favourite place for a pit stop, a lovely location and on summer weekends, refreshments can be had whilst watching a cricket match. Having taking your fill of this special place walk

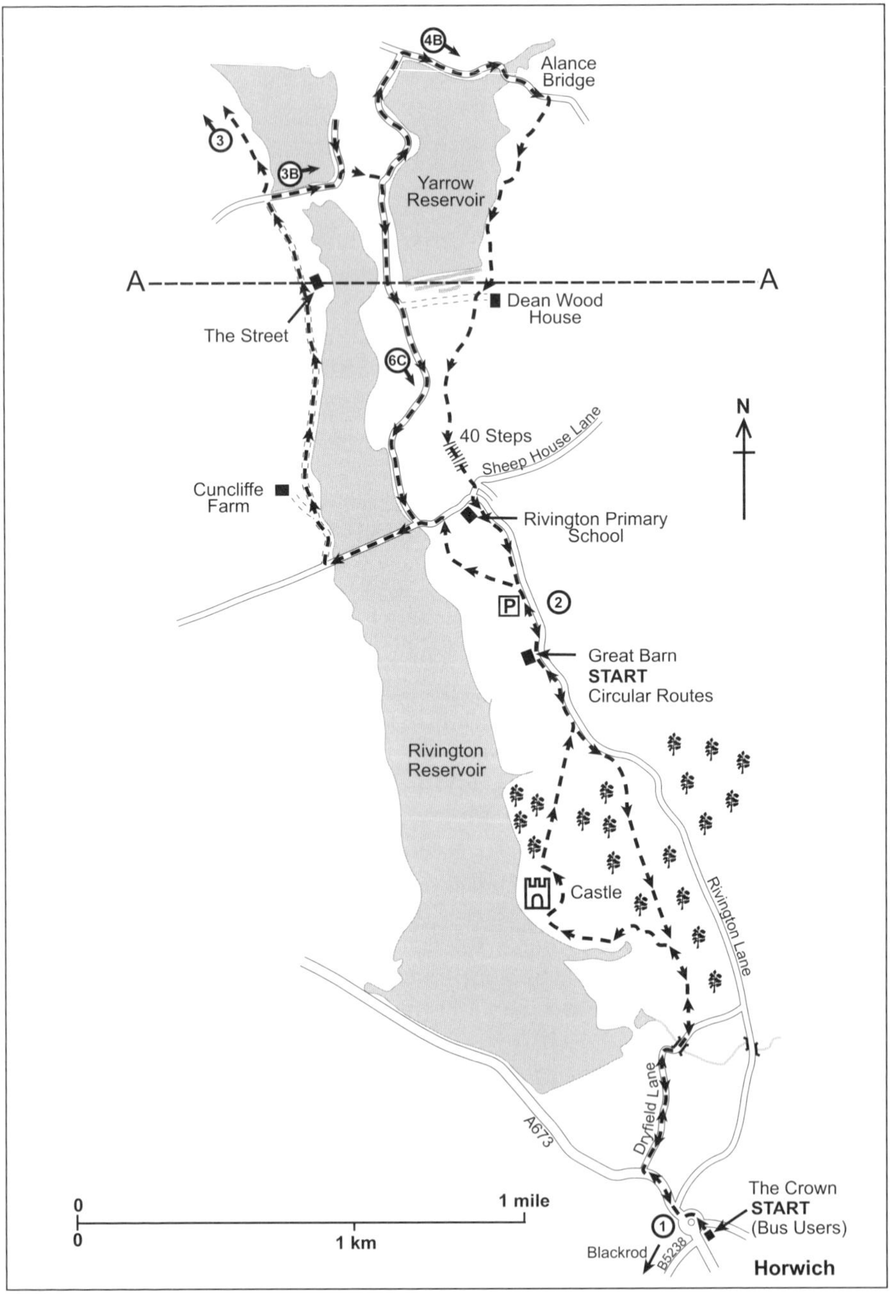

4B
Alance
Bridge
3
3B
Yarrow
Reservoir
A
A
Dean Wood
House
The Street
6C
N
40 Steps
Sheep House Lane
Cuncliffe
Farm
Rivington Primary
School
P
2
Great Barn
START
Circular Routes
Rivington
Reservoir
Castle
Rivington Lane
A673
Dryfield Lane
The Crown
START
(Bus Users)
0
1 mile
0
1 km
1
Blackrod
B5238
Horwich

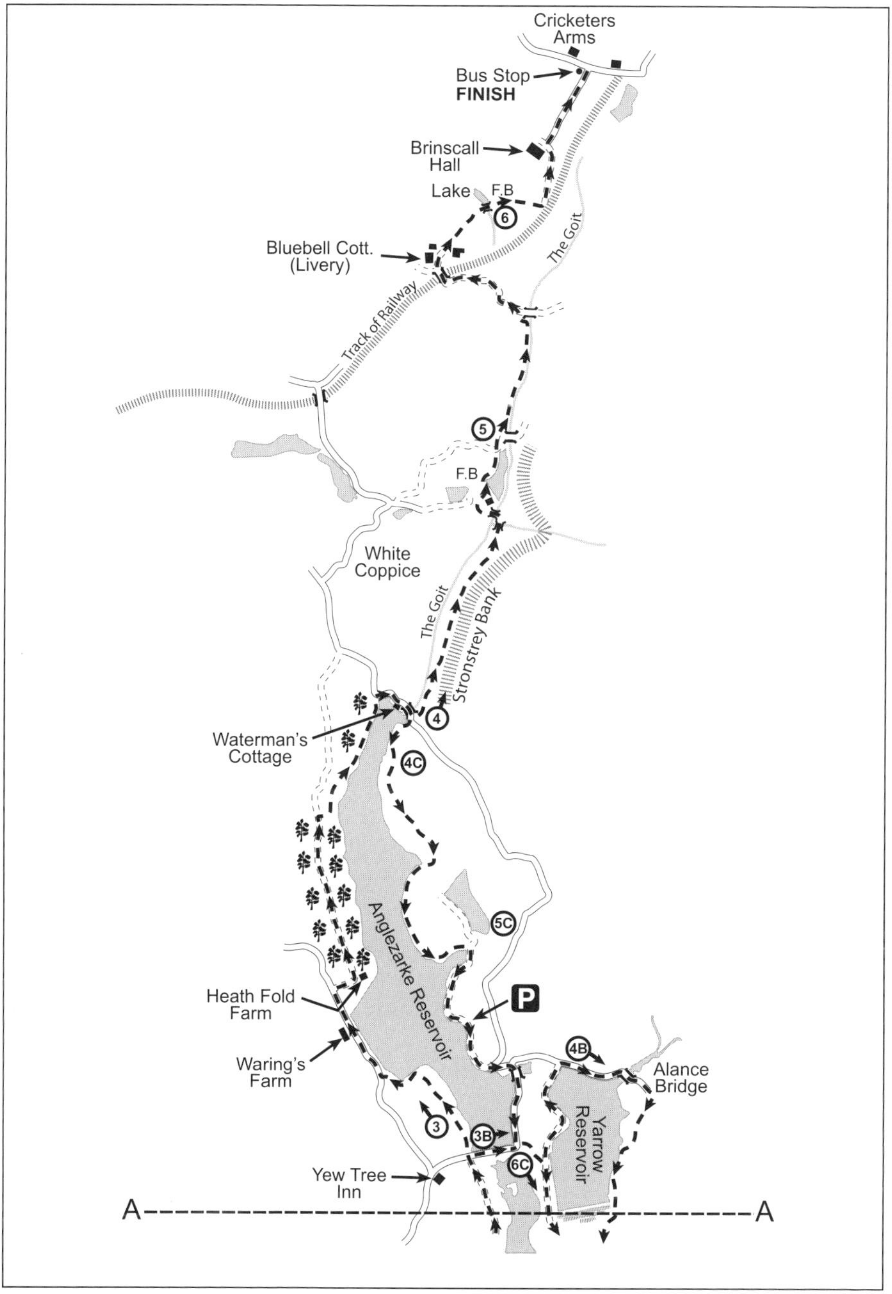

Cricketers Arms
Bus Stop
FINISH
Brinscall Hall
Lake
F.B
6
Bluebell Cott. (Livery)
The Goit
Track of Railway
5
F.B
White Coppice
The Goit
Stronstrey Bank
4
Waterman's Cottage
4C
5C
Anglezarke Reservoir
P
Heath Fold Farm
Waring's Farm
4B
Alance Bridge
Yarrow Reservoir
3
3B
6C
Yew Tree Inn
A
A

in front of the attractive cottages towards the small reservoir, turn left on a path to cross a small footbridge then turn right and follow the path to skirt around the reservoir to a track and a bridge over The Goit. Turn left before the bridge to follow this watercourse which is the feeder channel from the Roddlesworth Reservoirs near Abbey.

Footbridge over brook near White Coppice

5. Follow this attractive path for 600m to a gate and track over a bridge, pass through the gate and turn left onto the track, which climbs gently and zig-zags until it reaches the trackbed of a dismantled railway. Turn right to cross the trackbed on a stone bridge next to a farm. Bear right to pass through the farmyard and stables of Bluebell Cottage. The right of way lies beyond the large stable block on the right ,pass through a gate and cross a field keeping alongside a fence on the left. Cross a stile and cross another field to another stile which leads into a wooded area where the path emerges into an open area and a very tranquil scene with a small lake in a private garden. Cross a small footbridge and a stile then carry on through a boggy area alongside the left of the field to yet another stile which leads onto a farm track and turn right.

6. Follow the track between fields to a T-junction of tracks, turn left along a tree lined track. The track bends left to come out at Brinscall Hall. Turn right onto the tree lined road called Dick's Lane, in front of the hall, to eventually come out onto residential housing and School Lane in Brinscall. The bus stop for the bus to Chorley is on the left hand corner, and if in need of refreshment the Cricketer's Arms is diagonally across the road.

## Route B: 7 mile (4½ miles for car users) Rivington and Yarrow Reservoir circular

Bus users start the walk from point 1, and follow point 2; car users start from point 2. Then both continue on from point 3B.

3B. Turn right to cross the dam, then pass through a gate on the right onto a track, which passes near the overflow from the Yarrow Reservoir above.

Continue on the track which emerges onto another track around the reservoir, turn left and follow the track which climbs up to and over the spillway. After heavy rain this resembles a waterfall, then skirt around the reservoir before crossing a dam and joining Parsons Bullough Road.

4B. Follow the road for ½ mile passing over Alance Bridge over an inlet where the River Yarrow enters the reservoir. Continue until a waymarked kissing gate on the right, cross this and follow the path marked with yellow arrows across a field, there are good views from the path towards Rivington Pike and Winter Hill. Pass through a gate then cross a field. There are good views over the reservoir here towards the stone bridge over the spillway. The path then passes over two stiles in quick succession with a boggy area in between, stepping stones help to reduce muddy boots. The undiscernible path crosses a field parallel to the reservoir before passing alongside a drystone wall to another stile. Cross this onto a tarmacked track and turn right past a cottage and Deane Wood House, follow this down to where a brook passes under the track and pass through a kissing gate on the left to follow the lovely path alongside the brook. The path leaves the brook to a set of steps known locally as the forty steps, climb these, I think you'll find there are forty one!

Follow the path to emerge onto Sheep House Lane at Rivington. Turn right, then left, onto Rivington Lane and follow this back to the car park at The Great House Barn.

**Bus users** carry on, following the path alongside the road, then fork right on a waymarked track, then after crossing another track at a stone cottage bear right at a fork, then follow this track straight on through the park to come out at Dryfield Lane. Turn right to follow the road back to the A673 turn left for The Crown in Horwich and the bus stop.

## Route C: 10 mile (7 mile for car users) Anglezarke and Rivington Reservoir circular

Bus users start the walk from point 1, and follow points 2 and 3; car users start from point 2 and follow point 3.Then both continue on from point 4C.

4C. Continue on past the gates on the left and a few steps on cross a stile on the right, then shortly a footbridge, follow the well used delightful path as it winds its way alongside the Anglezarke Reservoir. It passes alternately through woodland and fields with a couple of stiles. Good views are to be seen over the reservoir, where the path enters a wooded area (which is full of bluebells in late spring). It joins a junction of paths at the foot of a dam. Turn sharp right onto a rough path which follows the edge of the reservoir around a wooded headland.

5C. The path emerges onto a tarmacked track, turn right and follow this down to the reservoir, follow the track alongside the reservoir then onto a road which leads up to a car park. Continue straight on to a junction of roads turn right and cross a bridge. Follow the road to a right hand bend at the dam.

6C. Turn left to pass through a gate on the left onto a track, which climbs alongside the overflow from the Yarrow Reservoir above. Continue on the track which emerges onto another track around the reservoir, turn right downhill alongside the dam. The track drops down to the Rivington Reservoir to emerge onto Horrobin Lane. Turn left to follow the lane then turn right at the Rivington Primary School. After passing the school and through the bollards, bear left to follow the broad track up to Rivington Lane. Turn right and follow the road back to the car park at The Great House Barn.

**Bus users** carry on, following the path alongside the road, then fork right on a waymarked track, then after crossing another track at a stone cottage bear right at a fork, then follow this track straight on through the park to come out at Dryfield Lane. Turn right to follow the road back to the A673 turn left for The Crown in Horwich and the bus stop.

## Historical Notes

**Lord Leverhulme** was a native of Bolton who made his fortune in soap manufacturing, landscaped a huge estate and built the castle as a scaled down replica of Liverpool Castle. The grounds were donated to the public, but looked after by the corporation of Liverpool. The reservoirs were at this time Liverpool's water supply.

### Great House Barn

The barn is on Rivington Lane, is Scandinavian in design, and is speculated to date from between 811 and 1300 AD with major renovation in 1702. The roof is spectacular with an internal oak framework.
More information at **www.bolton.org.uk/rivington.html**

More of the authors photographs can be found at:
**www.geograph.org.uk/search.php?i=46109230**
Press the tab key marked Map to get the locations

# WALK 14
# Ashurst Beacon and the Douglas Valley

*Linear and circular walks in the Douglas Valley along a canal towpath before a climb to a famous viewpoint over South Lancashire, followed by a gentle descent through pleasant countryside.*

| | |
|---|---|
| **Route** | **Parbold – Priors Wood Hall – Ashurst's Beacon – Walthew Green – Gathurst – Appley Bridge** |
| **Start/finish** | **Linear Route A: Start: Parbold Railway Station; Finish: Gathurst Railway Station**<br>**Linear Route B: Start: Parbold Railway Station; Finish: Appley Bridge Station**<br>**Circular Route C: Parbold Railway Station (car users at car park on Mill Lane)** |
| **Distance and grade** | **Route A: 6¾ miles – 725 ft (221m) ascent – Moderate**<br>**Route B: 5¾ miles – 660 ft (201m) ascent – Moderate**<br>**Route C: 7¾ miles – 646 ft (197m) ascent – Moderate** |
| **Map** | **OS Explorer 285 Southport and Chorley** |
| **Terrain** | **Mainly good well-marked paths with a couple of steep stretches and a few stiles. Some field paths can get muddy and there are a couple of stretches of quiet lane walking** |
| **Refreshments** | **The Windmill and other pubs and cafés at Parbold, the Prince William Inn on Beacon Lane, Sam's Bar and the Water's Edge at Appley Bridge; The Fox Inn at Roby Mill** |

## Directions to the walk

**Public transport:** Manchester walkers travel to Manchester city centre then catch a train from Manchester Victoria or Piccadilly stations, for a 2 trains per hour service to Parbold, Monday to Saturday. Hourly from Piccadilly on Sundays. Merseyside walkers travel to Ormskirk and catch either bus services 3A or 337 for an hourly service between Ormskirk/Parbold/Skelmersdale and Appley Bridge Monday to Saturday.

**By car**: **Sat Nav**: Postcode WN8 7NW will get you to the car park next to the canal in Mill Lane, Parbold (grid ref : SD 490105).
**Road directions**: From M6 exit at junction 27. Follow the A5209 for Parbold and Ormskirk. Parbold village is about 10km or 6 miles from exit. There is a fine viewpoint from a layby on the A5209 just past the Miller and Carter restaurant which gives views over Ashurst Beacon and the Douglas Valley. You may wish to see the famous Parbold Bottle just a 100m walk from the layby. After crossing the railway and then the canal, turn right into the village on Mill Lane, the car park is on the left directly after crossing over the canal bridge. Alternatively the Village Hall car park is on the left 200m after the railway level crossing.

## Directions from the walk

Manchester walkers return by train from either Appley Bridge which has 2 trains per hour service or from Gathurst for an hourly service.

There are many combinations of train and bus for Merseyside walkers to return home from Appley Bridge or Gathurst. Check Traveline for your best options. For car users walking the linear routes the best option is by train from either Gathurst or Appley Bridge.

## Walk Descriptions

The linear routes A and B follow the same route until Ashurst Beacon where the shorter route B heads down to Appley Bridge, whilst the longer route A passes through Roby Mill and the hamlet of Walthew Green then via Dean Wood to Gathurst.

The short circular route C follows the course of route B and then returns to Parbold via the Leeds Liverpool Canal. From Parbold the towpath is along a particularly pretty stretch of the canal before turning off past Priors Wood Hall. Farm tracks and gently ascending paths are followed before a steeper section up to Ashurst Beacon. I came face to face with a deer on Lees Lane on one memorable day's walking. There are great views over to Wales and Merseyside to the west and the Pennines to the east, Blackpool tower may be seen and on clear days The Lake District fells. A pub near the top can provide some sustenance if needed, before descending on good paths across open farmland with the West Pennine Moors always on view.

The longer route A to Gathurst follows a tree lined stretch of path that leads down to Roby Mill and The Fox Inn. A short stretch of road brings you to the hamlet of Walthew Green, a peaceful place that belies the fact the M6 and Wigan are just a couple of miles away. More paths and tracks and an ancient looking causeway lead down to Dean Wood, then alongside the River Douglas to Gathurst.

The shorter routes B and C follow a quiet dead end lane, then onto paths alongside brooks down to the River Douglas, passing duck ponds and a fishing lodge, and with lovely views and interest all the way to Appley Bridge. Circular route C continues along a beautiful stretch of the Leeds Liverpool Canal past Appley Locks to Parbold.

## Walk Directions

### Route A: 6¾ miles linear route to Gathurst Station

1. From the station turn right onto Mill Lane and walk to the canal bridge, cross and join the towpath on the left of the road. **Car users** join here from the car park next to bridge. Walk along the towpath for about one mile to bridge number 40 over the canal, leave the path to take a track down to a bridge over the River Douglas. Follow the track straight on until a junction of tracks, turn right to take a part concrete track which ascends gently past a small wood on the right. At the gate at the end of the track, a stile on the left leads to a field, keep to the right skirting the edge around the gardens of Priors Wood Hall.

2. A small gate in the wall leads to a path through a wooded area and a track that shortly joins the main farm track. It is worthwhile to have a pause to take in the medieval hall and its gardens. Carry on down this track which joins Lees Lane, turn right and follow this road to a road junction. Turn left to take the unmarked Hillock Lane. Walk up this road for about 300m, then take the public footpath signed track on the left. Follow this track which climbs steeply on slates and bricks made locally at Dalton Quarry.

3. Look out for a stile in the hedge on the left of the track, cross the stile into a field, keeping a line of trees by a bank to the right. Pass a metal gate with stile and waymarker. Pass through some kissing gates and cross a plank bridge then on to another stile and footbridge. Cross a boggy field then another stile and a footbridge over a brook, follow the path which brings you onto a dirt track. Follow the track which emerges onto a road.

4. Turn right on the narrow road (Long Heys Lane) and walk uphill for 250m, pass Ashleigh Farm and look out for stone steps set back in the embankment on the right leading up to a path. Follow the path along the edge of a field then cross a footbridge and a stile. Cross a field diagonally uphill and cross another stile. Continue along the path uphill to the Beacon at the summit.

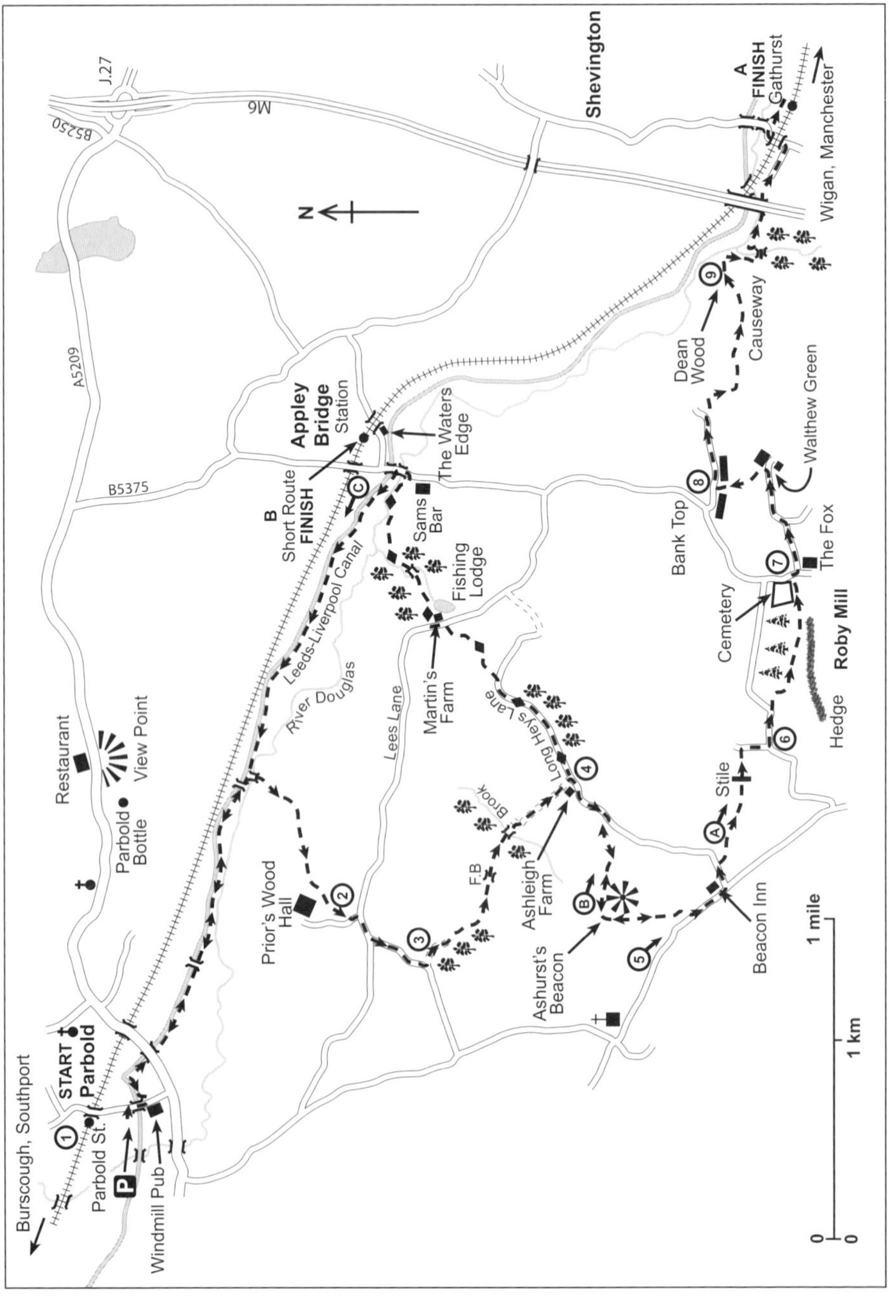

Burscough, Southport
1
START
Parbold
Parbold St.
P
Windmill Pub
M6
J.27
B5250
A5209
B5375
N
Shevington
A
FINISH
Gathurst
Wigan, Manchester
Restaurant
View Point
Parbold Bottle
Appley Bridge
Station
B
Short Route
FINISH
C
The Waters Edge
Sams Bar
Leeds-Liverpool Canal
River Douglas
Fishing Lodge
Martin's Farm
Lees Lane
Long Heys Lane
Prior's Wood Hall
2
3
4
F.B
Brook
Ashleigh Farm
B
Ashurst's Beacon
5
Beacon Inn
A
Stile
6
Hedge
Roby Mill
Cemetery
7
The Fox
Bank Top
8
Walthew Green
Dean Wood
Causeway
9
1 mile
1 km
0
0

**For the linear route (A) to Gathurst continue to point 5. For the routes (B and C) via Appley Bridge go onto point B.**

5. After exploring the area around the Beacon and taking in the grand vista with the aid of a toposcope to locate the landmarks, head directly south down a path to Beacon Road and follow the road past the Beacon Inn then turn left onto Long Heys Road. After 100m, before a left hand bend, look out for the hidden waymarked footpath on the right. Follow this hedge lined path which then emerges onto open farmland and descends steeply downhill for 400m between fields. At the foot of the hill a stone stile is crossed before a farm track. Turn right onto a track which joins Crow Lane.

6. Turn left to follow the road for 200m until a stile and a waymarked footpath on the right. Take the path diagonally left and head for a gap in a wooded area across a field. Pass through this gap and follow the path to the right to skirt around a formal plantation of conifers. This path descends gently between mature woods and a high hedge on the right. The area looks as if it was once the grounds of a stately home. The path finally ends at the

The stone stile at the foot of Ashurst Beacon Hill

back of housing where it dog legs left then right to emerge onto Roby Mill at St Teresa's Cemetery. Turn right along road to the Fox Inn.

7. Turn left into School Lane, follow this road which soon becomes a narrow lane, bear left at a no through road sign and keep straight on until the hamlet of Walthew Green, where a 'danger children playing' sign is passed. At a neat row of cottages on the left, a waymarker sign low down indicates a path which descends and bends left to follow a field boundary, then climbs up steeply between fields towards a gap in more housing.

8. The path ends on Ayrefield Road, turn right to follow the road which soon becomes a dirt track. Follow the track until it splits at a gate into Ayrefield House. Pass through the gate on the right into a small wooded area and follow the wall on the left for 50m. Follow the path right to where the path emerges at a gate onto open farmland. Continue to follow the path which appears to be an ancient causeway whose slabs may be seen on the field boundary, the path turns sharp left and gently descends downhill past a pond on the left until a wooded area.

9. Follow the path downhill through the woods, continue on steeply down following a fence on left, turn right at a gate on left. The path starts getting muddy here, carry on to reach a bridge over Dean Brook, cross this and turn left on a track which comes out on the bank of the River Douglas. The track passes under the M6 motorway bridge, then the railway appears alongside the track (this must be a unique place in Britain where a motorway crosses over a railway which in turn crosses a canal). This is followed to Gathurst Road. Turn left under the railway bridge, the end of the walk is the station approach road on the right.

### Route B: 5¾ miles linear route to Appley Bridge Station

Follow points 1, 2, 3 and 4 then on to B

B. From the Beacon return the way you came, down to Long Heys Lane, follow the lane downhill until a sharp right hand bend. Take the waymarked path on the left, the path descends steeply besides a brook with the sound of a waterfall, continue down to stepping stones,cross the brook and continue on, at a boggy patch the path has a by- pass route on the left, which soon returns to the main route. Cross a stile and continue past a duck pond with a gaggle of geese and a couple of donkeys, the path emerges onto Lees Lane. A fishing lodge lies opposite. Turn left past

Martins Farm and take a waymarked path on the right which starts on stone steps. Follow this delightful path alongside a brook through woods, then cross the brook and onto open farmland. Follow the path as it crosses the fields to the bank of the River Douglas, continue along the path which emerges at Appley Lane North. Turn left and follow the road across the river and the canal, then turn right for 150m to reach the station and the end of the walk.

### Route C: 7¾ miles Circular route from Parbold

Follow points 1,2,3,4 and B, then on to C

C. The circular route continues on from B until the bridge over the canal. Turn left here to follow the canal towpath after crossing the river. The towpath passes the unusual double Appley Locks, continue along the canal side to return to Parbold.

## Historical Notes

### Parbold Bottle

Parbold lies at the foot of Parbold Hill, where the famous Parbold Bottle, now restored, can be found from a small path leading off the A5209. This is a stone monument about 2m high, which closely resembles a giant bottle. It was built in 1832 to commemorate the Reform Act, and is visible from the Leeds Liverpool Canal. I have to thank Stan, a local walker whom I met on a recce walk for showing me the way to the Parbold Bottle.

The Parbold Bottle

### The Douglas Navigation

The River Douglas was made into a navigable canal before the construction of the Leeds Liverpool Canal made it redundant. The Navigation was mainly built to serve the collieries around Wigan, another factor was the supply of limestone for agriculture.

The navigation was in full use by 1741, and was about ten miles in length. It was continually improved to enable the use of larger boats with fixed masts.

Despite the opening of the canal from Liverpool in 1774, the navigation remained in use until 1782.

At Gathurst, the canal lock which joined the navigation has been filled in, but its copings are visible, and the lock house at Gathurst faces the river and not the canal, a reminder of the former importance of the keeper's job in controlling the river level.

Further information: **www.mikeclarke.myzen.co.uk/Douglas%20Navigation.html**

## Priors Wood Hall

There is a lack of detail relating to the early history of Priors Wood Hall in Dalton. It is thought to have connections with Burscough Priory. The Haydock family, one of whom was killed at Agincourt, held the property in trust for the Prior and a priest's hiding hole, a reminder of penal times, was found there. In the 1930s the house and its 119 acres was purchased by the Catholic Land Association, for £3,000. The aim was to make some contribution, however small, to the problem of unemployment then prevalent, by training a community that could work, and live off, the land.

Attributed to: **www.ourladysparbold.org.uk/historymenu.htm**

## Ashurst Beacon

The beacon at 173m is one of a chain of Lancashire beacons, which included Everton in Liverpool, to Lancaster Castle, built in the 16th Century by Sir William Ashurst to serve as an early warning system against invaders, particularly during the French Napoleonic war. It is a magnificent viewpoint over many counties. From the foot of the monument visitors can, on a clear day, see the mountains of Snowdonia, the Pennines, Blackpool Tower, the South Lake District mountains and the grand vista of Liverpool and the Mersey.

More of the authors photographs can be found at:
**www.geograph.org.uk/search.php?i=46115325**
Press the tab key marked Map to get the locations

# WALK 15
# Harrock Hill and Fairy Glen

*A choice of linear and circular walks passing through pastoral Lancashire countryside to visit a ruined windmill, a great viewpoint, a Bronze Age site and an enchanting waterfall in a famous glen.*

| | |
|---|---|
| Route | Parbold – Hunter's Hill – Harrock Hill – High Moor – Boar's Den Burrow – Fairy Glen – Appley Bridge – Leeds Liverpool Canal |
| Start/finish | Circular Route A: Parbold Railway Station (car users use car park at Parbold Village Hall)<br>Linear Route B: Start: Parbold Railway Station; Finish: Appley Bridge Railway Station |
| Distance and grade | Route A: 7½ miles – 813 ft (248m) ascent – Moderate<br>Route B: 7 miles for train users – 780 ft (238m) ascent – Moderate |
| Map | OS Explorer 285 Southport and Chorley |
| Terrain | Mainly good paths on firm surfaces, but some field paths can be muddy. Some short steep stretches and a few stiles. Some quiet road walking |
| Refreshments | The Railway, and other pubs and cafés at Parbold. Sam's Bar at Appley Bridge |

## Directions to the walk

**Public transport**: As for walk 14.

**By car: Sat Nav**: Postcode WN8 7DN will get you to the car park next to Village Hall at The Green off The Common, Parbold (grid ref: SD 490110).

**Road directions**: As for walk Number 14 to Parbold, the car park is on the left, 200m after the railway level crossing.

## Directions from the walk

As for walk 14.

## Walk Description

A great walk with outstanding views ranging from the Douglas Valley and Ashurst Beacon, the Lancashire plain towards Southport, and the West Pennine moors. The walk is especially attractive in late spring to view the bluebells in Fairy Glen. The highpoints are a ruined windmill and the great views from a trig point at the top of Parbold Hill. There follows a pleasant woodland farm track past Butteries Wood, then field paths lead on to an ancient barrow named 'Boars Den'. The route then descends through the appropriately named Fairy Glen with its wild flowers and waterfalls. The return leg for the circular route (A) follows tree lined tracks and paths and an attractive stretch of towpath of the Leeds Liverpool Canal back to Parbold. Alternatively a linear route (B) from Fairy Glen follows farm paths and tracks back to Appley Bridge station.

## Walk Directions

### Route A:

1. From the station turn left and cross the level crossing, walk up Station Road for 100m and turn right into Tan House Lane past a row of shops. Car users from the Village Hall car park turn right down Station Road for 100m and turn left into Tan House Lane. Walk up this pleasant road to the end. At the T-junction cross the road and follow the gated track next to a school on the right. Cross a stile and follow the path alongside a hedge and carry on by the side of the wood on the left. As the path gently ascends, the views open up towards Ashurst's Beacon. Cross a wooden footbridge and a stile. From here bear right uphill, the path crosses more open fields, a small copse is passed on the left of the path and then a stile to cross another field to reach a gate with stile on Stoney Lane.

2. Turn right along the road for a few yards the turn left to cross a stile onto a path before a house, keep to a fence on right, pass a stile amidst a muddy area. Keep on forward and walk up to a wall, keep the wall on left and follow it to the corner of the field. At this point the views open up westward over the Lancashire plain. Cross a stile at the corner of the field onto a track, turn right to follow the track, bear left at a quarry entrance, and then keep right to follow a bridleway past some stone farm buildings. Keep on uphill along the sandy track, a grand panoramic view opens out to the left over the Lancashire plain towards Southport. A kestrel was seen here hovering perfectly stationary over the hedgerow looking for prey. The path skirts the quarry on Hunger Hill, which is now disused and is in the process of being landscaped, until a car park is reached.

3. After perhaps a breather at the top of the hill, turn left downhill along Bannister Lane. Pass a large house called Hunters Meet, then a large patch of gorse comes into view. Continue on until the junction with Jacksons Lane on the right, turn up this single track road to a fork, keep left to follow the road and turn right at a gate at a waymarker sign and a sign for Bow Wood Barn. Cross the cattlegrid and follow the concrete track, bear right past a farm, where the track bends right cross the stepped stile on the left, then cross a field path uphill between young protected trees to another stile. Cross this onto an old sunken path which passes through gorse and dense bushes. The path emerges alongside a stone wall, continue to follow the path through bracken to a ladder stile over the wall. Cross the stile and follow the path between the fenced woodland and the stone wall, then at the end of the fence bear left to follow the path through dense woodland until the ruin of Harrock's Windmill comes into view.

A ladder stile on the path to Harrock Hill Windmill

Harrock's Windmill

4. Following exploration of the ruin, continue on past the ruin and bear right through the wood to a metal gate and cross the stile at the corner of a field. Follow the left field boundary towards the opposite corner, taking in the views over the West Pennine Moors, then turn right at the corner and follow the boundary alongside a tree plantation to a waymarker and gate. Turn left to follow the path alongside a field ascending gently towards the telecommunication masts seen in the distance. Pass through another gate and continue on to reach another tree plantation and a pass through a further gate, then follow the path between the plantation and a fence. At a junction of paths continue straight on to follow the field

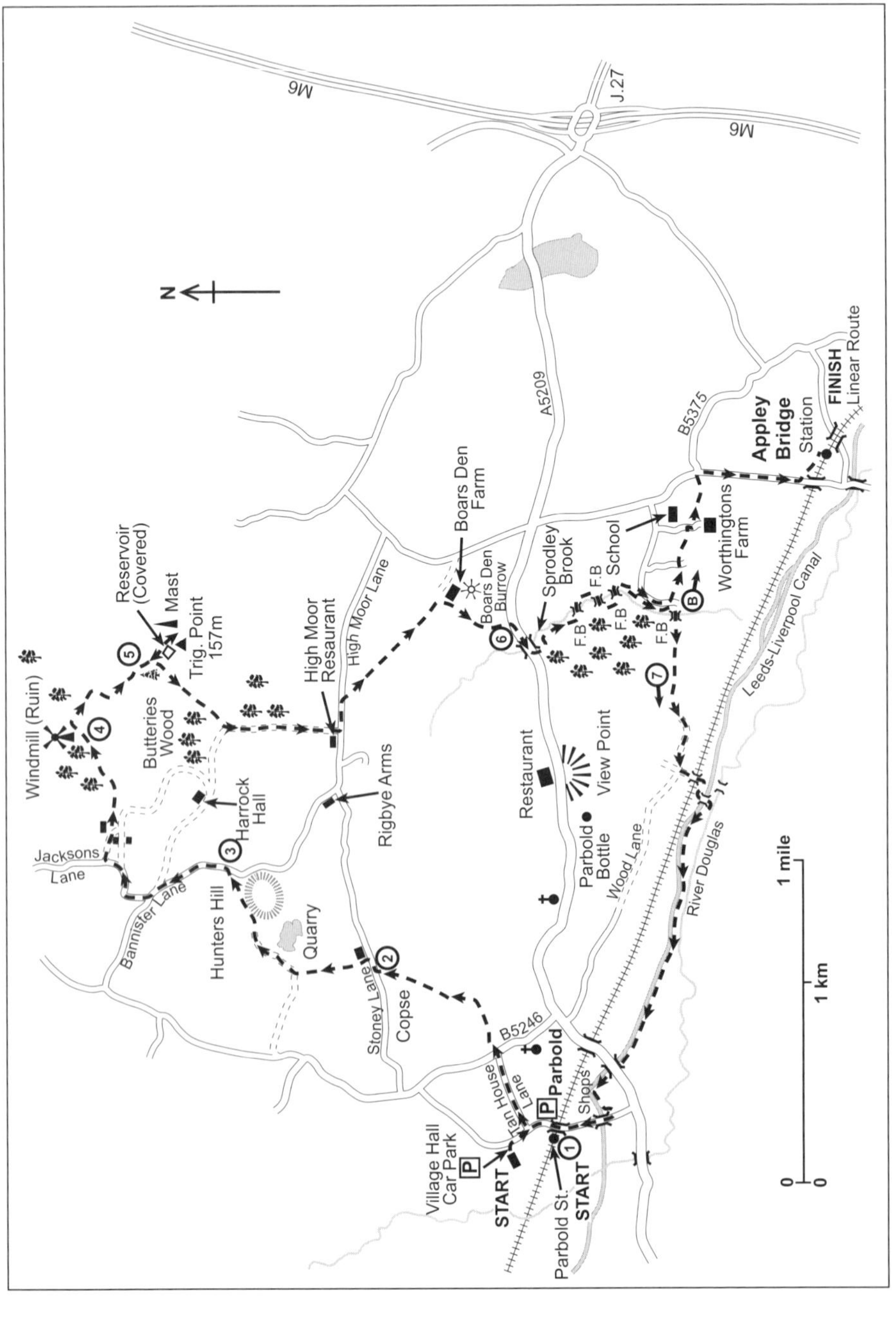

M6
M6
J.27
N
A5209
B5375
Appley Bridge
Station
FINISH
Linear Route
Leeds-Liverpool Canal
River Douglas
Worthingtons Farm
School
B
F.B
F.B
F.B
F.B
Sprodley Brook
Boars Den Burrow
Boars Den Farm
6
7
High Moor Lane
High Moor Resaurant
Reservoir (Covered)
Mast
Trig. Point 157m
5
Windmill (Ruin)
4
Butteries Wood
Harrock Hall
3
Jacksons Lane
Bannister Lane
Hunters Hill
Quarry
2
Stoney Lane
Copse
Rigbye Arms
Restaurant
View Point
Parbold Bottle
Wood Lane
B5246
Tan House Lane
Parbold
Shops
Village Hall Car Park
P
P
START
1
Parbold St.
START
1 mile
1 km
0
0

boundary alongside a mesh fence to a covered reservoir where the trig point is sited. This is the highest point of Harrock Hill at 157m (515 feet). The extensive views here, especially over the West Pennine Moors with Winter Hill and Rivington Pike most prominent, are worth taking in before returning to the tree plantation area at the junction of paths.

5. Turn left to go through an archway of bushes over the well made path alongside the plantation. The path descends between pastures and then a beautiful tree lined stretch next to Butteries Wood leads onto a gate and a concrete track from Harrock Hall. Bear left to follow the track downhill. Good views over Ashurst Beacon and the Douglas Valley are seen ahead as the track descends to High Moor Lane. The track ends next to High Moor restaurant, turn left to follow the road for 100m to a waymarked path on the right. Take this path to follow the edge of farm fields for 500m to a farm track, keep on to the farm and turn right at the gate to skirt round the farmhouse. Keep straight on where the farm boundary turns left and look out for the ancient barrow known as 'Boars Den' on the left. It is a small hillock of bare ground in the middle of a field. Follow the field edge around to a farm track, turn left and follow the track to a layby on the A5209.

High Moor Restaurant ,with the path waymarker in view just beyond

6. Turn right to follow this main road for 200m. Cross the road carefully and take the path on the left of the track entrance marked Fairy Glen, follow this path between masses of bluebells (in late spring) next to Sprodley Brook. Cross a footbridge over the brook and continue alongside the brook to another footbridge, cross this ignoring the path on the left which is also on a footbridge. Continue straight on, ignoring another path off to the left over another footbridge, the path then descends a flight of steps then emerges below a waterfall and a footbridge, cross this and the path follows the brook on the right in a small gorge. Ignore another path which crosses a footbridge off to the right, here there are wild garlic giving off their pungent smell in the shady damp woods. Continue on to a junction of paths.

**At the junction, the choice of linear or circular routes is made. The circular route continues at point 7 and the linear route at point B.**

7. Bear right down a flight of concrete steps, cross a footbridge then along a boardwalk, then climb the steps up to a ladder stile out of the wood to a field. As there is no clear path, cross straight across this field to reach a path at a gate on a corner of a plantation. Follow the boundary at the bottom of a field alongside the plantation, follow this path to a stile and fenced path. This path emerges onto a track, continue along the track which passes through a small wood and across a stream, then follow the path through a gate alongside the track in front of a white farm house. After passing through two more gates, turn left through a gate, and follow this track which soon crosses the railway and the canal at bridge 40. Turn right to follow the towpath for about one mile to Mill Lane Bridge 37 in Parbold. Climb up to the road and turn right to return to the railway station. (Car users continue on past the station to the Village Hall car park).

### Route B:

B. For the route to Appley Bridge from point 6 at the junction of paths, continue straight on uphill, pass through a squeeze stile, and follow the path to a farm track. Turn right then left at a waymarked path up stone steps. The path follows a field boundary above a farmstead, then reaches a lane by an ornamental well. Cross the lane up stone steps onto a waymarked path. Follow the path, then cross a stile into a field, cross this to emerge onto a track. Turn right and after a few metres take the waymarked gravel path as the track bends left. This path emerges opposite Skull House Lane, turn right down Appley Lane and follow for 500m to Appley Bridge station on the left.

## Historical Notes

### Boar's Den Burrow

This antiquity, thought to be a Bronze Age round barrow, is relatively undisturbed and consists of an earth and stone mound 66.5m (east to west) by 62m (north to south) with a maximum height of 2.5m. that suffered some plough damage in the past and is now used only as grazing land. If this round barrow were not marked on a map, despite being fairly extensive, it might be missed on the ground, mistaken as a natural lump in the middle of the field. See: **en.wikipedia.org/wiki/Wrightington**

## Harrock Hill Windmill

The windmill was built on the hill to catch the prevailing northwest wind coming off the Lancashire Plain. The windmill has a broad foundation, to allow for a basement to be dug into the sandstone to allow for carts to be driven under the mill for the loading of the grain. The historic records are not clear but it is thought to have been derelict ever since being destroyed by a fire in 1880.

Attributed to *Lancashire Evening Post* at:
**www.lep.co.uk/news/walk-harrock-hill-1-753508**

# WALK 16
# Billinge Hill

*A circular walk full of interest, visiting the highest point in Merseyside with great views, abundant wildlife, a popular lake, a small wooded ravine, and the historic remains of coalmining in a surprisingly rural landscape.*

| | |
|---|---|
| **Route** | **Garswood – Blackleyhurst – Billinge – Billinge Hill – Red Barn Road – Carr Mill Dam – The Goit** |
| **Start/finish** | **Circular Route A: Garswood Railway Station**<br>**Circular Route B: Beacon Road off Main Street in Billinge** |
| **Distance and grade** | **Route A: 9½ miles for train users – 682 ft (208m) ascent – Moderate/Hard**<br>**Route B: 6¾ miles for bus and car users – 570 ft (174m) ascent – Moderate** |
| **Maps** | **OS Explorer 275 Liverpool and OS Explorer 285 Southport and Chorley** |
| **Terrain** | **Good firm paths most of the way with a couple of stiles and gentle climbs. Some short stretches of quiet road walking** |
| **Refreshments** | **The Masons Arms on Carr Mill Road; Pubs and snack bar on Main Street, Billinge** |

## Directions to walk

**Public transport**: For the longer circular A route catch a train on the Liverpool to Wigan Line for the 2 per hour service Monday to Sunday to Garswood station. This station may be reached by Manchester walkers via Wigan Wallgate and Wigan North Western stations.

For the shorter B route catch the No 352 bus, which has a 4 per hour service Monday to Saturday, 2 per hour on Sunday from St Helens or Wigan to Billinge. Alight at the Stork Hotel on Main Street. Walk past the traffic lights and The Eagle and Child pub where the walk can be joined at Beacon road.

**By car**: **Sat Nav**: Postcode WN5 7HR will get you to the car park at Banke's Park on Main Street (grid ref: SD 533008).

**Road directions**: From the M6 Junction 23 (Haydock roundabout), follow the East Lancs Road (A580) west in the Liverpool direction for 3½ miles. At the Carr Mill traffic lights turn right onto the A571 towards Billinge for 1½ miles. At the mini roundabout in the centre of Billinge (Rainford Road) branch right and then carry on past a garage and follow the main road up the hill until two sets of lights next to The Stork Hotel. Carry straight on past Beacon Road for 100m, a car park at Banke's Park is on the left.

From Liverpool take the East Lancs Road towards Manchester, turn left on A571 for Wigan, at Carr Mill then follow directions above from the mini roundabout.

## Walk Description

The walk follows paths across farmland around Billinge where many stone buildings dating from the 18th century may be viewed, including St Aidens Church built in 1718. From here the route up Beacon Road is followed on a good path up to the highest point in Merseyside at 587ft. Billinge Hill has extensive views over Merseyside to the Welsh hills, Lancashire, and eastwards over Winter hill and Greater Manchester...bring your binoculars!

The descent of the hill on more farmland paths and tracks to Carr Mill Dam follows, where a variety of farmland birds and waterfowl may be seen. After a walk across the bridge of arches across the Dam, the route skirts around the Dam then above a wooded ravine following The Goyt before more field paths lead to the Masons Arms dated 1779. This is a real ale pub with a beer garden looking over farmland and has won awards by CAMRA for its beer and hospitality.

Rail users carry on the walk to Garswood across more farmland on easy flat paths and minor roads. This longer route is classified moderate/ hard for being longer than average. This route may be shortened by returning by bus to Garswood station from Billinge at Rainford Road.

## Walk Directions

Garswood Station

### Route A: For train users only

1. From the railway station, walk up the access road, turn left onto Station Road, and walk uphill until the Stag Pub on left is reached. Cross Garswood Road in front of the pub and take the waymarked footpath a

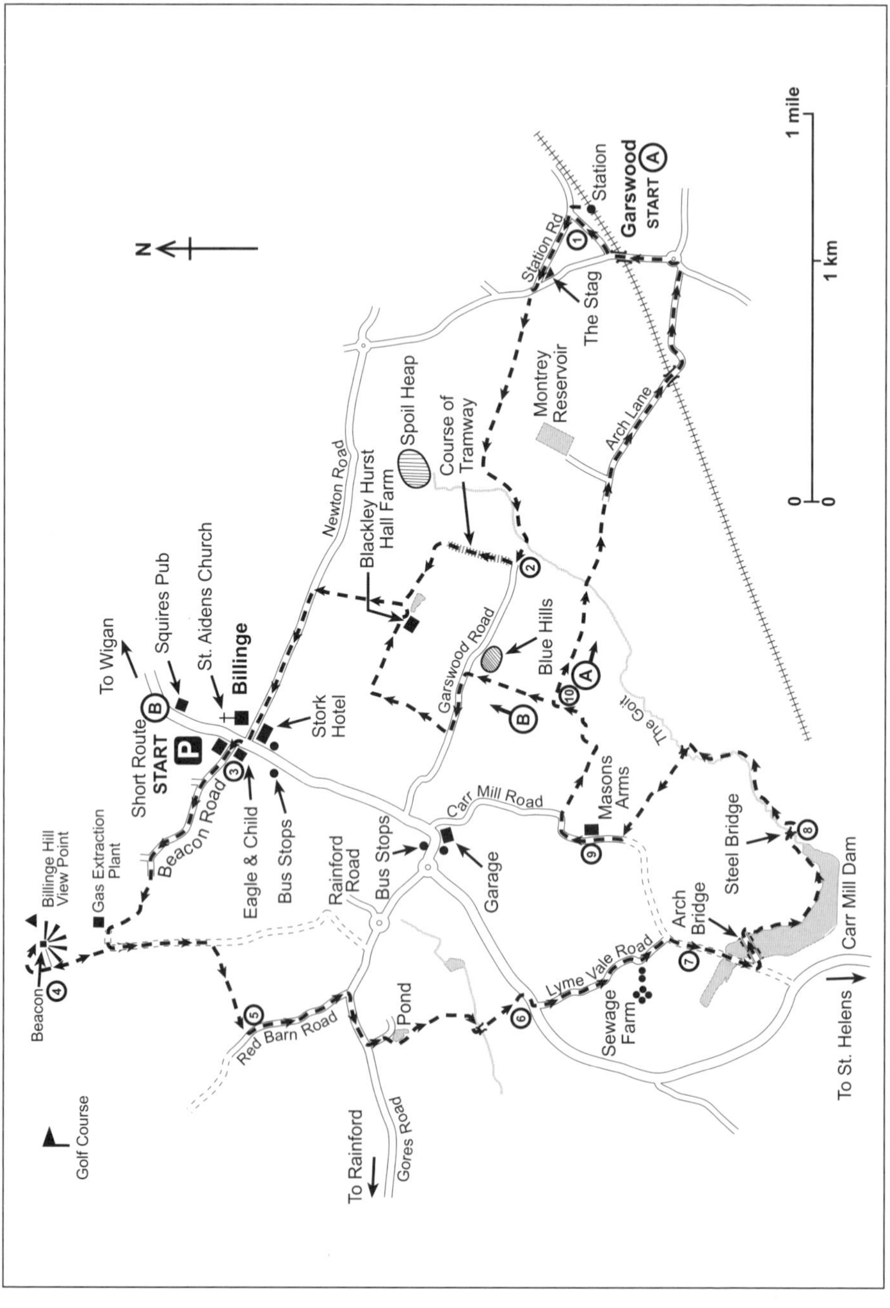
N
1 mile
1 km
0
0
Garswood
START A
Station
Station Rd
The Stag
Montrey Reservoir
Arch Lane
Course of Tramway
Spoil Heap
Newton Road
Blackley Hurst Hall Farm
Garswood Road
Blue Hills
The Goit
Masons Arms
Carr Mill Road
Steel Bridge
Carr Mill Dam
Arch Bridge
Lyme Vale Road
Sewage Farm
To St. Helens
To Wigan
Squires Pub
St. Aidens Church
Billinge
Short Route START
Stork Hotel
Eagle & Child
Bus Stops
Beacon Road
Gas Extraction Plant
Billinge Hill View Point
Beacon
Rainford Road
Bus Stops
Garage
Red Barn Road
Pond
Gores Road
To Rainford
Golf Course

few steps up from the road junction on the left. Follow this path uphill, it bends to the left on the brow, look out for spoil heaps on the right of old coal mines, now covered in vegetation. The path then descends alongside a brook before crossing it at a sharp right hand bend. The path climbs steeply and is joined by another path, turn right to take this path.

2. Follow this path, which is the trackbed of a colliery tramway, that transported coal from Blackleyhurst Collieries down to Blackbrook on the Sankey Canal. The path bends sharp left, carry on to pass a pond on the left and farmhouse until a farm track is reached, turn right on the track up to Newton Road. Turn left to follow the road into Billinge village. Cross the road (Main Street) at the lights where The Stork pub and St Aidens church lie opposite each other, then turn right passing another pub, The Eagle and Child and some shops.

**Bus and car users join the route here.**

3. Beacon Road is just yards away on the left. A snack bar is on the corner for refreshments and a rest before the ascent of Billinge Hill. Walk up Beacon Road, housing on both sides peter out and the Vicarage is passed before the road ends and a path continues with the views opening up to your left. The path emerges onto a tarmac road which is the service road for a gas plant that extracts the methane from the landfill site on the hill to convert to power for the national grid. Turn right after the plant up a waymarked path which climbs through a dense shrubby area to a gate. Pass through the gate and walk straight on before looping back to mount the top of the hill. The remains of an underground bunker, in use during the cold war by the Royal Observer Corps, can be seen next to the path. It is a good place to linger and take in the views and to visit the trig point and small tower built in 1788 as part of the Winstanley Estate. A beacon was used here to warn of the French invasion during the Napoleonic war. Beyond the boundary wall the landscaped landfill in the stone quarry can be seen. This has been planted with trees and shrubs to return the site back to nature.

4. Descend the hill (locally known as The Lump) the same way up until the tarmacked road is joined, turn right and follow the road downhill past a golf course on the right until a public footpath is reached,turn right on the path steeply downhill. The path follows a hedge alongside a field ending on Red Barn Road alongside Great Houghwood farm.

5. Turn left and walk along this quiet country road with great views over the farmland towards Crank Hill. Follow the road to the end where it joins the B2505 Gores Lane, turn right to follow the road downhill, then turn left at a gated track on the left. Pass through the gate to follow the track to a sign for Eddleston Waters Fishing Club. Turn right onto a path and bear right around the fishing lodge, then straight onto a path through a conifer plantation, turn right at a junction of paths and continue down alongside a field boundary and a wood. Turn left near a small pond on the left onto a farm track and remain alongside the wood and continue to follow a hedge, crossing a footbridge over a brook, then housing appears on the left until Birchley Road is reached.

6. Cross Birchley Road taking care as this is a major road (A 571) between Wigan and St Helens. Turn right for 100m, then turn left to take Lyme Vale Road, passing an old farmhouse. This road serves the farm and a few stone cottages and is a good place to see birds such as swallows, goldfinch, greenfinch, sparrows and others that nest and feed amongst the old buildings. Follow the road, it becomes a farm track after the last cottage. Continue on, a wooded area on the right is reached which surrounds a sewage treatment plant. Looking through the fence at a dip in the track next to a small brook, grey and pied wagtails may be seen seeking out grubs in the filter beds. The path climbs gently to join another track at a T-junction, turn right downhill along the track, passing the quaintly named Otterswift Farm on the right. Another good bird hotspot for swallows, swifts and house martins plus many other farmland birds.

7. Carry on down to a dip in the track where the top end of Carr Mill Dam is seen on either side. Turn left after the dip to skirt briefly around the woods on the Dam until the arched bridge on the left is reached. Cross this taking in the view of the dam and the waterfowl that abound here. Specialities are the great crested grebes that breed here, and a resident pair of swans whose nest is usually on view from the arches. If you are in luck a glimpse of a kingfisher may be seen. Turn right on the path at the end of the bridge and follow this path that skirts around the dam. The path crosses many small wooden bridges and the dam is in view all the time until an inlet forces the path inland to cross a large metal bridge over a brook called The Goyt.

8. Cross the bridge to climb up to a junction of paths, at a stone engraved 'The Goyt' turn left to take the path that follows The Goyt through a

Carr Mill Dam and the 19 arch bridge, with Billinge Hill in the distance

wooded area in a small ravine. This path winds its way uphill giving good views into the ravine below. The path climbs steeply then descends to another junction of paths in a wooded area. Turn left onto the path that follows The Goyt upstream across many wooden bridges as it twists and turns down to the dam. The path comes out at a small clearing where a junction of paths and a footbridge on the left spans The Goyt. Cross the bridge, continue uphill to follow the path alongside a hedge, ignoring paths joining from the left and the right, to keep straight on between fields until Carr Mill Road is reached. Turn right, the Masons Arms is 100m on the right.

9. After perhaps a refreshment stop at The Masons, carry on up Carr Mill Road, following a right hand bend in the road, take the path marked by a public footpath sign. Pass through a kissing gate to a path between a field and sports field. At a T-junction turn left following a farm track uphill. Following a double bend in the track, look out for another track on the right by a hedge.

**The shorter B route carries on up the hill at this point.**

10. Turn right to take this track and continue on to cross a small brook, then a gate and stile which emerges onto a tarmacked road. This is Arch Lane. Follow this road past Montrey Reservoir, a covered United Utilities water supply. Continue past a farm then over the railway bridge and on to the end of the road where it joins Garswood Road. Turn left to follow the road to a mini roundabout, keep left, go on to cross the railway bridge, then turn right along School Lane. At the end of this road turn right into station Road and the station is on the right.

### Route B: The short route for bus and car users

A path from the back of the car park leads onto Beacon Road, **bus users** walk to the lights opposite the church and turn into Beacon Road. Follow the directions from point 3 up to point 9 above, then carry on up the hill. Soon a blue/black slag heap (locally called the blue hills, the remains of mine workings) comes into view on the right where the path joins a T-junction. Turn left up a cobbled path. After about 100m a track on the right appears in a break in the hedgerow, take this and follow it uphill until it bends sharp right towards a farmstead on the right. This is Blackley Hurst Hall, turn left onto a track at the farm which leads uphill to the main road (Newton Road). Turn left and walk to the traffic lights on Main Street, turn right for the car park, or left for 100m for the No. 352 bus stop.

## Historical Notes

### Blackleyhurst Colliery

The colliery opened in the early 19th century and closed around 1880. At its height it consisted of 23 pits, all served by a roped tramway which lowered the coal wagons down to the Sankey Canal at Blackbrook.

### Billinge

The village still retains some of its old character. The main industries in this mainly agricultural and well wooded area were mining and nail making. Locally quarried Billinge stone can be seen in many of the town's older buildings, and there was also a thriving chair-making industry; Billinge chairs are rush-bottomed with high backs.
More information can be found at **www.wigan.gov.uk**

## The Stork Hotel

Mention must be made of the Stork Hotel, which has had a chequered history. From its humble beginnings as a farmhouse in 1718 the building has had many uses. Sited on the main road between Liverpool and Lancaster it was once used as a toll house for travellers on the road. Since then the Stork has been used as an inn, hotel and as a gaol used by Cromwell's troops during the English Civil War. Cromwell himself is believed to have stayed here on numerous occasions. It is also rumoured to be haunted by a cavalier and a highwayman!

More information can be found at **www.storkhotelbillinge.co.uk**

## Billinge Hill

The hilltop at 587 ft (179m) was used by the Royal Observer Corps and there was a bunker at the site, the top of the bunker can be seen 60 yards (55m) West of and below Beacon. The Beacon itself was used for aircraft observation during and after the war. The bunker would have been used in the event of nuclear war to monitor the location of nuclear blasts and the resulting fallout over Lancashire. The post opened in January 1960 and closed in October 1968.

The beacon has been lit to commemorate many special occasions, the last time was to mark the Queens Silver jubilee on 4th June 2012.

More information can be found at **en.wikipedia.org/wiki/Billinge_Hill**

## Carr Mill Dam

The lake known as Carr Mill Dam is the largest inland body of water on Merseyside and was expanded, in the mid 1700s, from being a small mill pond to a large reservoir to hold water to keep the Sankey canal topped up. The Dam is fed by two streams, the Goyt and the Black Brook, which both enter from the Billinge side of the Dam.

More information can be found at
**mysthelens.com/places/Carr%20Mill/carrmill.html**

**St Aidens Church** is on an original site which was established in 1539 as a place of worship. The present church was built in 1718 and enlarged in 1824 and further extensions were made in 1907.

More information can be found at **www.staidanbillinge.org.uk/history.htm**

More of my photos at:
**www.geograph.org.uk/search.php?i=48139423**
Press the tab key marked Map to get the locations

# WALK 17
# Historic Sankey Valley

*A circular walk along the quiet backwaters of the Sankey Valley which are full of historic and natural interest.*

| | |
|---|---|
| **Route** | **Earlestown – Bradley Lock – Sankey Canal – Sankey Viaduct – Newton Common Lock – Hey Lock – Winwick – Bradley Old Hall** |
| **Start/finish** | **Earlestown station (car users at car park on Bradley Road)** |
| **Distance and grade** | **6¼ miles – 193 ft (59m) ascent – Easy** |
| **Map** | **OS Explorer 275 Liverpool** |
| **Terrain** | **Mostly level paths on firm ground with no stiles, but some paths will be muddy after rain. Some stretches of road walking, mostly on quiet country lanes** |
| **Refreshments** | **Fiddle I'th Bag Pub at Burtonwood. A picnic area is near the end of the walk next the canal** |

## Directions to Walk

**Public transport:** Earlestown railway station is on the Liverpool Manchester line where there are frequent trains from both the Liverpool and Manchester directions.

Bus services to Earlestown from St Helens are routes No's 20, 34 and 141. From Leigh No 141 and from Warrington No 22. These routes entail a short walk to the railway station. Route 34A runs a 20 minute interval service from St Helens Monday to Saturday to Bradley Road where the walk can be started from the signed Sankey Valley car park.

**By Car: Sat Nav**: Postcode WA12 8QS will get you to Bradley Road at the junction with Valley View, the car park is 100m straight ahead (grid ref: SJ 576945).

**Road directions**: From the M62 motorway at junction 9, take the A49 towards Newton Le Willows. At the roundabout take the 2nd exit for Newton then at the traffic lights at the next junction turn left onto Hollins Lane, follow this road until sign for Alder Root Golf club, turn right onto Alder Root Lane. Follow the road under a railway bridge to Vulcan Village, turn left onto

Bradlegh Road. Follow the road over the railway bridge until Newton Community Hospital on the left, and turn left immediately after at the signed Sankey Valley, the car park is straight on. Join the walk at point 2.

## Walk Description

This walk visits many historic sites in the scenic Sankey Valley which is full of interest at every turn. Starting in the old industrial town of Earlestown, the route soon leaves the town to come out on a very scenic stretch of the historic Sankey Canal. Following the old towpath under Stephenson's viaduct, there is a visit to the remains of Newton Lock where the many iconic drawings and engravings were made of the view of the viaduct. Turning back, the route then follows part of the old disused canal which remains in water through to Winwick. At this point the canal is left and a break can be had at the quaintly named Fiddle I'th Bag pub. Having slaked your thirst the route continues down a quiet country lane to Bradley Old Hall, where a moat and listed 15th century gatehouse is visited. From here a track and path lead back to the canal and picnic area before the return to Earlestown station or car park.

## Walk Directions

1. At the entrance to the station turn left to follow Queen Street to the junction with Earle Street and turn left. Continue down Earle street to Junction Lane, turn left and follow this road which crosses the railway and enters a small industrial estate. After 150m turn left at a cross roads into Sankey Street. Take a path that appears alongside on the left, and follow this, continue on where the path parts company with the road. The path enters shrubbery and descends past a car park and comes out onto the Sankey Canal opposite a footbridge.

**This is where car users join the walk.**

2. A nature reserve is on the right, called Mucky Mountains named after the waste alkali from the Vitriol works that once occupied the site. Cross the bridge (Bradley Swing Bridge) that spans the canal and turn right to follow the canal. This is an attractive part of the canal which is still in water, continue up to Bradley Lock where the canal has been filled in. Following the towpath brings you past the site of Sankey Sugar Works, the last company served by the canal. It ceased production in 1959 and the canal subsequently fell into disuse in 1963. Carry on, as the magnificent viaduct comes into view. This is Stephenson's Sankey Viaduct, built in 1830, carrying

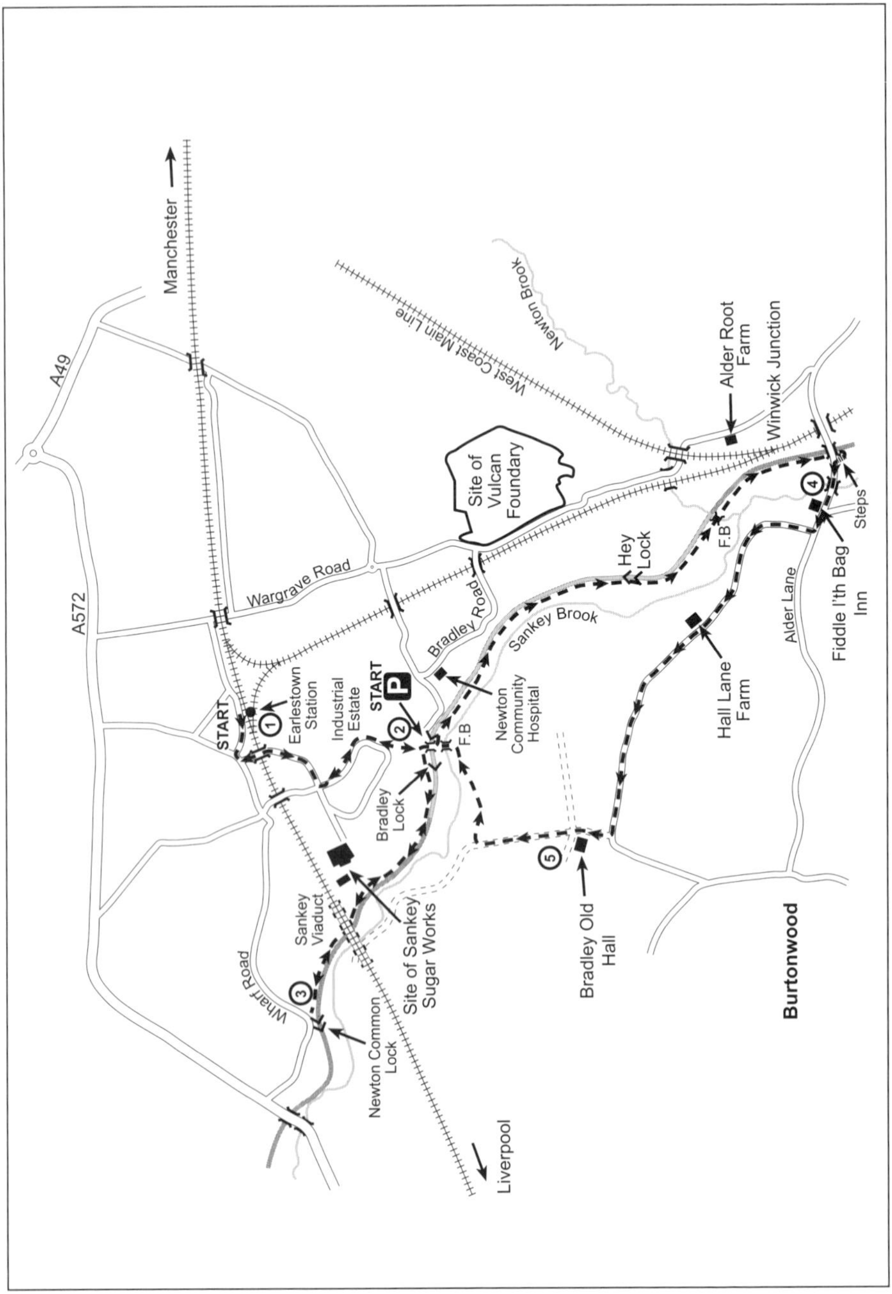
Manchester
A49
A572
Wargrave Road
West Coast Main Line
Newton Brook
Site of Vulcan Foundary
Alder Root Farm
Winwick Junction
START
Earlestown Station
Industrial Estate
START
P
Bradley Road
Newton Community Hospital
Sankey Brook
Hey Lock
F.B
Steps
Fiddle I'th Bag Inn
Alder Lane
Hall Lane Farm
F.B
Bradley Lock
Site of Sankey Sugar Works
Sankey Viaduct
Wharf Road
Newton Common Lock
Bradley Old Hall
Burtonwood
Liverpool
1
2
3
4
5

The Viaduct over the Sankey Canal from a drawing by I.Shaw

the first passenger railway over the first industrial canal in the world. As you pass beneath look out for the recess in the archway corner which once housed a roller to prevent chafing of the haulage ropes and stonework. Carry on the path until Wharf Road is reached, the site of Newton Common Lock and recent clearance work has exposed the chamber. This location is where a drawing based on engraving by I. Shaw was made.

Hey Lock on the Sankey Canal

3. The route now returns to Bradley Bridge and then goes on to follow the canal along its prettiest part with waterfowl and birdsong along the way. The Sankey Brook runs parallel with the path on the right. Soon the route reaches Hey Lock. Look for the date stone below the lower

lock gate inscribed Hey Lock 1886. This must be the renovation date of the lock. This is a favourite place for anglers, and fresh water mussels may be seen in the clear water, which proves the quality of the water. Continue along the bank then cross a footbridge spanning a conduit which carries Newton Brook over the course of the canal into Sankey Brook. The canal is filled in here. Follow the path on its course to a road bridge, pass under the bridge and take the steps on the right up to the road (Alder Lane), turn left to follow the lane to the Fiddle I'th Bag pub on the right.

4. After a break at the pub carry on to Hall Lane on the right, and follow this quiet narrow country lane. After passing Hall lane Farm the lane swings left, follow on to the junction with Bradley Lane turn right down this lane to another junction of tracks, turn left and soon Bradley Old Hall is on the left with its Ivy covered Gatehouse. The moat and fishpond is all that remains of the original 15th century manor. There is supposedly a bed called the Kings Bed inside where the Duke of Gloucester, later King Richard III, slept on his way travelling north to take on the Scots. The buildings have a great air of antiquity, but they are not open to the public, so please respect privacy.

The medieval gatehouse at Bradley Old Hall

5. Return to the junction of tracks and turn left to continue down Bradley Lane to where it bends sharp left, then turn right onto a path alongside a field. Follow the path to come out onto a footbridge across the Sankey Brook. Cross over and the Sankey Canal is joined once again, a picnic site is alongside the canal on the left, otherwise the return to Earlestown Station is straight across the swing bridge and up the path to retrace your steps up Sankey Street, Junction Lane and Earle Street back to the station.
   Car users return to the car park next to the path.

## Historical Notes

### The Sankey Canal

The canal was built by Henry Berry, Liverpool's second dock engineer. It was the first to be built in England and followed the course of the Sankey Brook.

It was originally built in 1757 to carry coal from St Helens to the Liverpool chemical industries, which in turn spread rapidly down the length of the canal thus creating the growth of industrialisation of both Widnes and St Helens.

The canal is a broad canal, built to accommodate 'Mersey Flats' - sailing barges used on the Mersey, Irwell and Weaver rivers, they were sea going craft that were able to sail around the local coasts. Their masts meant the necessity for swing bridges on all roads passing over the canal. The first railways crossed in a similar manner, except for Stephenson's magnificent viaduct carrying his railway between Manchester and Liverpool, which allowed for a 70 foot clearance for the Flats' masts.

The final use of the canal was very different - raw sugar flowing in the opposite direction from Liverpool for refining at the Sankey Sugar works at Earlestown near the railway viaduct. The canal closed in 1963 when this traffic ceased in 1959. The canal north of here had closed in 1931.
More information can be found at **www.scars.org.uk**

## The Sankey Viaduct

The railway viaduct was completed in 1830 by George Stephenson for the Liverpool & Manchester Railway Company. It is the first major railway viaduct ever built and remains in operation to this day, built using local sandstone and brick. The viaduct is 183m (600 ft) long, with nine arches of 15m (50 ft) span and 21m (70 ft) high.
More information can be found a
**www.transportheritage.com/find-heritage-locations.html?sobi2Task=sobi2Details&sobi2Id=710**

## Bradley Old Hall

The hall is actually a farmhouse which stands on the site of a 15th century moated manor house, though only the gatehouse, moat and fishpond survive. The gatehouse was built about 1460, and was probably restored in the early 19th century. The moat forms an island on which the buildings stand which are accessed via a modern causeway from the gatehouse. The manor belonged to the Legh family until the 19th century.
More information can be found at
**www.burtonwood.org/stories/burtonwood.html**

More of the authors photos at:
**www.geograph.org.uk/search.php?i=53286115**
Press the tab key marked Map to get the locations

# WALK 18
# South Mersey Waterfront

*An all season linear walk along Liverpool's historic waterfront with great views, and a visit to the newly restored Festival Gardens.*

| | |
|---|---|
| Route | Albert Dock – Brunswick Dock Marina – Dingle – Festival Gardens – Otterspool Promenade – Cressington |
| Start/finish | Start: James Street Station, Liverpool. Car users at car park at Albert Dock<br>Finish: Cressington Station (or at St Michael's Station for the shorter route) |
| Distance and grade | 5¾ miles – 138 ft (42m) ascent – Moderate<br>Shortened route: 3¾ miles – 111 ft (34m) ascent – Easy |
| Map | OS Explorer 275 Liverpool |
| Terrain | Firm level surfaces all the way, with no stiles, but there are a few stretches of road walking |
| Refreshments | Many facilities at Albert Dock, Britannia pub/restaurant at the old Festival Gardens, the Otterspool pub/restaurant on Otterspool Promenade |

## Directions to the walk

**Public transport:** Travel to Liverpool city centre then catch a train from Merseyrail Wirral line at Lime Street station to James Street Station. Or if preferred, walk from Lime Street ½ mile through town centre and Liverpool 1 to Albert Dock.

**By Car**: **Sat Nav**: Postcode L3 4AA will get you to Albert Dock.

**Road directions**: From the end of the M62 motorway continue onto Edge Lane for the city centre, after 1½ miles turn left onto Durning Road, then straight onto Tunnel Road, and turn right onto A562 Upper Parliament Street. After 1½miles check signage for Albert Dock and turn right onto Chaloner Street. In about ½ mile signs for Albert Dock indicate turning left onto Gower Street, follow the sign for car parks.

As the car park location is random, walkers are best joining the route at the waterfront near the Liverpool Arena at point 1.

## Directions from the walk

Catch a train at Cressington or St Michael's station to Liverpool Central, then a short walk to Lime Street for trains/buses home.

## Walk Description

This walk can be done in any season, as it is along the seafront of the Mersey estuary on firm level paved paths. It is best done during high tide to maximise the chance of seeing shipping making their way to the Manchester Ship Canal, Tranmere Oil Terminal, Garston and Cammell Lairds. Starting at Albert Dock, with all its attractions, the route follows the waterfront past the Liverpool Arena, luxury maisonettes, the old south ferry basin, and marina. Then across the lock entrance and on to the circular Chinese restaurant at Columbus Quay. From here there is more luxurious housing and the Riverside Drive on the site of The Dingle oil jetty and 'Cast Iron Shore'. A break can be made at the Britannia pub, and a shortened walk can made shortly after here by passing through the restored Festival Gardens and returning from St Michael's Station where a short detour can be made to visit St Michael's church (the cast iron church). The full walk is along Otterspool Promenade and through the leafy suburban Grassendale and Cressington Park estates. The whole route has views over the Mersey with points of interest along the way, a walk were binoculars come in handy.

## Walk Directions

1. From James Street turn right to The Strand, cross this major road at the lights and turn left to follow the side of Canning Dock, turn right at the entrance to the Albert Dock estate, and follow the Salthouse Quay left around the Salthouse Dock, a marina in the dock on the left is for canal boats from the Leeds Liverpool Canal, which is linked across the Pier Head to the north docks. Cross the bridge over the entry into Albert Dock, seen on the right, then turn right at Duke's Dock to come out onto the waterfront next to the Liverpool Arena.

   ### Car users join the walk here.

   Duke's dock was named after the Duke of Bridgewater and the dock was used by barges brought across the Mersey from his canal at Runcorn for

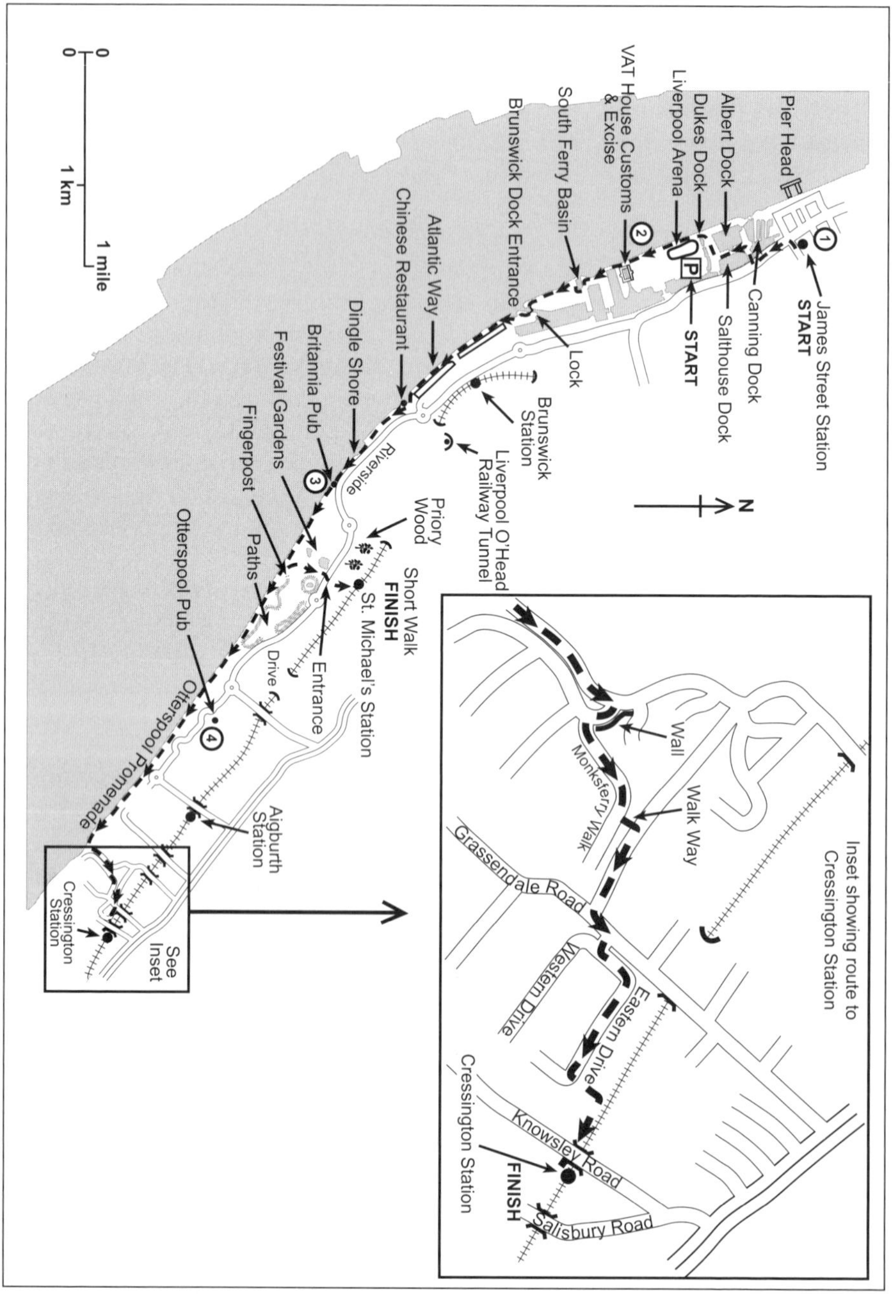

Pier Head
James Street Station
START
Canning Dock
Albert Dock
Salthouse Dock
Dukes Dock
Liverpool Arena
START
VAT House Customs & Excise
South Ferry Basin
Brunswick Dock Entrance
Lock
Brunswick Station
Atlantic Way
Chinese Restaurant
Dingle Shore
Liverpool O'Head Railway Tunnel
Riverside
Britannia Pub
Festival Gardens
Priory Wood
Fingerpost
Short Walk FINISH
St. Michael's Station
Paths
Entrance
Drive
Otterspool Pub
Otterspool Promenade
Aigburth Station
Cressington Station
See Inset
N
0
0
1 km
1 mile
Inset showing route to Cressington Station
Wall
Walk Way
Monksferry Walk
Grassendale Road
Western Drive
Eastern Drive
Cressington Station
Knowsley Road
FINISH
Salisbury Road

transhipment in an enclosed warehouse. This was sadly demolished to make way for the Arena. In the distance the two cathedrals can be seen, The Liverpool Roman Catholic (locally known as 'Paddies Wigwam') on the left and the Anglican Cathedral to the right. Further along is the tall red building of Cain's Brewery.

2. Walk along the seafront, passing the new Customs and Excise building which occupies part of Queen's Dock, then pass the marina and around the small south ferry basin once used by small boats as a refuge at high tide. Continue on past luxury apartment blocks to the locks into the marina at Brunswick Dock. These locks used to be the main entrance for ocean going ships, only one of the two entrances are in use and this has been halved in width as only small boats use it. Follow on to the long Atlantic Way, with good views of oil tankers berthed at Tranmere Oil Terminal on the opposite shore of the Wirral. A granite marker half way along marks the administry boundary of the dock estate. At the end of Atlantic Way just before the circular Chinese restaurant, look through the

The marina at Brunswick Dock with the Anglican cathedral in the background

boundary fencing where in the distance can be seen the Liverpool Overhead Railway tunnel entrance in the redstone rock, this was the extension to Dingle station. After passing the restaurant on the site of Herculaneum Dock entrance locks, the route continues onto the site of Dingle Oil terminal, and the 'Cast Iron Shore', then onto the promenade to the Britannia Inn. From the Britannia pub continue along the Otterspool Promenade.

Otterspool Promenade

The full walk continues at point 4 along the promenade, but a visit to the restored Festival Gardens is a must as it is just off the promenade before continuing along past recreation grounds, picnic areas and The Otters Pool pub.

Walkways in the Festival Gardens

3. For the shorter walk, after 600m take a left turn at a finger post pointing towards St Michael's station, go up an asphalt track into the Festival Gardens, bear left then right to pass under a footbridge and cross a curved boardwalk that bridges the picturesque landscaped water gardens. The path emerges onto the paved entrance drive, turn right to reach Riverside Drive. Cross the road onto a track, bear left off this to follow a short path past Priory Wood which comes out at St Michael's Station. To visit St Michael's church (The Cast Iron Church) carry straight on over the railway bridge and turn right onto Alpass Road, the church is 100m on the left.

4. Continue along the promenade until it ends where the path turns inland onto Beechwood Road, take a look at the fine houses overlooking the river of the Cressington Park estate before following this road. At a sharp left

bend, turn right in front of a tall brick wall, and then turn left onto Monksferry Walk. This area is the Cressington and Grassendale estates, the leafy suburbs built for the well-heeled gentry of 19th century Liverpool. Follow this road for 100m, take a paved path back onto Beechwood Road, then turn right and follow the road to a T-junction with Grassendale Road, turn left and follow this road for 100m, and turn right into Eastern Drive (at no through road sign ). Follow this road to the end and take a hidden passageway on the left which comes out onto Knowsley Road. Cressington Station is across the road on the right.

## Historical Notes

### The Cast Iron Shore

The shore at Dingle is more commonly known as the Cast Iron Shore or the 'The Cazzy'. It got its name from the days when the Mersey Foundry was in operation in the 19th century on a large site near Grafton Street in the Dingle. The leeched ferric oxide from the plant stained the beach along the shoreline. The church at St Michael's which may be visited on the walk was constructed from iron forged at the Mersey Foundry.
More information can be found at:
**http://gerryco23.wordpress.com/2010/11/18/the-dingle-digging-into-the-past/**

### The Festival Gardens

These gardens were built on the site of the Herculaneum Dock to revitalize Liverpool's tourism in the 1980s. It was a huge success with over 3 million visitors but It fell into decline until it was decided to redevelop the site by turning it partly over for housing. The redevelopment has restored the Chinese and Japanese gardens, as well as the lakes, watercourses and the woodland sculpture trails.
More information can be found at:
**www.liverpoolfestivalgardens.com/image_gallery.html?FID=Restored**

### The Marina

The marina is part of the south docks complex of Brunswick and Coburg docks which fell into disuse in 1975 when the locks were left open and gradually silted up. The marina was constructed and the renaissance of the south docklands began in 1980s.

## Otterspool Promenade

The promenade was constructed using the household waste from Liverpool in the 1950s. Likewise the Festival Gardens were constructed in the 1980s.

## Tide Tables

For maximum interest this walk is best done during high tide. The following website gives the tide tables for Liverpool:
**www.ntslf.org/tides/tidepred?port=Liverpool**

More of the authors photographs can be found at:
**www.geograph.org.uk/search.php?i=46135709**
Press the tab key marked Map to get the locations

# WALK 19
# Speke to Spike Island

*A scenic walk along the Mersey estuary, with its varied birdlife and historic interest, and a visit to the 'chocolate box' village of Hale.*

| | |
|---|---|
| Route | Dungeon Lane – Hale Head – Hale – Pickering Pasture – Widnes West Bank – Widnes/Runcorn Bridge – Spike Island |
| Start/finish | Start: Speke, Hale Road/Dungeon Lane<br>Finish: Widnes Waterloo Road (car user's return to Speke by bus) |
| Distance and grade | 7¼ miles – 331 ft (101m) ascent – Moderate<br>3¼ miles (shortened route) – 203 ft (239m) ascent – Easy |
| Map | OS Explorer 275 Liverpool |
| Terrain | Mainly good level paths that may be muddy at times, with a couple of stiles. Some short stretches of road walking |
| Refreshments | There are pubs and a coffee shop in Hale. Toilet facilities are at Pickering Pasture. Public facilities are available if time allows a visit to the Catalyst Science Discovery Centre in Mersey Road, Widnes |

## Directions to walk

**Public transport: By train**: Catch a direct train to Liverpool South Parkway from any of the lines from Wigan North Western, St Helens, Huyton, Liverpool Lime Street and Central Stations, Manchester Piccadilly and Oxford Road, and Southport. From here bus No. 80 (80A on Sunday) makes a short journey to Eastern Avenue on the Speke estate. A short walk south to Hale Road will bring you to the start of walk at Dungeon Lane.

**By bus**: Local buses to Speke estate are 80, 81, 82, 82A runs from Runcorn, No 89 runs from St Helens and Huyton.

Walkers on buses 82A and 89 alight on Hale Road and make for Dungeon Lane, all other bus routes run through the Speke estate and alight on Eastern Avenue, then walk south to Hale Road for the start of walk at Dungeon Lane.

**By car**: **Sat Nav**: Postcode L24 1WG will get you to Hale Road, Dungeon Road is off this road towards the River Mersey. A dirt car park is on the left 300 yards down the road (grid ref: SJ 449821).

**Road directions**: From the M56 at junction 6 take the A5300 to Liverpool Airport. After 2½ miles take the 2nd exit of the roundabout onto Speke Road/A562. Follow Speke Boulevard/A561 for 2½ miles.Turn left onto Western Avenue and at the end at T-junction turn left into Hale Road. Dungeon Lane is ½ mile on right.

## Directions from the walk

At Widnes, Waterloo Centre bus stop, bus No. 82A (2 per hour service) will take you back to Hale Road, Speke.

Walkers on the shortened route return to Speke on the same bus from Hale Village.

The bus No. 61 (3 per hour service) and bus No. 79C (4 per hour service) routes go direct to Liverpool, via Huyton and Hough Green respectively, in one direction, and to Runcorn in the opposite direction. Walkers travelling to Manchester catch No. 110 bus (3 per hour service) for Warrington Central and change for trains to Manchester.

## Walk Description

This walk is without doubt one of the best scenic walks in Merseyside. The paths follow the Mersey estuary from Speke round Hale Head and up to Widnes and Spike Island. The views across the river estuary are extensive, directly opposite are the hills of Frodsham and Helsby, with the flares of the huge Stanlow oil refinery evident. On the landward side it is mostly farmland, and the village of Hale is a delight with thatched cottages. It is the resting place of the famous 'Childe of Hale' giant who is buried at St Mary's church.

Aircraft will be frequently seen and heard, but this doesn't detract from the views and as the Mersey estuary is a magnet for all kinds of wading birds, especially in the winter, large flocks of dunlin can be seen, and out on the mud banks curlew, black tailed godwits and grey plover. Teal and shelduck may also be seen in the mud gullies at low tide.

Hale Point lighthouse is the highlight of the walk, this is occupied, but inoperative since 1958. From here the route follows a path inland to Hale village where the walk may be shortened by catching a bus back to Speke. Further on upstream the River Mersey bends sharply then narrows towards the Widnes-Runcorn gap. The full route continues after a short bus ride then follows the path along the bank of the river on the National Trans Pennine Trail, from Pickerings Pasture crossing Ditton Brook and the remains of the

West Bank dock entrance, then on to Spike Island at the entrance to the Sankey Canal.

## Walk Directions

1. Walk from Hale Road to Dungeon Lane then down the lane until the road turns sharp right. This lane lies under the flightpath for John Lennon Airport, plane spotters use the car park on the lane. A track leads off left to follow the river bank. Shortly there are some steep wooden steps down to negotiate before resuming along the path. Follow the well defined track towards Hale Head taking in the views over the estuary with Stanlow Oil Refinery, then Helsby and Frodsham Hills prominent on the opposite side of the river.

2. Soon the lighthouse on the headland is reached. The view is beautiful, and depending on the state of the tide, there can be many wading birds to be seen. After lingering awhile continue around the headland where the great

Hale Head Lighthouse

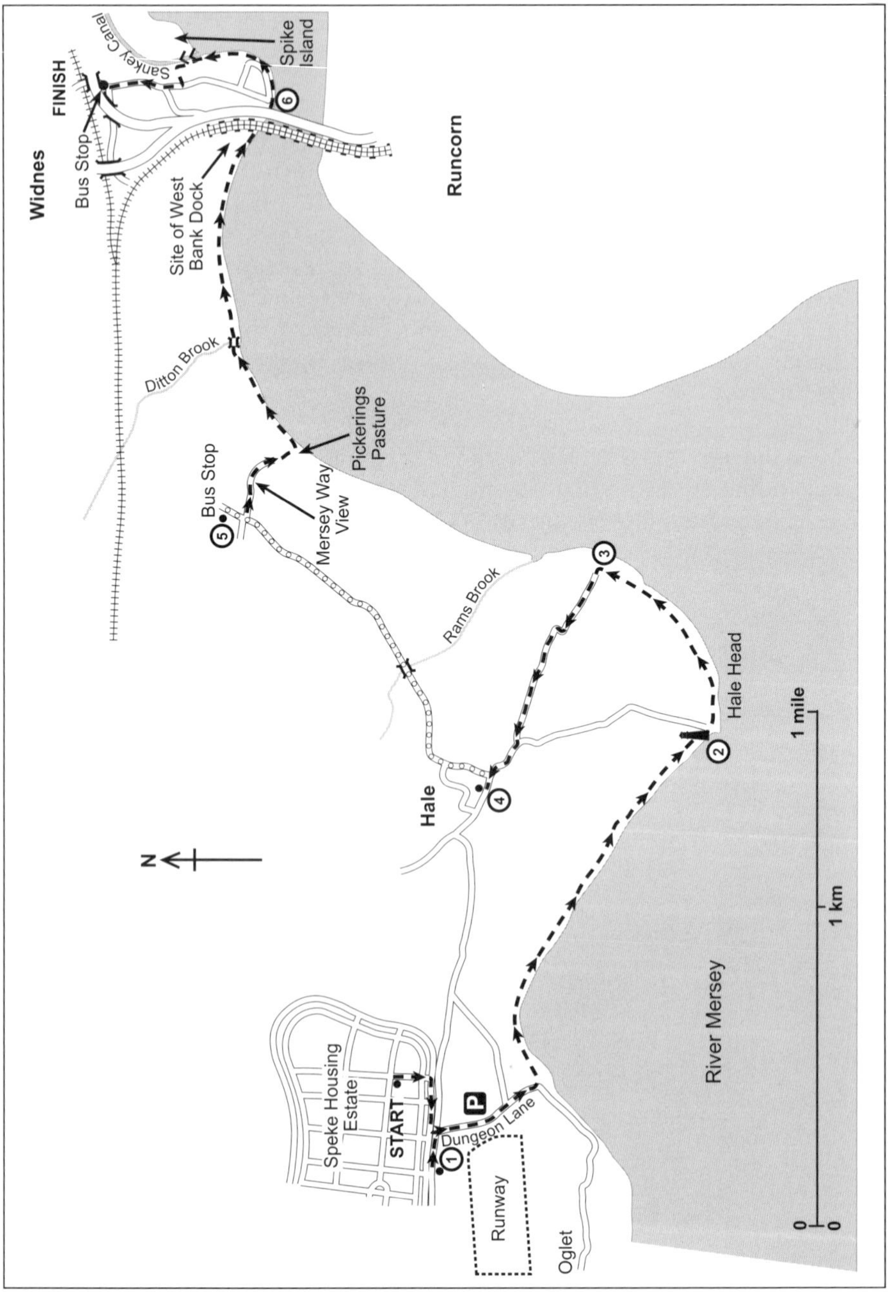
Widnes
FINISH
Bus Stop
Sankey Canal
Spike Island
Site of West Bank Dock
Runcorn
Ditton Brook
Pickerings Pasture
Bus Stop
Mersey Way View
Rams Brook
Hale Head
Hale
N
Speke Housing Estate
START
Dungeon Lane
P
Runway
Oglet
River Mersey
1 mile
1 km
0
0
1
2
3
4
5
6

chemical works Ineos ChlorVinyls Runcorn Site, more commonly known as Castner Kellner, across the river becomes very prominent. There are bench seats along the route to take in the view.

3. Where a gate and signpost is reached turn left inland, following the track until a farm road is reached. This road leads to Hale village, where St Marys church and 'The Childe of Hale' is buried. A carved wooden effigy stands nearby to show how he may have looked. The thatched cottages and memorial on the village green make for a picture postcard scene. There are two pubs and a teashop for refreshments.

'The Childe of Hale' carved effigy in Hale Village

4. At this point walkers have the choice of either returning to Speke or continue on to Widnes. Bus No. 82A (2 per hour service) goes back to Speke along Hale Road. Walkers wishing to continue can also get the same bus in the opposite direction towards Halebank. They could walk this 1½ mile road walk but it's best to linger awhile in this lovely village and catch a bus to the next stretch of the route.

5. Alight from the bus at Mersey View Way for Pickering's Pasture. Walk down this road and soon the visitor centre is reached. This is Pickering's Pasture Local Nature Reserve, walk towards the River Mersey to meet the Trans Pennine Trail running along the waterfront. Turn left towards the Runcorn Widnes Bridge in the distance. Cross Ditton Brook on the white bridge and climb the zig-zag wooden steps on the far side. Further along the path, industry on the left appears. Eddy Stobart's transhipment hub from rail to road is based here. Then the path crosses the entrance to West Bank Dock, where lock gates can still be seen which is all that remains of a port for sea going coasters carrying mainly coal, sand, chemicals and wood pit props. They were closed and filled in during the 1960s.

The view of the Widnes-Runcorn bridges from the closed West Bank Dock lock entrance

6. Passing under the rail and road bridges the path joins a road. At the Mersey Hotel, turn off the road and down onto the Lower Promenade. Here you get a good view of the bridge which is actually the same design as the Sydney Harbour Bridge (although only ⅔ of the size), There are pictures of the construction of the bridge and the previous famous Transporter Bridge on the walls of the Mersey Hotel. The old power house for the transporter bridge is passed before continuing round the promenade. Walk onto Terrace Road for as short distance before a sign for Spike Island indicates the way, follow the path and then the lock entrance to the Sankey Canal comes into view. Walk alongside the canal. A short detour across the lock gates onto historic Spike Island is rewarding, with interpretation boards showing the railway yards and dock up until the 60s.

   Continue along the canal bank to the boat club and turn left to join upper Mersey Road, turn right and follow the road to Waterloo Road, turn right and follow the road for 250m to a motorway bridge, where the bus stop is situated for the return journey.

## Historical Notes

**Dungeon Lane** derives its name from the Old English *Dunge* or *Denge*, meaning land of, or next to, the marsh. The same name is mentioned on walk number 21 at Thurstaston.

**Hale** village is famous for 'The Childe of Hale' who lived here more than 300 years ago. His real name was John Middleton, born in Hale in 1578. Even before he was 20 years of age, his height reached a staggering 9 foot 3 inches.

The white washed walls of Childe's cottage still stand today with its sloping thatched roof. In the gable end that face onto Church End/Church Road, you can see two windows high up; there is a legend that when the childe slept, he had to have each foot hanging out of each window in order to lie the full length of the cottage.

### Ditton Brook

The entrance to the brook once was a hive of industry, with an iron foundry and wharfs where Mersey flats (a type of flat bottomed sailing barge) were trading to many ports in the estuary between Warrington and Liverpool, carrying mainly coal and salt.

### The Widnes- Runcorn Transporter Bridge

The transporter bridge that once spanned the river was operated by means of a suspended gondola which carried vehicles and pedestrians. This was electrically driven and took 2½ minutes to cross the river. The driver was sited in a cabin on top of the gondola from which he had an uninterrupted view in all directions. It was powered by electric motors on the trolley supplied by a power house built within a tower on the Widnes side of the river.

### Spike Island

The Sankey Canal terminus at Spike Island was first built in 1833 when the St Helen's Canal Company extended its canal from Fiddler's Ferry on the Mersey to Widnes. The dock was also next to the St Helen's & Runcorn Gap Railway site at Widnes. Its importance maybe due to it being the first dock built by a railway company in the country. The dock was mainly used to transfer coal from the local coalfields to Liverpool and other parts of the region. A steady decline followed the demise of the coal industry until closure in the 70s.

More of the authors photographs can be found at:
**www.geograph.org.uk/search.php?i=46135837**
Press the tab key marked Map to get the locations

# WALK 20
# Neston and Parkgate

*A scenic circular walk along the Dee estuary with birdlife and historical interest, together with visits to Parkgate and the quaint hamlet of Gayton.*

| | |
|---|---|
| **Route** | **Neston – Wirral Way – Gayton – Parkgate – Old Quay – Harp Inn** |
| **Start/finish** | **By train: Neston Railway Station**<br>**By bus: Brook Street bus stop, Neston**<br>**By car: The Old Baths car park next to the Boathouse Inn at Parkgate** |
| **Distance and grade** | **7½ miles – 318 ft (97m) ascent – Moderate**<br>**5½ miles shortened route – 183 ft (56m) ascent – Easy** |
| **Map** | **OS Explorer 266 Wirral and Chester** |
| **Terrain** | **This walk is mainly on level, good footpaths with few stiles, but there may be a short stretch of marshy ground. There are a couple of stretches of quiet lane walking** |
| **Refreshments** | **Many facilities at Neston and Parkgate, The Harp Inn at Little Neston** |

## Directions to the walk

**Public transport: By train**: Travel to Liverpool city centre, and then catch a Merseyrail Wirral line train from Lime Street station to Bidston on the West Kirby line. A connecting hourly train at Bidston takes you to Neston on Monday to Saturday. Very infrequent service on Sunday, so please check Traveline for best option.

**By train and bus**: From Lime Street Station take a short walk to Victoria Street where the No. 487 Arriva bus has a ½ hourly service to Neston. Monday to Saturday, No. 488 bus on Sunday has an hourly service.

**By Car**: **Sat Nav**: Post code CH64 6RN will get you to The Boathouse on The Parade, the car park is at the end of the track past the pub (grid ref: SJ 274790). The walk starts at point 5.

**Road directions**: From the M53 motorway at junction 4 take the A5137 towards Heswall onto Brimstage road. After 3 miles join A551 and then at the roundabout take the first exit onto A540 towards Chester. After ½ mile turn right onto B5135 Boathouse Lane for Parkgate. The Boathouse is 2½ miles on the right on a sharp left bend. Turn right onto small road at the side of pub to reach the car park. The start of the walk is at point 5. (The route is ½ mile shorter for car users.)

## Walk Description

Great views over the Dee estuary and an abundance of birdlife, especially in spring, together with a visit to a pub in a beautiful setting on the edge of the Dee marsh, makes this a really satisfying walk. The start is in the centre of Neston where the tree lined Wirral Way is joined. The full route follows the cobbled road through the quaint hamlet of Gayton, then onto a particularly pleasant path alongside the salt marsh with great expansive views over the Dee estuary before arriving at Parkgate. The famous popular front is walked before the ruins of the Old Quay are visited. From here the route follows the old shore line to the isolated but characterful Harp Inn and Denhall Quay. After perhaps a refreshment break the route returns briefly to The Wirral Way and Neston town centre.

## Walk Directions

1. From the railway station walk down to Raby Road and turn right under the railway bridge to High Street, then turn left and then first right down Parkgate Road past the water fountain. Bus users alight at Brook Street bus station and walk ahead past Tescos, at the crossroad go straight across the High Street into Parkgate Road. Follow this road until immediately past the library on the left and take a walkway which comes out onto a residential road, cross this and take another walkway opposite which comes out onto the Wirral Way.

2. Turn right and follow the tree lined way to a car park, bear right through the car park and pass a World War II pillbox, then down steps onto the road, cross over the road to 'The Ropewalk' opposite. Walk down the road a few metres, then take the cobbled path (which once was the platform approach to the Parkgate railway station) on your right, next to an electricity substation. This brings you back onto the Wirral way, turn left to follow the path for 400m to a road bridging the path.

   You can shorten the walk here by taking the track that passes over the

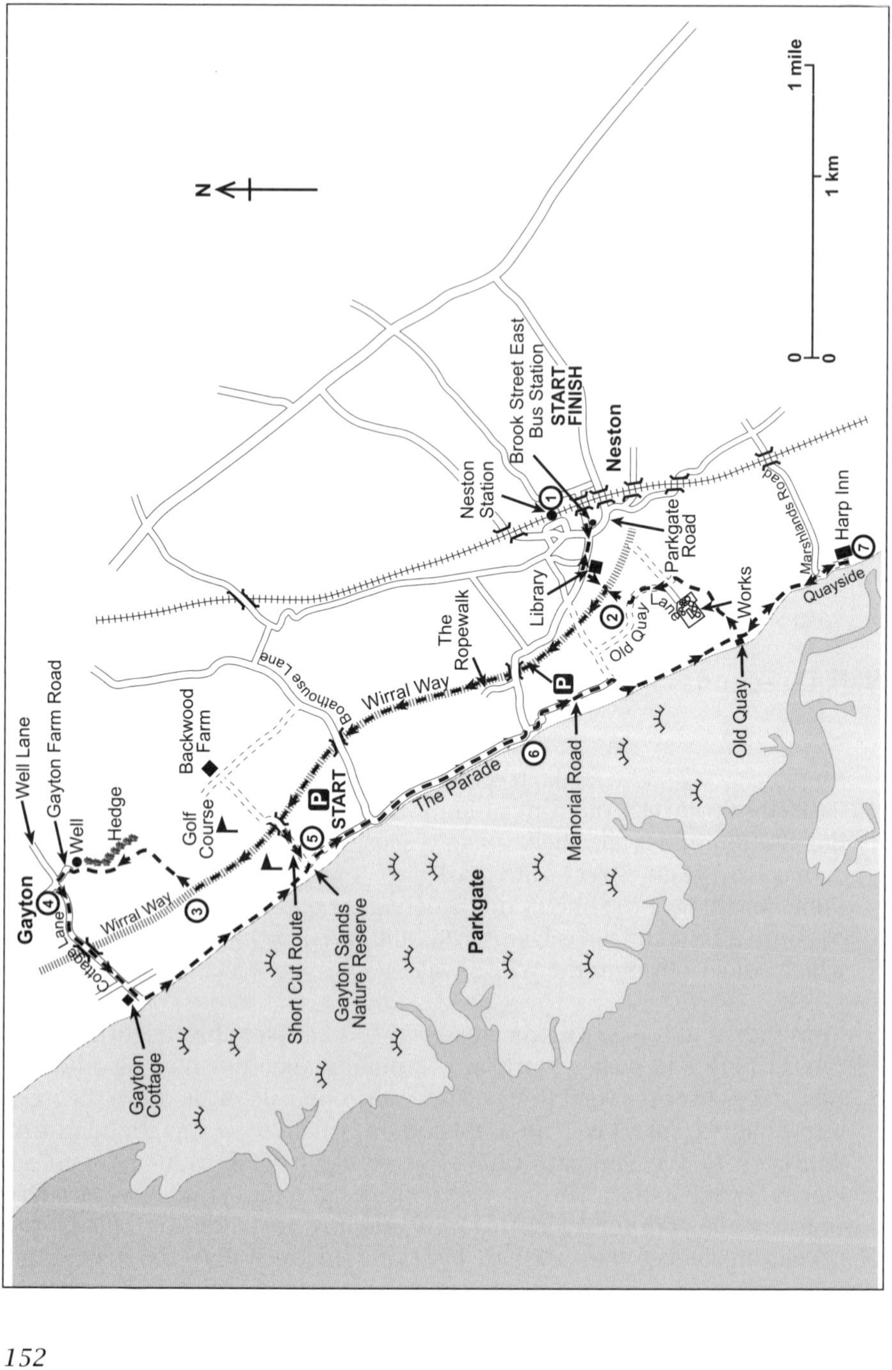

N
1 mile
1 km
0
0
Brook Street East
Bus Station
START
FINISH
Neston
Neston
Station
Parkgate
Road
Library
The
Ropewalk
Wirral Way
Boathouse Lane
Old Quay Lane
Works
Marshlands Road
Harp Inn
Quayside
Old Quay
Manorial Road
The Parade
Parkgate
START
Backwood
Farm
Golf
Course
Hedge
Well
Well Lane
Gayton Farm Road
Gayton
Cottage Lane
Wirral Way
Short Cut Route
Gayton Sands
Nature Reserve
Gayton
Cottage

path at Backwood Hall Bridge (marked under the bridge arch) back to the Old Baths car park and The Boathouse Inn.

Continue on for about ½ mile, first alongside some residential areas, then through farmland and a golf course. Ignore a couple of the golf club's access crossings which cross the Wirral Way, and continue on until the public right of way signposted for Gayton, this crosses the golf course and the Wirral Way.

3. Turn right through a metal kissing gate and walk straight across the fairway between blue marker posts to a line of trees, pass through these then cross another two fairways to a large hedge and steps up to a T-junction of paths. Turn left to follow the path which lies within a tunnel of dense holly bushes. The path joins a track, continue to follow this and look out for the ancient Gayton Well in the bank on the right, probably used when the track was a major turnpike to Chester. The track leads onto Gayton Farm Road. Bear left and follow the cobbled road into Gayton past an ivy clad cottage with a very attractive garden. The road ends at Well Lane, turn left and after a few yards turn left into Cottage Lane.

Cottages in timeless Gayton Village

4. Follow this past the Heswall Golf Club and some attractive gardens, carry on to the end, passing over the Wirral Way to the edge of the estuary where grand views open up. Take the path on the left up past some very old worn sandstone steps. This is a pleasant path with extensive views over the Dee estuary towards the Clywidian hills of Wales. The path passes alongside a golf course and skirts the saltmarsh before emerging at the Old Baths Car Park at Parkgate.

**Car users start and finish their walk at this point.**

5. Walk on past the Boathouse and then along the promenade of Parkgate. The shore here is now acres of marsh grass; until the middle of the 20th century there was a sandy beach up to the sea wall. On very high spring tides the sea may encroach the marsh grass, when there is a chance of

seeing raptors such as kestrels, peregrines, short eared owls and merlins – our smallest bird of prey. The high tides drive the rodents living on the marsh out of hiding, providing easy picking for the birds.

6. At the end of the promenade, where the road turns left, carry straight past the Old Quay pub onto a path that swings left between gardens to arrive at Manorial Road. Turn right and follow this road to the end, a short path leads onto another road, continue on to a junction, turn right onto a path on the corner of Old Quay Close. Follow the path to the marsh shore and turn left to skirt marshlands along the path which leads on to the Old Quay. The path crosses a few streams on boardwalks and a footbridge before emerging at a stone wall and stile that are the remains of a quay that predated Parkgate as a port. Carry on to where the path joins a track then onto a gate, pass through onto a road and keep straight on. This rough road leads on to the Harp Inn, a popular pub which has lovely views and spectacular sunsets. You are likely to see egrets fishing in the briny lagoons of the marshland. A little further on is an information board giving the history of Neston Colliery and Denhall Quay, only traces

The stone stile at Old Quay

of sandstone blocks remain now nearly two miles from the sea.

7. Having wrenched your way from this very special place, return the way you came to the Old Quay, then turn right onto a broad path between fields, passing through a couple of kissing gates to emerge onto a narrow road, 'Old Quay Lane'. Follow the road for 150m until a waymarked path on the right, follow this path to the Wirral Way.

The Harp Inn on the Dee estuary near Neston

**Car users turn left along Wirral Way and follow on from point 2.**

Cross this track to the path that was followed at the start of the walk back to the library on Parkgate Road. Turn right and follow the road to Brook Street for the bus to Liverpool or turn left along High Street and right onto Raby Road for the railway station and the train to Bidston, and the Wirral Line to Liverpool Lime Street.

## Historical Notes

**Parkgate** was once a thriving port, it being the main seaport for Ireland but it lost out to Holyhead when the shorter less hazardous route was opened up. The rapidly silting up of the river together with improved roads through Wales helped its demise. The last boat from the port was in 1811.

**The Harp Inn** was formerly miner's cottages, a result of the Neston Colliery which was in operation nearby until 1928. The mines were dug under the estuary and very wet conditions were endured bringing up poor quality coal. More information can be found at:
**www.bbc.co.uk/liverpool/content/articles/2009/04/20/neston_colliery_feature.shtml**

More of the authors photographs can be found at:
**www.geograph.org.uk/search.php?i=46194565** and
**www.geograph.org.uk/search.php?i=46194992**
Press the tab key marked Map to get the locations

# WALK 21
# Wirral Country Park and Thurstaston Common

*Linear and circular walks taking in a great variety of scenery of the estuary, heathland, a sandstone hilltop and wooded parkland.*

| | |
|---|---|
| **Route** | **Heswall – The Wirral Way – The Dungeon – Thurstaston – Thurstaston Common – Royden Park – Frankby** |
| **Start/finish** | **Linear Route A: Start: Heswall bus station; Finish: Frankby Village**<br>**Circular Route B: Wirral Country Park Visitor Centre, Thurstaston** |
| **Distance and grade** | **Route A: 6½ miles for bus users – 436 ft (133m) ascent – Moderate**<br>**Route B: 6 miles for car users – 446 ft (136m) ascent – Moderate** |
| **Map** | **OS Explorer 266 Wirral and Chester** |
| **Terrain** | **Mainly on good well marked paths with few stiles. A few short steep stretches, and some care needed on slippery paths following wet weather, and in navigating on Thurstaston Common. There are stretches of quiet lane walking** |
| **Refreshments** | **Many facilities at Heswall,The Cottage Loaf Inn, Thurstaston, and Farmers Arms public house at Frankby, tea room at Royden Park in season and bank holidays, and there is a café at Thurstaston Visitor Centre** |

## Directions to the walk

**Public transport:** Travel to Liverpool city centre where the Nos. 471 and 472 buses from Victoria Street, has a 10 minute frequency service Monday to Saturday; 15 minutes on Sunday to Heswall bus station.

**By Car**: **Sat Nav**: Postcode CH61 0HN will get you to Station Road at Thurstaston, the car park is at the end of the road (grid ref : SJ 239835).
**Road directions**: From the M53 motorway at junction 3 take the A552 towards Heswall, then at the traffic lights at Arrow Park turn left towards Heswall. After 1 mile at a roundabout take the 2nd exit onto B5138 towards Heswall then after 200m turn right onto Thingwall Road, follow the road 1½ miles then turn right toward West Kirby. Follow the road to a crossroads, go straight on then at another T-junction turn right onto Station Road, the car park is off a left turn at the café and visitor information sign for the Wirral Visitor Centre.

## Directions from the finish of the linear walk

From Frankby bus No. 437 has a 10 minute frequency service Monday to Saturday, 15 minutes on Sundays to Liverpool town centre.

## Walk description

Arguably the walk with the best views on the Wirral, the linear route starts from Heswall down to the front via the quaint High Street giving good views over the Dee estuary. There follows a stretch alongside the marshy shoreline on a well-defined but occasionally muddy path, then up to The Wirral Way along firm ground of the Hooton to West Kirby Railway track bed. From here there is a steady climb where the views open up over the River Dee. Then on to The Dungeon where steep steps take the path across a brook in a small ravine. Thurstaston with its magnificent church is visited before a short climb through heathland up to the viewpoint on Thurstaston Hill. The path then follows the fine sandstone ridge with great views over the Dee and Welsh mountains. The path passes through gorse and heather before descending into woodland and Royden Park. A miniature steam railway runs in high season and bank holiday weekends.

The circular route follows much of the linear route, but starts on the Wirral Way at Thurstaston next to the Dee estuary, where a cliff top path passes a noted birdwatching viewing spot over the feeding grounds of the mudflats. At Royden Park the route returns through the wooded Thurstaston Common alongside Greasby Brook and passes the famous Thor's Stone.

## Walk directions

### Route A: The linear route

1. Alight at Heswall bus station, walk back up Telegraph Road to the traffic lights, turn left to walk down The Mount out of the village centre. Follow

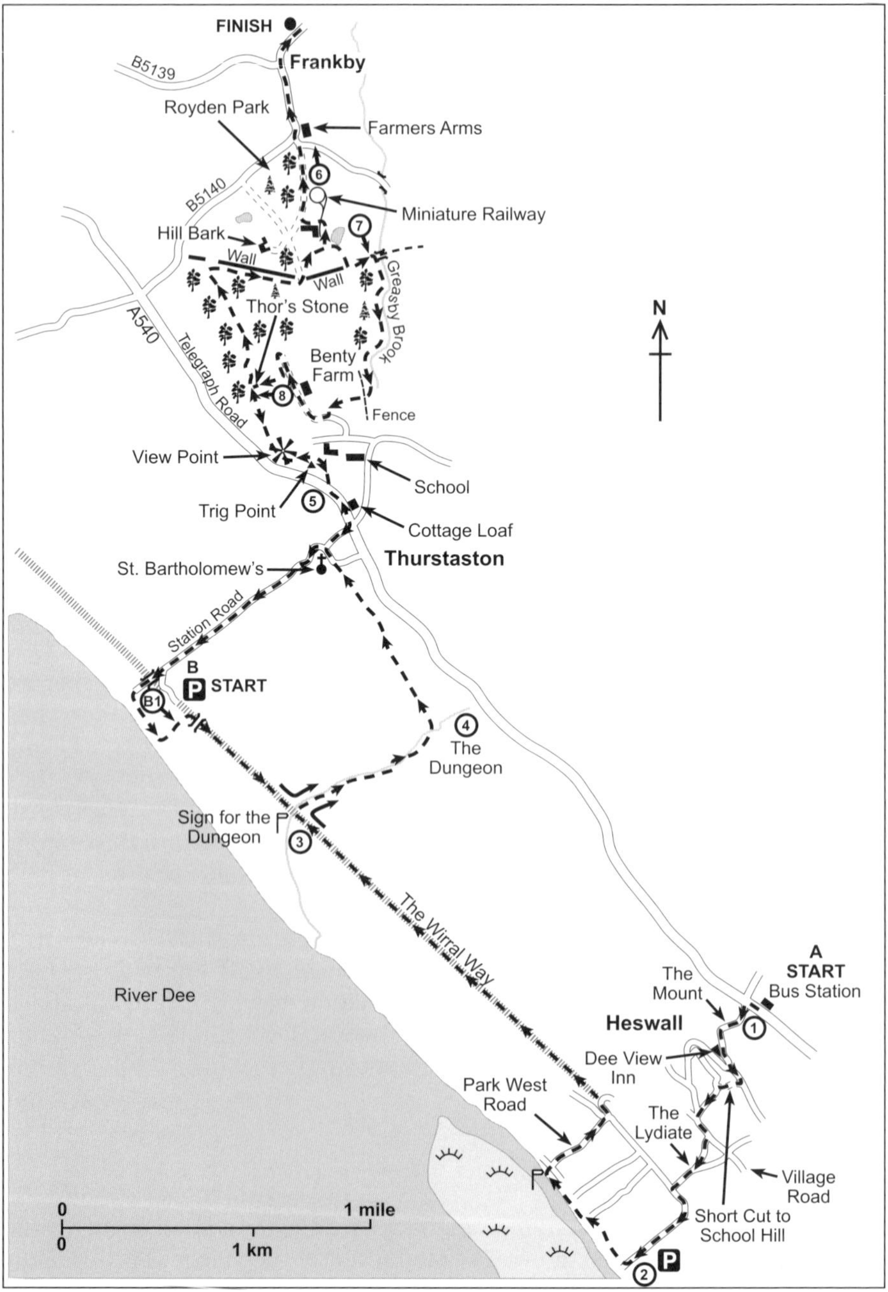
FINISH
Frankby
B5139
Royden Park
Farmers Arms
B5140
Miniature Railway
Hill Bark
Wall
Wall
Greasby Brook
Thor's Stone
A540
Telegraph Road
Benty Farm
Fence
View Point
School
Trig Point
Cottage Loaf
Thurstaston
St. Bartholomew's
Station Road
B
START
The Dungeon
Sign for the Dungeon
The Wirral Way
River Dee
A
START
Bus Station
The Mount
Heswall
Dee View Inn
Park West Road
The Lydiate
Village Road
Short Cut to School Hill
N
0
1 mile
0
1 km

the road until the Dee View Inn is reached. This is indeed a very fine viewing place over the marshland, the Dee estuary and to the Welsh hills beyond. Opposite the Inn a path leads down to School Hill, follow this narrow road downhill until Village Road and the Black Horse pub is reached, turn left through the village. Look out for The Lydiate, a restricted access road on the right, turn down this road, past some fine old sandstone buildings. Upon reaching Station Road turn right, the Dee estuary is straight ahead, carry on passing the site of the Heswall railway station, of which no trace remains, and turn left at Riverbank Road. Follow this road, passing the entrance to the Wirral Way on the left, to the car park at the end.

2. From the car park, follow the well defined path north along the shoreline, the path drops down to the marshland, continue for 300m where a raised concrete embankment and signpost comes in view. Climb the steps at the signpost to gain Park West Road. After taking in the extensive view walk up this road until the junction with the Wirral Way is reached. Turn left and follow this pathway which is the trackbed of the Hooton to West Kirby railway for 1½ miles. Look out for a signpost which shows the way to The Dungeon, turn right and follow this path.

3. The pathway climbs steadily between fields and hedges until a deep ravine with many steep steps are met in the middle of a copse. This is the Dungeon. Descend to cross the brook then ascend more steps, turn right at the top and continue upwards through the woodland, look out for the waterfall on the right. Follow the path until meeting a farm track, at a signpost on a T-junction of paths, turn left for Thurstaston.

4. Follow the track passing a fir tree plantation on the left and Thurstaston church soon comes into view. The St Bartholomew's church and its bell tower nearby is well worth a good look to appreciate the radiant sandstone of which they are built. Turn right into Station Road immediately after the church, then shortly left onto Telegraph Road, heading for the Cottage Loaf public house across the road. Passing the Cottage Loaf pub, look out for the National Trust sign on the right for Thurstaston Common, and pass through the gate.

5. Follow the path bearing left and after 100m towards higher ground on one of many paths through the heather to make your way up to a viewing point. This must be the grandest view on the Wirral, looking over the Dee

estuary towards the Welsh mountains. A toposcope indicates all the significant locations seen from the viewpoint. Having taken in the view, follow the sandstone path through the heather and gorse northward along the ridge. Continue straight on ignoring paths to the left into woodland until a wall is reached with a National Trust sign. Turn right to follow the ill-defined path through the woods alongside the wall which separates Royden Park and the large mansion called Hill Bark from the Common. The mansion soon comes into view and may be seen from a long gap in the wall. Continue along the line of the wall, where the wall resumes turn left and cross a field diagonally towards a wall and the buildings of Royden Park, turn right on a path leading to the entrance of the miniature railway.

The toposcope on Thurstaston Hill

The miniature railway may be visited and ridden, whistles will be heard if the trains are running. At the gated entrance turn left to follow the path between a small lake (Roodee Mere) and the railway line around to a level crossing. Cross this and follow the path around the buildings where a small walled garden that has sculptures, pond and plants can be visited. There are public conveniences and a tea room here.

**Car users on the circular route carry on to point 7 from here.**

6. From here walk past the car park and turn right to follow the entrance drive to Hillbark Road and cross the road for the Farmers Arms. A popular pub with a beer garden and good pub grub. Having had a break continue down Hillbark Road to Frankby Road, turn right and the bus stop is on the left in the village.

## Route B: The Circular Route

B1. From the car park entrance turn left, cross the bridge and turn left through a gate onto a path which crosses a field, then pass through a gap in a large hedge to another field. On the left are hummocks of grass covering what was the site of an anti-aircraft battery, keep right to follow the cliff top path. Sea birds and waders probing the mud and sandbanks may be seen here, the numbers varying according to season and tide. The greatest numbers are seen in winter at high tide. Shelduck, oystercatchers, knot and dunlin are amongst the most frequently seen. Follow the path through a shrubbery then onward to a gap in another large hedge where numerous grass paths radiate out in a recreation area. Turn left to follow the line of the hedge and shrubbery to the corner of the field and bear right to follow the grass path along the boundary to a gate leading onto the line of The Wirral Way. This path is a bridleway which runs parallel with the main path, turn right and follow the path southward. Just before a bridge cross over to the main cycle/walkway then pass under the bridge and carry on for 250m. Look out for the signpost for The Dungeon and turn left and continue on at point 3, follow through to point 5, then on to point 7.

7. From Royden Park garden turn back to pass the entrance of the miniature railway and the sidings to follow the path waymarked Thurstaston Woods into the woodland, follow the path back to the wall then turn left to follow the wall to where it ends. The path then descends to a brook and a footbridge, don't cross the bridge but turn right and follow the gravel path alongside the brook through the wood. Continue straight ahead at a crossing of paths, and go straight on past a bench. Follow the path as it bears right to follow a fence in an area of bracken. Continue to follow the fence to a kissing gate on the right with a National Trust sign. Pass through this gate to follow the path through a pleasant area of silver birch then a small heathland to a nifty stile with wooden bars that lift to allow easy access for dogs and the less agile to pass. The path emerges onto a wide gravel track, turn right and follow the track past Benty Farm. Shortly after the farm, look out for a path joining the track from the left at a sharp angle and turn almost back on yourself to follow this path which skirts around a boggy area to a gate in a wall. Pass through this, then straight on to reach Thor's Stone.

8. Having examined this huge buttress of red sandstone, the favoured return route is via the crest of Thurstaston Hill to savour the great view once again. Carry on in the same direction up the sandy path between the heather and gorse over a small hill then follow the path through a small silver birch wood which emerges suddenly back to the great expansive views over the Dee. Turn left and follow the ridge uphill where the viewing

The cliffs on Thurstaston shoreline near the Visitor Centre

point and trig. point can be appreciated before passing and descending, bearing to the right to emerge at the car park on Telegraph Road, carry on left through the picnic area then onto the road passing the Cottage Loaf pub. Turn right onto Station Road then at a T-junction right again, follow the road as it swings left then it's a ½ mile walk down the road to return to the car park at the visitor centre.

## Historical Notes

### West Kirby to Hooton Railway

The railway closed to passengers in 1956. In 1882 the Liverpool ship owner Thomas Ismay, founder of the White Star Line, had a mansion in Dawpool at Thurstaston, it is thought that his influence caused the railway to be built almost a mile away from the village as it mainly runs alongside the river Dee. The platforms of the station can be seen from the car park and the road bridge.

### Thurstaston Church

This beautiful church was designed by John Loughborough Pearson, also the architect of Truro Cathedral, and was built entirely of local sandstone. It was consecrated in 1886. Although nothing remains of the earlier Norman church, the tower of the second one still stands in the churchyard and the sandstone of the old building was used to construct a wall enclosing the new churchyard.

St Bartholomew's Church at Thurstaston

## Thurstaston Common

The common is a site of Special Scientific Interest (SSSI) and a local nature reserve, much of which is owned by the National Trust. Thurstaston Hill, at 298ft (91m) is one of the highest points on the Wirral. Thor's Stone is a large sandstone mound which as legend has it, was thrown by the Norse God, Thor. In reality the sandstone rock has been eroded by the elements as well as many visitors wanting to climb to its small summit and leaving their carved initials for posterity.

## Bark Hill

The house was originally built in 1891 on Bidston Hill for Robert William Hudson, the soap manufacturer, and was modelled on Little Moreton Hall near Congleton, an Elizabethan half timbered house. Incredibly it was moved to its present location in 1930 by Sir Earnest Royden, due to the encroachment of urban development, which even in the 1930s was spreading into the countryside. It is now owned by Hoylake Urban Council and has been converted into a home for the elderly.

More of the authors photographs can be found at:
**www.geograph.org.uk/search.php?i=48139022**
Press the tab key marked Map to get the locations

# WALK 22
# West Kirby and Caldy

*A circular walk with a mixture of coastal and hill paths on National Trust heathland, with great views and abundant birdlife.*

| | |
|---|---|
| Route | Hoylake – Red Rocks – West Kirby – Wirral Way – Caldy – Caldy Hill – Ashton Park |
| Start/finish | By train: Start: Hoylake Railway Station; Finish: West Kirby Station<br>By car: Charles Road car park, Hoylake |
| Distance and grade | 6½ miles – 318 ft (97m) ascent – Moderate |
| Map | OS Explorer 266 Wirral and Chester |
| Terrain | Good well marked paths with no stiles. A few short steep stretches and some quiet road walking |
| Refreshments | Many pubs and tearooms in West Kirby, The Ring o' Bells on Village Road, an unpretentious family pub /restaurant with real ale and good pub grub |

## Directions to the walk

**Public transport**: Travel to Liverpool city centre, and then catch a train on the Merseyrail Wirral Line to Hoylake, four per hour service Monday to Saturday, two per hour on Sunday.

**By car**: **Sat Nav**: Postcode CH47 2AB will get you to Charles Road Hoylake, near to the station where there is a free car park. There are other street car parks, and the station car park if using a train to return from West Kirby (grid ref: SJ 217889).

**Road directions**: Leave the M53 at junction 2, then leave the motorway at junction 2A, go round the roundabout, take the 2nd exit and turn left for Moreton. At the next roundabout take the 1st exit for the A553 to West Kirby. After about 4 miles turn left at a roundabout onto Station Road then left just before the railway crossing. Turn left into Albert Road, Charles Road is on the right.

## Walk Description

A walk with a great variety of scenery around the coast line and the high ridge of Caldy Hill at the western point of the Wirral. Starting in Hoylake, the route goes down to the seafront and along the shoreline (tide permitting) to arrive opposite the Red Rocks off Hilbre Point. This is a great place for sea bird spotting, many wading species including terns may be on view. Turning south round the point, the route goes over the rocks to a nature reserve with a boardwalk through a reed bed and sand dunes where more birds such as skylarks and stonechats may be heard if not seen! The walk then skirts the marine lake, before a short section of the Wirral Way, then on through the attractive village of Caldy, with distinctive red sandstone and Tudor style buildings. A short climb up to Caldy Hill takes us through a National Trust beauty spot where, in spring, there are acres of heady scented golden gorse. Here there are fine views in a mixture of heathland and wooded areas where an abundance of species of birds such as nuthatch, woodpecker, jay, and a variety of warblers and tits may be seen. From here the route passes a column which once acted as a beacon for shipping, then the Ring o' Bells pub is passed before returning to West Kirby Station via another section of the Wirral Way through a park. Car users have a choice of completing the walk along the footpath to Hoylake or let the train take the strain!

## Walk Directions

1. From the station turn right down Station Road to an attractively floral roundabout. Carry straight on and walk down The Kings Gap past The Green Lodge Hotel on the left to the end at the foreshore. Turn left and walk along the shore (tide permitting).The alternative when there is an exceptional high tide is to retrace your steps and turn right at the Green Lodge Hotel to the end of Stanley Road. Make for the point opposite the Red Rocks, stay near the shore line, then walk up the rocky point where there are usually sea birds to view, before heading off to round the corner of Hilbre Point.

2. There are alternative routes to follow, either through the nature reserve which follow boardwalks over reed beds, or along the shore line which give more open panoramic view over the Dee towards Hilbre Isle. The nature reserve is host to the natterjack toad and birdlife such as the stonechat and skylark, either way has its merits, both take you on to the marine lake. Public conveniences and an ice cream kiosk are located at the end of the tarmacked footpath around the lake, follow this right

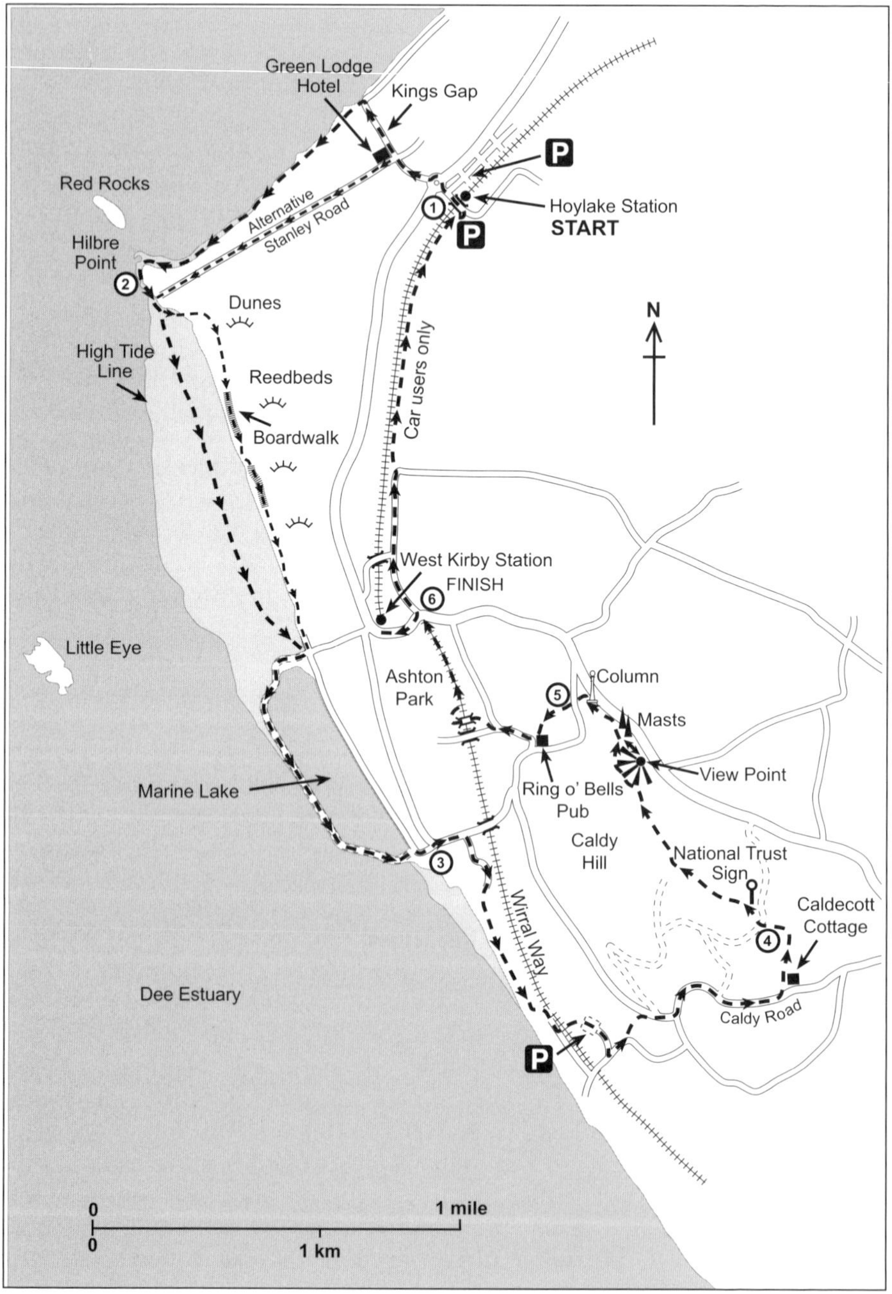
Green Lodge Hotel
Kings Gap
Red Rocks
Alternative Stanley Road
Hoylake Station
START
Hilbre Point
Dunes
Car users only
N
High Tide Line
Reedbeds
Boardwalk
West Kirby Station
FINISH
Little Eye
Ashton Park
Column
Masts
View Point
Ring o' Bells Pub
Marine Lake
Caldy Hill
National Trust Sign
Caldecott Cottage
Wirral Way
Caldy Road
Dee Estuary
0
1 mile
0
1 km

Red Rocks at high tide off Hilbre Point

around to the far end, sailboarders are often to be seen practising their skills as you walk round the lake.

3. Walk straight up inland along Sandy Way and turn right into Macdona Drive. Follow this road to the end where it meets a grassy cliff top, follow the path along the top with great views over the Dee. Keep straight on until the path turns inland to a kissing gate which is on the Wirral Way. Turn right to follow this through a car park to Croft Drive, turn left to follow the road for 200m and take a marked bridleway on the left where the road bends right. Follow the bridleway which comes out onto Caldy Road. Turn right into the village and follow the main road round the sharp left hand bend past a memorial and church. Restricted pavements through the village means care is needed when crossing the road. Turn left onto a waymarked bridleway about 100m past Caldy Wood at Caldecott Cottage. This path leads into the very attractive wooded estate on Caldy Hill. The path comes out on a road called Kings Drive, bear left and follow this for 150m.

4. Where the road bends left at a road junction, take the path opposite marked by a National Trust sign 'Caldy Hill' pass through a gate, then

pass through a gap in a wall, carry straight on, ignoring a path on the left. The path passes through gorse and a seating area, then through a second sandstone wall. The path passes a boundary wall on the left, carry on straight ahead ignoring paths left and right, then over an outcrop of sandstone rock where there is another seat with a great view over Hilbre Island. The path then descends for 150m past a firebeaters stand and a waymarker, carry straight on slightly uphill passing three more seats and more gorse and heather. From here the path descends gradually, passing a small pond then a fenced off private garden of a large white house. After passing a fire hydrant, look out for a path merging from the right, the tall radio masts are abreast of the path junction. Turn right onto the path almost back on yourself and climb 100m up to the brow of the hill where there is a stone plinth with a viewing platform, take in the great views before returning back to the junction and carry on over a natural stone step. Carry on and bear right at a junction of paths then pass a large stone post among dense gorse and heather. After about 300m you arrive at the Mariners Column. An old millstone at its base came from an old mill which once stood here.

Caldy Village

The Mariners Column on Caldy Hill

5. After taking in the fine views, turn left to descend the steps at the back of the column and cross a road to enter a path leading down to an old stone stile and Rectory Lane. At this point you can either turn left for a few metres to visit The Ring o' Bells pub/restaurant for refreshments, or turn right down Rectory Lane to continue on back to the station. If a visit

to the pub has been your choice, retrace your steps to Rectory Lane and re-join the route to go down the road to a junction and Ashton Park gates. Walk through the gates, straight on along a tree lined track to a footbridge, cross over this bridge which spans the Wirral Way. Keep right and pass a playground on the left to join the path onto the Wirral Way, follow the path to Grange Road. (Car users not returning by train go to point 6.) Turn left and West Kirby railway station is 120m on the right.

6. Car users cross Grange Road and walk down Orrysdale Road opposite and go straight onto Anglesey Road to gain the footpath alongside the railway back to Hoylake station and the car park.

## Historical Notes

**The Kings Gap** is derived from William III's army embarkation point at the anchorage in 'Hoyle Lake', the once deep water pool that lay off this coast. The army was being sent to Ireland to fight James II at the battle of the Boyne in 1689.

**Caldy Hill** is part of a ridge of sandstone rock that extends from Heswall in the south to Hilbre Island in the north. The land is owned and cared for by the National Trust, and is one of the highest points on the Wirral at 260 feet (79m), where a toposcope helps to identify the locations of the superb views over the Dee Estuary, Hilbre Island and the Irish Sea and, weather permitting, the more distant views of the mountains of Snowdonia.
More information can be found at: **www.cheshirenow.co.uk/caldy_hill.html**

**The Beacon on Caldy Hill** stands on the site of an old mill that was used as a landmark by mariners navigating into the River Mersey. It was destroyed in a storm in 1839 and the present 60ft (18m) column was erected in 1841 by the trustees of the Liverpool Docks by permission of the landowner John Shaw Leigh, who also gave the stone for its construction.

More of the authors photographs can be found at:
**www.geograph.org.uk/search.php?i=48139182**
Press the tab key marked Map to get the locations

# WALK 23
# Crosby and Sefton Coast

*A simple linear coastline walk with a mixture of promenade walking and sand dune paths, always with great sea views and abundant birdlife.*

| | |
|---|---|
| **Route** | **Crosby Marine Gardens – Crosby Promenade – Coastguard Station – Alt Estuary – Hightown** |
| **Start/finish** | **Start for all routes: By train: Waterloo Station in Crosby, Liverpool; By car: At car park on Cambridge Road at Crosby Finish: Full route: Hightown Railway Station; Shortened route: Hall Road Railway Station; Extended route: Formby Railway Station** |
| **Distance and grade** | **Full Route: 4¾ miles – 75 ft (23m) ascent – Easy<br>Shortened Route: 3 miles – 70 ft (21m) ascent – Easy<br>Extended Route: 8½ miles – 105 ft (32m) ascent – Moderate** |
| **Maps** | **OS Explorer 275 Liverpool; OS Explorer 285 Southport and Chorley** |
| **Terrain** | **Good firm level paths most of the way with no stiles, but some sand dune paths have a few short steep stretches. Some stretches of quiet road walking** |
| **Refreshments** | **Many facilities on South Road, Waterloo including the Marine pub, Hightown Hotel on Alt Road next to Hightown Station, and The Railway near Formby station** |

## Directions to walk

**Public transport:** Travel to Liverpool city centre, then catch a train on the Merseyrail Northern Line at Central Station Liverpool, 4 trains per hour service. Travellers to Liverpool Lime Street Station walk to Central Station.

**By Car**: **Sat Nav**: Postcode L22 1RR will get you to Cambridge Road in Waterloo, the car park is at the end of the road near the Marine Lake (grid ref: SJ 317977).

**Road directions**: From the end of the M57 and M58 (junction 7) motorways take the A5036 for Seaforth, continue for 3½ miles to a roundabout and flyover, take the second exit for the A565 to Southport then at the next junction, where Antony Gormley's Other Place car park is signed, turn left and follow the road to the car park. As the walks follow linear routes, car users return by train from Hightown, Hall Road, or Formby stations to Waterloo station.

## Directions from the walk

Catch a train at Hightown, Hall Road or Formby stations to Liverpool Moorfields station then catch any Wirral Line train to Liverpool Lime Street station for local train/bus network for connections home.

## Walk Description

The Merseyrail Northern Line parallels the coast all the way up to Southport, which enables walks from station to station along scenic coastal paths with many permutations of routes possible according to ability, weather conditions, or simply as you see fit as the day progresses. This walk and walk 24 may be shortened or extended and even joined up, the nearby railway makes it easy to be flexible in your plans.

This is a good walk for any season, on well used flat paths, and some sand dune walking with plenty of interest, following the coastline where shipping may be seen making their way into and out of the Mersey. The first part of the walk is along a promenade where Antony Gormley's statues standing in the tidal beach will be seen. Controversial when first installed, for they are so lifelike from a distance, it was thought they may be seen as people in distress as the tide rose around them. But they are now an accepted and much loved part of the landscape. Birds such as oystercatcher, redshank, dunlin and cormorant are among many that may be seen at the Marine Lake and along the shoreline. At high tide a great show of wheeling birds taking off en masse is a grand spectacle that may be observed as the tide encroaches on their feeding grounds.

At the end of the promenade is the coastguard station, sadly under threat of closure, the station monitors shipping movements in one of Europe's busiest shipping areas. This is also a favourite site for fishermen after flatfish, sea bass, cod and whiting. The sea water quality has vastly improved in the last twenty years and as a consequence increased the chances of a good catch. The walk may be shortened here by returning via Hall Road Station. Beyond the promenade the route continues along the coast on a bank built up with land-fill to reduce coast erosion and is backed by low sand dunes and rough grassland. It is home to skylarks and meadow pippets. Further on the path leads you through sand dunes past a sailing club and the River Alt estuary, with more water fowl before joining the road to Hightown Station.

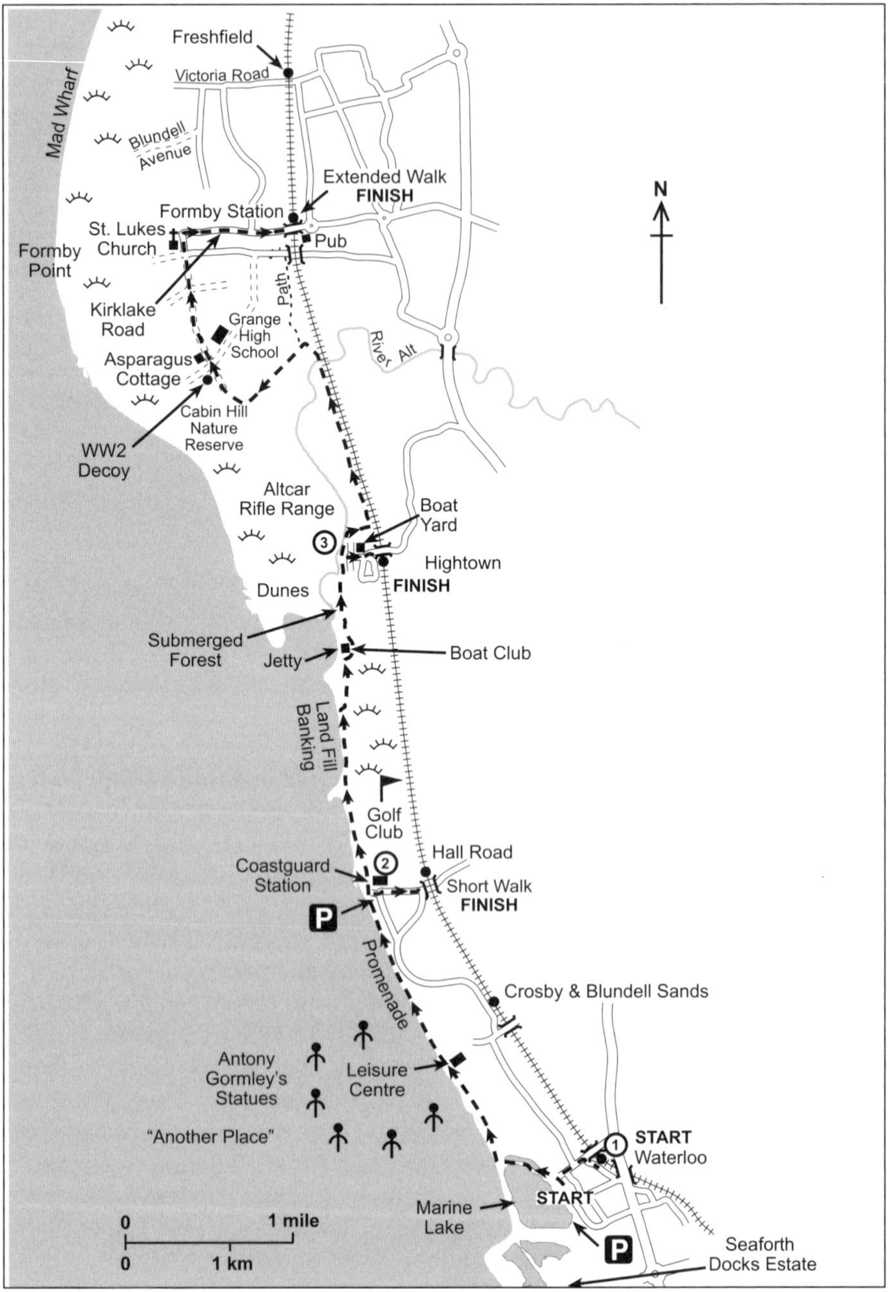

Mad Wharf
Freshfield
Victoria Road
Blundell Avenue
Extended Walk
FINISH
N
Formby Station
St. Lukes Church
Pub
Formby Point
Path
Kirklake Road
Grange High School
River Alt
Asparagus Cottage
Cabin Hill Nature Reserve
WW2 Decoy
Altcar Rifle Range
Boat Yard
3
Hightown
FINISH
Dunes
Submerged Forest
Jetty
Boat Club
Land Fill Banking
Golf Club
Hall Road
2
Coastguard Station
Short Walk
FINISH
P
Promenade
Crosby & Blundell Sands
Antony Gormley's Statues
Leisure Centre
"Another Place"
1
START
Waterloo
START
Marine Lake
0
1 mile
0
1 km
P
Seaforth Docks Estate

## Walk Directions

1. From the station turn left onto South Road and follow this to the entrance of the promenade, carry on into the attractive Marine Gardens, bear right to pass between the marine and boating lakes.

   **Car users join the route by leaving the car park at its furthest point where a path continues on to join the path between the two lakes.**

The boating lake at Crosby with offshore wind farm seen between the sand dunes

   Sea birds may be seen at the lake especially in bad windy weather when they can be found seeking shelter. Notice the smart looking 'villas 'overlooking this area, these were favoured by retired sea captains and ship owners who liked to observe the shipping movements into the Port of Liverpool. To the left can be seen the container port at Seaforth Docks with its huge wind turbines.

   Turn right and follow the promenade, at high tide the shipping activity is at its greatest, with vessels navigating close to the coast following the narrow deep water channel into the Mersey. Further out to sea may be seen the vast array of wind turbines off the Wirral and Welsh coasts. At low tide it is possible to walk out on the sand to get up close to Antony Gormley's statues and perhaps have your photo taken with one. Continue on past the futuristic looking Crosby Leisure Centre then on to the end of the promenade and the coastguard station.

   At the coast guard station the promenade finishes, **the walk can be shortened here** by walking up the road beside the coast guard station to Hall Road and continue onward to the Hall Road railway station.

2. To complete the full route, pass through a squeeze gate and continue to follow the asphalt path along the coast. The path follows the bank which consists of what seems to be builders rubble used to protect the coast from erosion. The sand dunes of Formby point lie in the distance ahead, soon after passing a pumping station, the moorings of the boat club are seen. At

The coastal sea defences at Crosby Coastguard Station

a small artwork called *The Pebble* the path turns inland into the dunes and as it bends sharp right, turn left to follow a grassy path into the dunes. At a fork bear right, the path winds through growths of creeping willow, sedges and sea-buckthorn. There are many paths in the dunes from here; the way forward is to follow straight ahead, parallel to the dunes on the coast to your left, keeping the houses of Hightown and masts of the yachts in the distance ahead. Soon the path emerges onto a track leading to the Blundell Sands Yacht Club where a board points the way to a viewpoint. At low tide the rotted remains of tree trunks of a submerged forest may be seen, which are around 4,000 years old. Continue on the path indicated by the Sefton Coast Marker through the dunes which is marked by white topped posts. The path emerges alongside the Alt estuary to a boatyard. The river Alt rises at Huyton and is a modest 15 miles in length, it meanders across the Lancashire Plain before emptying into the Irish Sea. The path joins a road, follow the road and at a junction (to extend the route to Formby continue onto point 3) turn right in front of a boat yard and follow the road to a roundabout, then straight on to Lower Alt Road to the Hightown Station and if in need of refreshment, the Hightown Hotel.

**Car users** must catch a train towards Liverpool and alight at Waterloo Station then turn left to follow South Road to the entrance of Marine Park, pass through and turn left to reach the car park.

3. **To extend the route** a further 3¾ miles to Formby station, continue on the road beside the River Alt past the No Through Road sign, then follow the marked Sefton Coast Footpath (SCP) alongside the railway beside the Altcar rifle range, crossing the footbridge over the River Alt. Then follow a broad gravel path alongside a ditch to a junction of paths where a sharp left takes the SCP (waymarked with a yellow arrow) alongside a ditch and boundary fence, and a small plantation of conifers. This path is called Hoggs Hill Lane, follow this to a junction with another path and turn right to pass a small wood. This area is called Cabin Hill Nature Reserve and abounds in wildlife. Nesting lapwings and skylarks may be seen. Continue to follow the path past the remote Asparagus Cottage, and then school playing fields. The path turns into a rough track before it's joined by a

High tide at the River Alt estuary, viewed from Blundell Sands Yacht Club

tarmacked road, continue ahead along this attractive tree lined road to a junction with Lifeboat Lane and carry straight on to St Lukes Church Road, pass the church and turn right to follow Kirkland Road which leads to Formby Station. Refreshments may be had by crossing the railway bridge, descending the steps on the right where a few steps brings you to The Railway pub (seen from the railway bridge)

More of the authors photographs can be found at:
**www.geograph.org.uk/search.php?i=46196626**
Press the tab key marked Map to get the locations

# WALK 24
# Formby Point

*A walk of contrasts, following woodland, shoreline, sand dune and heathland paths, all with great views, and a wealth of flora and fauna.*

| | |
|---|---|
| Route | Formby – Cabin Hill – Formby Point – Red Squirrel Reserve – Sefton Coastal Footpath – Fisherman's Path – Freshfield Dune Heath Reserve – Freshfield |
| Start/finish | Start: Formby Station Railway Station (car user's park free with a rail ticket from Freshfield)<br>Finish: Freshfield Station |
| Distance and grade | 7 miles – 98 ft (30m) ascent – Moderate<br>Shortened route: 5½ miles – 69 ft (236m) ascent – Moderate |
| Map | OS Explorer 285 Southport and Chorley |
| Terrain | Mostly level path with no stiles, but some paths through sand dunes can be steep in places and care in navigation is needed. Some stretches of quiet road walking |
| Refreshments | The Railway near Formby station, The Freshfield Inn near Freshfield Station and ice cream vans, in season at car parks |

## Directions to walk

**Public transport:** Travel to Liverpool city centre, and then catch a train on the Merseyrail Northern Line at Central Station Liverpool, 4 trains per hour service. Travellers to Liverpool Lime Street Station walk to Central Station.

**By Car**: **Sat Nav**: Postcode L37 4AL will get you to Duke Street Formby, carry straight onto a cobbled road where the main road bends left, then follow sign for car park by turning right under a road bridge (grid ref: SD 292070).

**Road Directions**: From the end of the M57 and M58 (junction 7) motorways take the A5036 for Seaforth, then after 400m turn right onto A5207. Follow the signs for Formby, turn right onto the A565, and follow for 4 miles. Turn left onto the B5195 and take the second exit at a roundabout and the first exit at a mini roundabout onto Duke Street, then at a second roundabout take first exit. Turn right at a grassy island past a row of shops, then straight onto a cobbled road where the main road turns left. Follow the sign for the car park by turning right under a road bridge.

## Directions from the walk

Catch a train at Freshfield station to Liverpool Moorfields station then catch any Wirral Line train to Liverpool Lime Street station for local train/bus network for connections home.

## Walk Description

This walk is one of great variety and is especially good for nature lovers, rich in flora and fauna. As this is a deservedly popular venue it's best appreciated in spring or autumn in the quieter months and when wildlife is most active.

Starting at Formby station the suburban roads are shortly followed by tracks leading through woodland accompanied by birdsong and the distant rumble of surf on the beach. The route passes a small nature reserve before passing through the dunes to reach the beach where a grand vista opens up scanning, from the south, the Liverpool skyline, Seaforth Dock cranes, the mountains of Wales from Moel Famau to the Carnedds, then the Great Orme jutting out to sea, and on a clear day Anglesey can be seen. Closer is the great array of wind turbines off the Wirral and Welsh coasts, and the gas rigs off the Fylde coast.

The walk along the beach is a delight with a feeling of wide open spaciousness. It is especially attractive at high tide when the surf breaking on the beach adds to the drama, and wading birds and gulls can be seen at close quarters all along the beach. Dunlin, redshank, oystercatcher, sanderling and knot may be present depending on the season. A pair of shelduck landed within 100m of me as I passed. The route follows the coastline around the Formby Point where the view towards Blackpool with its tower and big dipper opens up, before heading inland on part of the Sefton Coastal Path through a variety of habitats where stonechats, skylarks and meadow pipits may be seen. In summer the area is alive with dragonflies and butterflies. The route follows winding paths through pine forest, the home of the endangered red squirrels, mixed woodland, wild flowers, grassland and dunes. Finally the route follows the Fisherman's Path back to Freshfield, crossing a small heathland before ending at Freshfield Station.

## Walk Directions

1. From the Southport bound station platform a path leads off to Ennerdale Road, follow this onto Kirklake Road, turn right and follow the road, turning sharp left to continue on the road past St Luke's Church. At the next road junction carry straight onto a rough track which passes a stable and woodland on the right. At another junction of tracks continue forward passing a waymarker for the Sefton Coastal Path (SCP), the track passes through woodland full of birdsong in spring, a flock of long tailed tits were seen here flitting between the branches.The route passes Grange High School sports field, and Asparagus Cottage, named after the growing of this vegetable in the area until recent times. The path becomes sandy and the woodland is left for more open landscape. At a junction of tracks, waymarkers and information boards show this is Cabin Hill, a small nature reserve where nesting skylarks and lapwings may be heard or seen.

2. Turn right to follow the track (Hoggs Hill Lane) past a ruined world war decoy building, which was used to confuse the Luftwaffe on their bombing

Kirklake Road,Formby

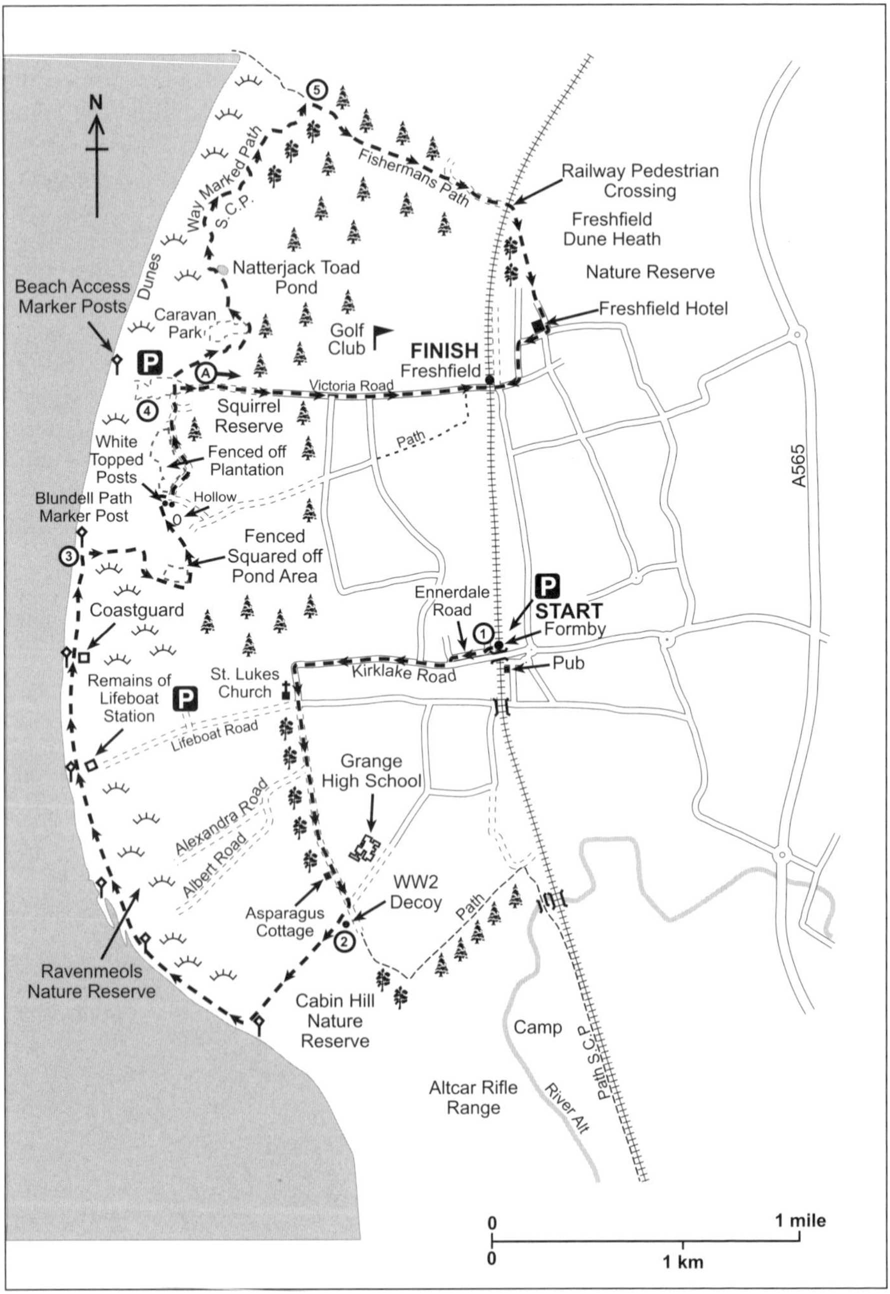
N
Beach Access
Marker Posts
Dunes
Way Marked Path
S.C.P.
Fishermans Path
Railway Pedestrian
Crossing
Freshfield
Dune Heath
Nature Reserve
Freshfield Hotel
Natterjack Toad
Pond
Caravan
Park
Golf
Club
FINISH
Freshfield
Victoria Road
Squirrel
Reserve
Path
White
Topped
Posts
Fenced off
Plantation
Hollow
Blundell Path
Marker Post
Fenced
Squared off
Pond Area
A565
Ennerdale
Road
START
Formby
Pub
Coastguard
Kirklake Road
St. Lukes
Church
Remains of
Lifeboat
Station
Lifeboat Road
Grange
High School
Alexandra Road
Albert Road
WW2
Decoy
Asparagus
Cottage
Path
Ravenmeols
Nature Reserve
Cabin Hill
Nature
Reserve
Camp
Path S.C.P.
Altcar Rifle
Range
River Alt
0
1 mile
0
1 km

The Formby sand dunes near the Blundell Path marker post

raids on Bootle Docks. The track reduces to a sandy path as it approaches the dunes, where a climb is necessary. At the brow of the dune it becomes clear there is a second line of dunes before the beach is reached. The path splits up into many routes, just keep on until breasting the second line of dunes where the grand vista of Liverpool Bay can be appreciated before descending down to the firmer sand of the tide swept beach. Turn to the right and follow the tide line past the beach access markers for Ravenmeols Nature reserve, Alexander Road then Lifeboat Road, where the remains of the first lifeboat station in Britain can be seen; it was closed in 1918.

The constantly shifting sand dunes have to be maintained to prevent erosion of the coastline and fence pailings and brushwood used to halt the sand shifting inland may be seen. Continue along the beach past the small coast guard station at Formby Point then at the marker for the Blundell Path, turn to walk inland between the massive dunes along a sand gulley.The Nicotine trail is close to here, named after the dumping ground in this area of tobacco waste from the once a major industry in Liverpool. Tell tale signs of these dumps can be seen in spring, where the grass is greenest is where the waste is adding nutrient to the sandy soil.

3. Pass through the dunes, looking out for a small square fenced off area on the right, keep right of this and walk up a hummock of old dune where the next objective can be seen on an indistinct path at 45 degrees left towards a plantation of conifers in the distance. A pair of Wheatear were sitting on a post here, not flying off until quite close up. Descend left to the path which meanders first on sand then grass.

   The path comes to a shallow depression were there are many stumps of chopped down trees. Skirt around right and left of this then climb past weather bent shrubs, then turn right onto a sandy path towards a corner of the fenced off plantation of conifer forest. Follow the path alongside the fence inland, white topped markers are alongside the path, continue to a broad path and turn left to follow this path through a forested area to a junction of paths with a marker post with an Asparagus sign. Continue ahead, bear left where it divides and follow the path which is marked by SCP yellow arrowed posts, the path soon emerges at the National Trust car park.

   **This is where the squirrel reserve may be visited and the shorter route is taken to return to Freshfield Station at point A.**

4. Cross the car park and follow the tarmacked track to the caravan site, just before the gate entrance turn right to take a path, marked with a cycle symbol, round the perimeter fence of the park. Pass through an area of weather beaten trees, and pussy willow, the path emerges onto a broad path at the corner of the fenced caravan site. Turn left onto the path, keep straight on past a recreation area at a junction of paths. Follow the path through the wooded area and old sand dunes which are held in check by trees and undergrowth. A waymarker for the SCP is passed, ignore paths going off right and left, follow the SCP posts past a large encroachment of sand dunes which have killed off the trees on the left. At a junction of paths bear left to follow the SCP path back into the dunes. Soon a small pond with natterjack toad information is passed on the right, then at a bench seat a right turn is made to follow the SCP.

   Pass through a line of fencing, then through a low bushy area, the path returns to grass as it passes through are large growth of orange berried sea buckthorn and continues on past a gate leading on to the golf course. The path then enters a mixed woodland area where it meanders pleasantly through the woods of conifers and silver birch filled with bird song. All too soon the path emerges onto the broad Fisherman's Path.

The Fishermans Path leads to Freshfield

Turn right to follow the path to a gate, pass through this and cross the golf course, taking care to look right for flying balls! The path ends at a railway crossing, take note of the warning signs and cross carefully. At the opposite side, take the path off to the right that diverges from the railway line alongside a fence past a small heathland. The path enters a small wood before crossing a bridleway, then passes behind a residential area and emerges onto Rimmers Avenue. At the end of Rimmers Avenue is the Freshfield Hotel with real ale and good pub grub. This makes for a refreshing break at the end of the walk. It is but a short walk to Freshfield Station by way of following straight on past the pub onto Gregsons Avenue, turn left into Argarmeols Road and turn right into Victoria Road, Freshfield station is on the right.

To visit the National Trust Red Squirrel Reserve and/or shorten the walk, turn right at point (A) at the NT car park and follow Victoria Road for about 300m to the reserve entrance, or continue on to Freshfield Station.

More of the authors photographs can be found at:
**www.geograph.org.uk/search.php?i=46533453**
Press the tab key marked Map to get the locations

# WALK 25
# Cheshire Sandstone Trail

*Linear and circular walks, with great views from an elevated woodland route, which follow paths through the beautiful rural Cheshire landscape.*

| | |
|---|---|
| **Route** | **Frodsham – Overton Hill – Woodhouse Hillfort – Alvanley Cliff – Austerson Old Hall – Manley – Mouldsworth** |
| **Start/finish** | **Route A: Start: By train: Frodsham railway station; By bus: Bus stop opposite the Bears Paw pub on Main Street, Frodsham**<br>**Finish: Mouldsworth railway station**<br>**Route B: By car: At car park on Simons Lane, Overton Hill, Frodsham** |
| **Distance and grade** | **Route A: 6 miles for train/bus users – 862 ft (263m) ascent – Moderate**<br>**Route B: 5 miles for car users – 869 ft (265m) ascent – Moderate** |
| **Map** | **OS 267 Northwich and Delamere Forest** |
| **Terrain** | **Mostly good level paths with a few stiles, but there are some steep stretches with many steps. Can be muddy in places. There are some short stretches of quiet road walking** |
| **Refreshments** | **Many pubs and cafés in Frodsham including The Bears Paw at the start of the walk. The Ring o' Bells and The Bulls Head at Overton and The Goshawk pub at Mouldsworth (real ale, good food and terrace)** |

## Directions to walk

**Public transport**: **By bus**: Merseysiders travel via Runcorn (Palace Fields) to connect with number 21, 36 or X30 buses half hourly service to Frodsham. Bus number 329 from St Helens to Warrington connects with the X30.

Greater Manchester walkers travel via Warrington to connect with number X 30 bus to Frodsham. The following services give a direct link to Warrington: Bus number 5 starts in Altrincham, number 28 starts from Leigh, number 360 from Wigan.

**By train**: Merseysiders travel via Warrington Bank Quay to connect with trains to Frodsham. Trains run hourly from Liverpool via Huyton to Warrington Bank Quay and hourly from Hough Green to Warrington Central, a short walk from Warrington B.Q. Alternatively Merseyrail trains from Liverpool Lime Street connect with trains to Frodsham at Chester which is also an hourly service. For Manchester walkers there is an hourly service from Manchester Piccadilly via Warrington to Frodsham.

**By car**: **Sat Nav**: WA6 6HG will get you to the car park on Simons Lane, Overton Hill, Frodsham (grid ref: SJ 519766).

**Road directions**: From the M56 Junction 12, follow the A56 towards Chester, after 1½ miles turn left at traffic lights in Frodsham onto the B5152 and pass under the railway bridge. Carry on for 600m, then at a junction on the right with Manley Road, signed Heathercliffe Hotel, turn right and follow this road until a junction on the right signed Forest Hills Hotel and The View Night Club. Turn onto the road (Simons Lane), the car park is ½ mile on the right.

## Directions from finish of walk

Merseyside walkers catch a train from Mouldsworth station to Chester (hourly service Monday to Saturday, 2 hourly on Sunday). Then catch the Merseyrail Wirral lines 15 minute frequency service back to Liverpool Lime Street for train /bus connections homeward.

Greater Manchester walkers catch a train, again an hourly service Monday to Saturday, 2 hourly on Sunday service from Mouldsworth in the opposite direction to Altrincham and Manchester Piccadilly for train/bus service connections homeward.

## Walk Descriptions

### Route A: The Linear Route

This linear route starts in the pretty tree lined Frodsham Main Street, where the northern part of the Sandstone Trail starts. The route passes through the attractive suburb of Overton, with St Lawrence's Church and the Ring o' Bells pub, before ascending a steep sandstone path up through woodland to the top of Overton Hill. The view from here over the Mersey estuary and Hale Head is outstanding, where much of the route of the Walk 19 can be seen. Following on, the route skirts around the wooded sandstone buttresses then descends down steps into the eerie Dunsdale Hollow. From here the path passes the banked up Iron Age hill fort of Woodhouses, then descends through Snidley Moor Wood and past a scout camp. The route then follows a stretch edging the wooded Alvanley Cliff with lovely views over the Cheshire

Plain towards the Welsh Clwydian range of hills. The half-timbered Austerson Old Hall is passed, then at Simmonds's Hill a field path off Manley Road is followed towards Manley Old Hall. Then a succession of tracks, paths and lanes through the rustic Cheshire landscape lead on to the hamlet of Manley and Mouldsworth railway station.

### Route B: The Circular Route

The circular route starts on Beacon Hill and follows the North Cheshire Way through the beautiful grounds of Heathercliffe Hotel to the War Memorial on Overton Hill, and then continues on the linear walk route above to Snidley Wood. Paths and lanes with many kissing gates and more great views lead on to join the Delamere Way, which follows restricted byways (green lanes) and then on through the rural Cheshire landscape on paths back to the car park.

## Walk Directions

### Route A: The Linear Route

1. **If arriving at Frodsham by bus**, alight on the High Street outside Morrison's then continue ahead to the traffic lights and turn left onto Church Street. **Rail users join the route here** from the station access road. Continue under the railway bridge for 250m then take the path up the steps on the right waymarked the Sandstone Trail. The path emerges at St Lawrence's Church, cross Church Road, and continue to follow the way-marker sign past The Ring O' Bells pub and Bulls Head pub up Bellemonte Road. Another way-marker on the right indicates the route up a short road onto the path, bear left up the steps, then climb the zig-zag path which ascends up through woods to the summit of Overton Hill and the War Memorial. From here is a stupendous view over the Mersey Estuary and the Liverpool waterfront. A toposcope helps get your bearings and the identification of the landmarks.

The war memorial on Overton Hill with the Castner Kellner works and Mersey estuary in view

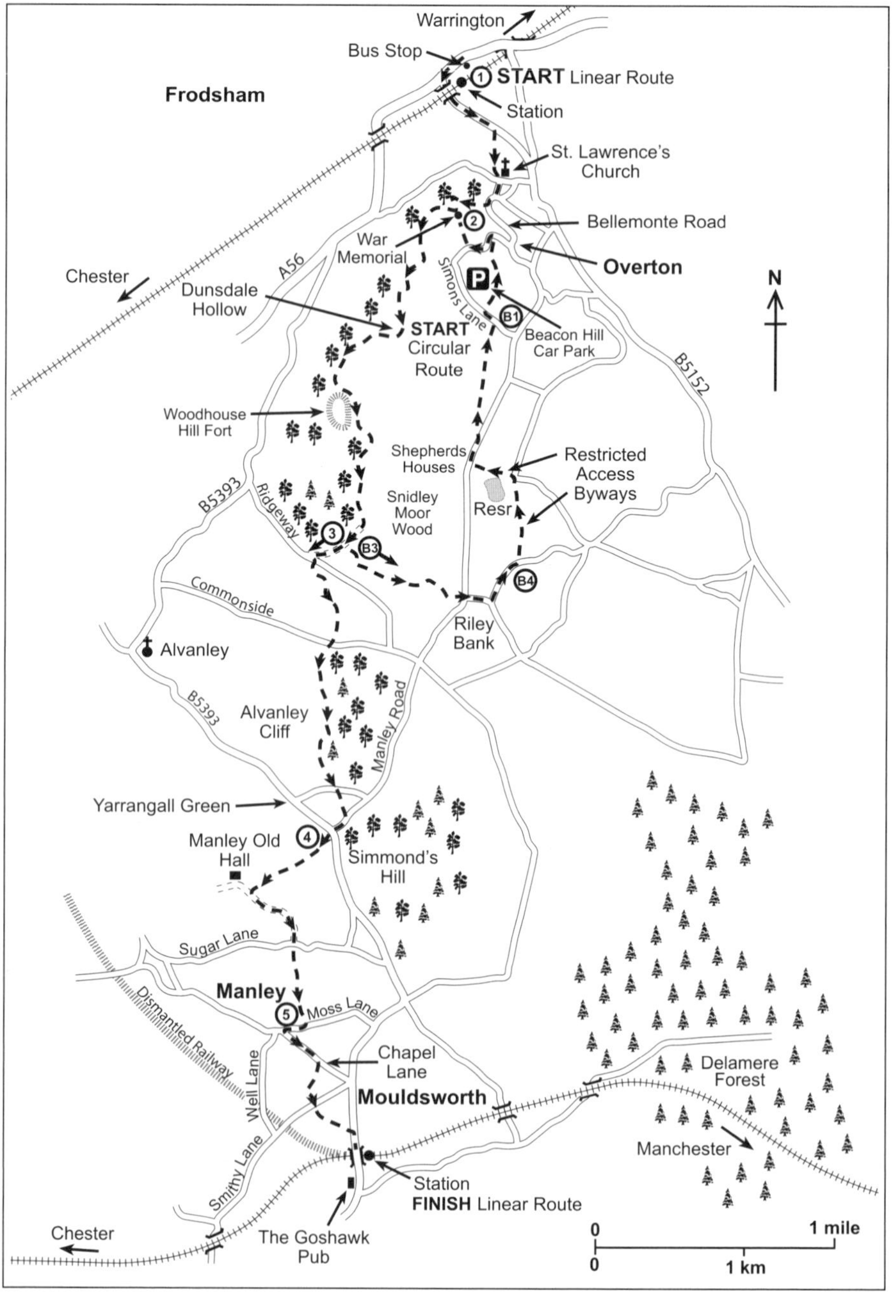
Warrington
Bus Stop
1 START Linear Route
Frodsham
Station
St. Lawrence's Church
2
Bellemonte Road
War Memorial
Overton
Chester
A56
Simons Lane
P
N
Dunsdale Hollow
START Circular Route
B1
Beacon Hill Car Park
B5152
Woodhouse Hill Fort
Shepherds Houses
Restricted Access Byways
Resr
B5393
Ridgeway
Snidley Moor Wood
3
B3
B4
Commonside
Riley Bank
Alvanley
B5393
Alvanley Cliff
Manley Road
Yarrangall Green
Manley Old Hall
4
Simmond's Hill
Sugar Lane
Manley
5
Moss Lane
Dismantled Railway
Well Lane
Chapel Lane
Mouldsworth
Delamere Forest
Manchester
Smithy Lane
Station
FINISH Linear Route
Chester
The Goshawk Pub
0
1 mile
0
1 km

2. Having caught your breath and soaked up the airy atmosphere, the route is by way of the path past the toposcope which follows the edge of the hill on a terraced path through woodland full of birdsong. The path meanders around the buttresses of rock until the Baker's Dozen metal steps lead down into Dunsdale Hollow. Follow the waymarker sign for Delamere Forest and climb the rising steps cut into the living rock on the right to lead out onto a wooded, terraced path with more great views over Helsby Hill and the Mersey estuary. Continue past a bench and information board with Ice Age information and follow the signposts for the Sandstone Trail. Keep right to follow a low walled path then on past the ramparts of the Woodhouse Hill Fort. The path comes to a T-junction, turn right downhill through the woods then on down a sunken track. This is the Woodland Trust's Snidley Wood. Continue onward through the beautiful wood to where the path descends gently onto a grassy stretch through a hollow at the foot of a field.

3. The path bears right onto a track leading to lane called The Ridgeway. Turn left then shortly turn right, up steps at the waymarker for Delamere

Helsby Hill viewed from Overton Hill

The Sandstone Trail passes through a hollow near Snidley Wood

Forest. Follow the path through Ridgeway Wood, cross a brook, and then follow the field boundaries to emerge onto a road at a kissing gate called Commonside. Cross the road to pass through another kissing gate, and then follow the path which passes below Alvanley woods along a lovely stretch with great views over the Cheshire Plain towards the Welsh Hills. The path bears right to skirt the grounds of the half-timbered Austerson Old Hall, then emerges onto Yarangall Green. Cross the green and pass through a metal kissing gate almost opposite. The path passes between fields and a small copse to emerge at a kissing gate onto Manley Road. Turn right to the road junction with the B5393.

4. From here the route parts company with the Sandstone Trail. Cross the road to a stile opposite, next to a gate, cross this and follow the faint field path towards Manley Old Hall seen in the distance. Keep near to the left of the field, passing a stone house then following the left hand field boundary through a gate, and continue onto the path towards the farm.

The path drops down to this sizeable Victorian farm house, at the left corner of the farmstead perimeter. Turn left into the next field, then right alongside a tall conifer hedge to emerge at a stile onto the farm access track and turn left. Follow the track to Sugar Lane, cross and pass through a crude stile nearly opposite. Follow the field boundary on the right, continue on and cross a second field, then follow a narrow path to emerge at a stile onto Moss Lane.

5. Turn right and follow the road to a T-junction then turn left, follow this road (Chapel Lane) for 250m to a ladder stile and gate just before the old Methodist Church (now a day nursery). Cross the stile and follow the gravel path to a stone stile, cross this and continue on across a field passing through a gate continue on to emerge at a gate onto a track. Turn left to follow the track which emerges onto the well-manicured, hedged Smithy Lane. Turn right for a few steps then take the waymarked track on the left, signed Rose Bank Farm. Follow the track to where it bends sharp right, then continue straight onto a public path past the farm and pass between fields to emerge onto the B5393 (Station Road). Turn right and follow the road to Mouldsworth Railway Station, and a little further is The Goshawk pub.

## Route B: The Circular Walk

B1. Leave the car park and turn left, follow the road to a gate marked Overhill Cottage, turn left and follow the track (The North Cheshire Way) past the cottage and continue on a path on the right of the track into the grounds of Heathercliffe Hotel. The grounds are especially attractive in late spring with a wonderful display of rhododendrons. The path joins a road where there are excellent views over the Mersey estuary, with the Runcorn Bridge and Fiddlers Ferry power station prominent. Turn left uphill then shortly right through the ornate gates of the Memorial Fields and follow the path which leads onto the Memorial and the spectacular views over the Mersey estuary.

**Follow the directions for the linear walk at point 2, up to Snidley Wood.**

B3. Look out for a metal kissing gate on the left, go through the gate to leave the Sandstone Trail and follow the grassy path to the right and pass another kissing gate, then carry on through the miniature valley through mixed woodland up the hill. Rabbit burrows may be seen on the left of the path. A further kissing gate is passed then a steep stretch is climbed before the path crosses a field path (a friendly horse may greet you here!) to a kissing gate and Manley Road. Cross over and go down the road directly opposite past Riley Bank Farm, keep left at a junction, then as the road curves right take the path on the left marked with a restricted byway sign.

B4. Follow this path to a road and another signed restricted byway, turn left and follow this track which is lined with bluebells and wild flowers in spring, back to Manley Road. Turn right to follow the road for 100m, to a waymarked kissing gate on the left. Pass through and bear right and cross the field, then cross a track and continue up steps to another path opposite where there are good views to the west over the Mersey estuary. Follow this path alongside a field bounded with tall conifers then continue on alongside a hedge next to a golf course where the path emerges onto Simons Lane. Turn left and follow the road back to the car park.

## Historical Notes

**Woodhouse Hill Fort** is an Iron Age hill fort. Woodhouse Hill has steep cliffs on the western sides, providing a natural defence. It is defended by a rampart to the north and east where the ground slopes more gently. Excavations in 1951 showed that the rampart was originally four metres high and revetted with stone on both sides. A number of small rounded stones, believed to be slingstones, have been found on the site.
See: **en.wikipedia.org/wiki/Woodhouses_hill_fort**

The half-timbered **Austerson Old Hall** is an Elizabethan building circa 16th century with 17th century additions. It was transported from Austerson, Crewe and Nantwich Borough in the 1980s. The reconstruction was carried out wherever possible using original timbers, old brick and tile.
More information at:
**www.britishlistedbuildings.co.uk/en-57170-austerson-old-hall-alvanley-**

More of the authors photographs can be found at:
**www.geograph.org.uk/search.php?i=46221227** and at
**www.geograph.org.uk/search.php?i=46221183**
Press the tab key marked Map to get the locations